CITIZEN INDIANS

Citizen Indians

NATIVE AMERICAN INTELLECTUALS, RACE, AND REFORM **LUCY MADDOX**

Cornell University Press   Ithaca and London

First published 2005 by Cornell University Press

Printed in the United States of America

Library of Congress Cataloging-in-Publication Data
Maddox, Lucy.
  Citizen Indians : Native American intellectuals, race, and reform
/ Lucy Maddox.
    p. cm.
  Includes bibliographical references and index.
  ISBN 0-8014-4354-7 (cloth : alk. paper)
    1. Indians of North America–Politics and government.
2. Indians of North America–Intellectual life.   3. Indians of
North America–Government relations.   4. Indians, Treatment of–
North America–History.   5. Indian activists–North America–
History.   6. Indians in literature.   7. Social reform–United
States–History.   8. United States–Social policy.   9. United
States–Race relations.   10. United States–Politics and government.
I. Title.
  E78.T77M33 2005
  305.897′073–dc22   2004030154

Cornell University Press strives to use environmentally responsible
suppliers and materials to the fullest extent possible in the
publishing of its books. Such materials include vegetable-based,
low-VOC inks and acid-free papers that are recycled, totally
chlorine-free, or partly composed of nonwood fibers. For further
information, visit our website at www.cornellpress.cornell.edu.

Cloth printing 10 9 8 7 6 5 4 3 2 1

CONTENTS

ACKNOWLEDGMENTS

I am grateful to the Graduate School of Arts and Sciences at Georgetown University for a senior faculty research grant that allowed me to complete this project. I also owe thanks to the many people who have helped to support, encourage, or improve this book. Among them, special appreciation goes to Robert Allen Warrior and Frederick Hoxie for careful, astute readings; to my students at Georgetown and at the Bread Loaf School of English for sharing their intellectual energy and insights; to the reference librarians and the ever-helpful staffs of the Manuscripts Reading Room and the Prints and Photographs Division at the Library of Congress; to Sheri Englund at Cornell University Press for clear-eyed direction; to John Raymond for helpful editing; to librarian extraordinaire Chris Brady, who kept me supplied with information, passwords, and maple syrup; to Jim Maddox for continuing to think this was a good idea; to the eleven o'clock club for keeping it all in perspective.

A NOTE ON SOURCES

All of the collections of papers cited in the notes to this book are available on microfilm, and all include materials that were indispensable to the research for the book. The papers of the Society of American Indians include copies of Arthur C. Parker's correspondence on matters relating to the SAI as well as copies of circular letters sent out by the organization, membership lists, and programs for the annual conferences. The papers of Carlos Montezuma contain copies of correspondence between Montezuma and a number of people important to this study, especially Gertrude Bonnin and Richard Henry Pratt. The papers of the Indian Rights Association include annual reports and pamphlets published by the association. The papers of James McLaughlin include his reports to the Commissioner of Indian Affairs on the Wanamaker expedition of 1913.

CITIZEN INDIANS

INTRODUCTION

GOING PUBLIC

Among the special events offered on the opening day of the 1893 World's
Columbian Exposition in Chicago was the appearance of Potawatomie chief
Simon Pokagon, who had been invited by fair organizers to deliver a special
Chicago Day address and to perform a ceremonial ringing of a replicated Liberty Bell. Pokagon, whose father had signed the 1832 treaty that ceded the site
of Chicago to the whites, used the occasion to address white America in ways
that must have surprised and perhaps dismayed those who had asked him to
participate. Rather than joining in the general celebration of American
progress and achievement, Pokagon took the opportunity to separate himself,
as a representative American Indian, from the underlying ideological prem-
ises of the fair:

> In behalf of my people, the American Indians, I hereby declare to you, the
> pale-faced race that has usurped our lands and homes, that we have no
> spirit to celebrate with you the great Columbian Fair now being held in
> this Chicago city, the wonder of the world. No; sooner would we hold the
> high joy day over the graves of our departed than to celebrate our own fu-
> neral, the discovery of America. And while . . . your hearts in admiration
> rejoice over the beauty and grandeur of this young republic and you say,
> "behold the wonders wrought by our children in this foreign land," do not
> forget that this success has been at the sacrifice of *our* homes and a once
> happy race.

Pokagon continued throughout his address to speak as the representative
of all displaced American Indians, concluding with an image of the Indian future meant to make clear to fairgoers the dark underside of Chicago's exuberant celebration of American progress: "And so we stand as upon the seashore,
chained hand and foot, while the incoming tide of the great ocean of civilization rises slowly but surely to overwhelm us. . . ."[1] This prognostication led at
least one apparently unfazed listener to hear in the speech not a plainspoken
rebuke to Pokagon's white audience for the rapaciousness of their history but
only the "resigned" valedictory of the "chief of a vanishing tribe and race."[2]

The appearance of Pokagon, a "real" Indian chief with strong connections to the history of Chicago, seemed designed primarily as a kind of curiosity, an added draw for those who might attend the spectacle of opening day at the fair. The major focus of the fair's planners was on the potential of its exhibitions and performances to educate fairgoers and, simultaneously, to celebrate American cultural and scientific achievements. Indian people and their histories played a significant role in these aspects of the fair as well; among the displays designed to contribute to the grand educational mission in Chicago were three Indian exhibits: an ethnographic display of objects sent by the Smithsonian Institution and two "live" exhibitions. One of the "live" exhibits, organized by Frederick Ward Putnam, director of Harvard's Peabody Museum of Archaeology and Ethnology, consisted of a series of replicated Indian villages; the other was an Indian school exhibit, including a model school, organized by Thomas Jefferson Morgan, the Commissioner of Indian Affairs. In Putnam's village exhibit, Indians from various tribes were established in replicas of traditional dwellings and given "typical" tasks to do; visitors to the fair were able to wander among these replicated villages and observe "traditional" Indian life at first hand. Morgan's model schoolhouse was occupied by delegations of Indian students from several Bureau of Indian Affairs (BIA) schools who demonstrated the "civilized" accomplishments—reading, writing, the performance of skilled manual labor—that had been made possible by their education at the hands of the BIA. The program of the Chicago fair also included regular performances of Buffalo Bill's Wild West Show, with a large cast of hired Indian participants, who enacted scenes from frontier history—buffalo hunts, Indian attacks—culminating in the grand finale, Custer's heroic "last stand."[3]

When Henry Adams attended the Chicago fair, in the course of a search for answers to his questions about the direction of American history, he was struck by the immensity of the fair and the scale of its grand ambitions, reflected in the sheer number and variety of exhibits designed to inform the public: "Education ran riot at Chicago," he wrote. Adams found himself dizzied by the seeming chaos of "vague and ill-defined and unrelated thoughts and half-thoughts and experimental outcries" making up the educational "riot" that characterized the fair for him. His response to the confusion and disorder was to try to sort it all out by posing the right questions:

Chicago asked in 1893 for the first time the question whether the American people knew where they were driving. Adams answered, for one, that he did not know, but would try to find out. On reflecting sufficiently deeply, . . . he decided that the American people probably knew no more than he did; but that they might still be driving or drifting unconsciously to some point in thought . . . and that, possibly, if relations enough could be observed, this point might be fixed. Chicago was the first expression of American thought as a unity; one must start there.[4]

While Adams did not include any of the Indian exhibits and performances in his meditations on the meaning of the fair, his response to the exposition as a whole—his questions about whether the mass of seemingly random exhibits actually could be seen to constitute a unified vision of the orderly movement of American experience toward some fixed point—applies as well to the varying ways that Indians were represented at the fair.

The very fact of the Indians' presence as part of a series of demonstrations, all carefully planned and orchestrated by white scientists, entrepreneurs, educators, promoters, and government officials, suggests the extent to which Indian people were, by 1893, being positioned within various, and often widely divergent, discourses of American progress. There was no *single* Indian exhibit at the Chicago fair, no *single* representation of Indianness. Instead, the different representations of Indian life, including Pokagon's prognosis for the future, offered fairgoers several ways of locating Indian people in relation to the political and cultural centers of American civilization, emblematized by the "White City" that was the architectural center of the fair: as the extinct bequeathers of curious artifacts; as themselves living artifacts of largely ethnographic interest; as mythologized antagonists in the frontier struggle for control of the country, now definitively concluded (as Frederick Jackson Turner famously declared during the course of this fair); as the tragic remnants of a vanishing race; and as more or less docile trainees in white America's grand benevolent project of uplift and civilization. These representations clearly did not fit together comfortably or coherently; Morgan's school exhibit was, in fact, specifically designed to *contrast* as much as possible with both the ethnographic exhibits and the Wild West Show. To consider the very heterogeneity of these representations of Indians in Chicago in 1893 is one useful way to begin to understand both the complexity of the issues that had been collapsed into the "Indian problem" in turn-of-the-century America and the multiple efforts, on the part of non-Natives, to define the place of the Indian within the material and ideological spaces of America.

The Indians on display at Chicago in 1893 might have been curiosities, but they were definitely not anomalies. Buffalo Bill's show had first opened in 1883, with Indian performers, and was immediately followed by a number of other, less famous Wild West shows. The 1876 Philadelphia Centennial Exposition had included its own displays of Indian life; Indian people had been occasional participants in local historical and civic pageants since the beginnings of the American pageant vogue in the early 1880s; and individual Indians, such as Sarah Winnemucca, Susette La Flesche, and Pauline Johnson, had taken to the lecture-reading circuit before 1893, often performing or lecturing in full tribal regalia.[5] In fact, instances of what one critic has called "red-white cultural interaction of the performer-audience type" can be traced back at least to the early years of the nineteenth century.[6] For the purposes of this study, however, the Chicago exposition offers a useful starting point to examine the proliferation of Indian performances that increased in number and kind after 1893 and continued well into the twentieth century.

The staged exhibitions, of which Chicago provided multiple examples in 1893, can seem entirely manipulative and demeaning to the Indian participants when viewed from a twenty-first century perspective; they may seem somewhat less so, however, if we recognize that they were not only exhibitions *of* Indians; they were also performances *by* Indians—forms of address to white Americans who were ill equipped to recognize Indianness as anything but a performative role. Significantly, these proliferating performances allowed Indian people to embody roles that before had been largely discursively constructed, and in embodying them to alter them. That pattern of embodied performance is discernible, I will argue in the chapters that follow, in the multiple forms of address that Indian people used to reach white audiences, including the address of Indian intellectuals to white elites.

Philip Deloria has commented on the performative practices adopted by some Indian intellectuals and activists in this period—his two major examples are Charles Eastman and Arthur C. Parker—who were willing to "don a literary headdress," evoking and miming white constructions of Indianness in order to reconstruct them for their own purposes. Deloria acknowledges the pedagogical impulse behind these performances, but he also finds them problematic and troubling. "Although they might alter Indian stereotypes," he notes, "native people playing Indian might also reaffirm them for a stubborn white audience, making Indianness an even more powerful construct and creating a circular, reinforcing catch-22 of meaning that would prove difficult to circumvent."[7] Deloria's discomfort is certainly understandable. At the same time, however, if engaging in forms of performance was seen by these earlier intellectuals as a political necessity, then examining the nature of Indian performance in its historical context is, for contemporary intellectuals, a scholarly necessity and perhaps a means of moving beyond discomfort.

Understanding the extent to which Indian people were performing their histories, their successes and failures, their political appeals, and their individual and collective identities before a largely white American public is, as this book will argue, important to understanding the nature and form of American Indian intellectual activity from the 1890s through at least the first two decades of the twentieth century. Indian people had to position themselves on the literal as well as the figurative stages of American public life, through strategic moves, as a way of both inserting their embodied selves into the national consciousness and establishing their claim to a place on those stages. Kathryn Shanley has written that "for Indians [today], developing a sense of belonging within mainstream institutions will be the prerequisite to redefining that space—actual and intellectual—as Native American."[8] Earlier Indian intellectuals were also, of necessity, concerned to redefine public and institutional spaces by first establishing their ability, and their right, to inhabit those spaces alongside other Americans.

Robert Allen Warrior argued in 1992 that "American Indian intellectual production from [the twentieth] century needs to be read with a critical eye toward both the historical circumstances from which it emerges and the political associations of its producers." Warrior followed through on his own challenge in his 1995 book, *Tribal Secrets,* in which he used the examples of Vine Deloria Jr. and John Joseph Mathews to analyze "the ways American Indian intellectuals write about and speak to each other about the role of intellectual work in the social, political, economic, cultural, and spiritual struggle for an American Indian future." Understanding writers like Deloria and Mathews, Warrior argued, requires understanding "how much the work they produced was guided by the political landscape they inhabited."[9] Warrior's insistence on the importance of locating Native writers and intellectuals within the larger political and social history of the United States constitutes one perspective on the question of how best to contextualize Native productions—how to define and demarcate the *traditions* within which the significance of those productions is most apparent. Warrior's turn to a national, historically specific context is not, of course, the only option. An alternative perspective is represented in the criticism of Elizabeth Cook-Lynn and Craig Womack, both of whom focus on Native literature and for both of whom the "Americanizing" of Native literary productions implies a dangerous weakening of the specific and local political aims of Native writing. Cook-Lynn has urged scholars of American Indian literature to "work toward a new set of principles that recognizes the tribally specific literary traditions by which we have always judged the imagination."[10] Womack takes a similar position, arguing that "Native literature, and the criticism that surrounds it, needs to see more attention devoted to tribally specific concerns." Consequently, Womack proposes a critical methodology that, among other things, "roots [Native] literature in land and culture. This criticism emphasizes unique Native worldviews and political realities, searches for differences as often as similarities, and attempts to find Native literature's place in Indian country, rather than Native literature's place in the canon."[11]

My purpose here is not to argue for the superiority of one position over the other, or even to set the two positions in opposition to each other, since I don't believe they are oppositional. For one thing, Cook-Lynn and Womack are specifically concerned with the ways of reading and writing about Native literatures, while Warrior's reference is to a broader and less well-defined range of productions, some of them coming from individuals who might not define themselves primarily as writers. Although he focuses on a later generation of Native intellectuals than the ones I am considering in this book, Warrior's perspective is more immediately relevant to my own concerns here, and my analysis is therefore more deeply indebted to his work, since I wish to locate turn-of-the-century Indian intellectuals within both a pan-Indian (rather than tribally specific) context and a national context. I wish, that is, to view them as both Indian intellectuals and American intellectuals—and to spell out as clearly as possible the significant problems they faced as a result of inhabiting both positions.

There are many ways in which the term *Indian intellectual* might be applied or understood. At one end of a spectrum of meanings, the term might apply very broadly to the many organic intellectuals who have always provided various kinds of leadership, often at the local level. At the other end of the spectrum the term may convey a much more specialized meaning, as it does in Margot Liberty's *American Indian Intellectuals*, which considers only Native contributions to the field of ethnography. In my own use of the term in this book, which focuses on the late nineteenth century and the early years of the twentieth, I refer specifically to those individuals who were concerned with pan-Indian issues, particularly with the host of issues and problems—both practical and theoretical—arising from the wardship status of Indians, and who addressed them in a public way, especially through writing. Within this fairly limited range, I focus primarily on the public nature of the intellectual work of these individuals, on their engagements with an audience that was likely to find Indians in general exotic and to perceive the idea of the Indian intellectual as oxymoronic.

My effort therefore is to situate the political positions of these intellectuals within the context of the Progressive politics of the period, especially the politics of race and reform, and at the same time to consider the ways in which the *productions* of Indian intellectuals were shaped by trends in both elite and popular culture during the period. Most especially, I wish to argue that Indian intellectuals were, to a large extent, responding to the American public's persistence in placing Indian people, individually and collectively, in performative roles. Rather than always refusing those roles, Indian intellectuals often adopted and sometimes co-opted them, working to take the control of performance away from the white managers, and in the process tacitly acknowledging that the best way to gain the attention of the people who had power over Indian lives was through carefully orchestrated performances.

In the preface to his 1928 book *My People the Sioux,* Luther Standing Bear described the volume as "a message to the white race; to bring my people before their eyes in a true and authentic manner." In a book published five years later, *Land of the Spotted Eagle,* Standing Bear began with a quite different sense of the capacity of a white audience to understand Native authenticity, noting this time that "the inner life of the Indian is, of course, a closed book to the white man." At the end of that book, Standing Bear reiterated his conviction that "the white man does not understand the Indian for the reason that he does not understand America."[12] Standing Bear's language points to the difficulty faced by any Native person (including those who came before him) who addressed Indian issues in a public way. Standing Bear knew that the Native "message" needed to be heard by a white audience that had been given too much of what he considered the untrue and the inauthentic; at the same time, he recognized that the white audience was incapable of fully understanding Native ideologies, individual Indian subjectivities, or the centrality of Indian histories and cultures to the formation of the country. The white audience, as Standing Bear perceived it, understood only its own creation, the figure that Gerald Vizenor has called the *indian*—a simulation, in Vizenor's terms, that functions only as a sign of the absence of the real Native.[13] Standing Bear's statements about the limitations of the white audience frame and condition his text; this time, the "message" to the white audience includes a caution about the audience's rush to find the "authentic" Indian, in a text or an ideology, and a strong intimation that the Standing Bear of the text is, to some extent, a fabrication produced through the collaboration of Native writer and white reader.

As a result of this perceived gap between Native knowledge and white understanding, I would argue, the nature of the "message" offered to white audiences by Standing Bear and other Native writers, intellectuals, and activists of the period was, of necessity, performative. In approaching Native productions this way, I am indebted to Vizenor for his characterization of modern Indian cultural productions as working to "contravene the absence of the real with theatrical performances"; for Vizenor, these performances are another form of simulation, but one that is creative and oppositional, yielding a new body of tribal stories.[14] I am also indebted to James C. Scott for his notion of the "hidden transcript" that often underlies and motivates the self-representations of subordinate populations to inquiring others in positions of power. Scott argues that powerless groups often have "a self-interest in conspiring to reinforce hegemonic appearances"; their public behavior can thus take the form of a performance, presented to the members of a dominant group who are also performing the public roles required by their positions of mastery. It is in the interest of the subordinate group, according to Scott, "to produce a more or less credible performance" that will, "by its accomodationist tone, provide convincing evidence for the hegemony of dominant values, for the hegemony of dominant discourse." The visible public transcript functions in part to conceal the hidden transcript from those in power.[15] Scott's perspective on the performative function of the discourse of the disempowered can help us to better understand some of those Native statements and behaviors that have been seen at times as simply and unambiguously accomodationist, or even assimilationist, rather than as deliberate and nuanced means of negotiating with those in power.

For the period that is the focus of this book, a period that corresponds roughly with the years that have been characterized by historians (in increasingly contested ways) as the Progressive Era, the need for Native spokespersons to communicate with white audiences, especially those white elites with access to forms of political power, was pressing and acute. By the end of the nineteenth century, American Indians had come under scrutiny from a number of sources, including missionaries and lay reformers, producers of popular media, the rapidly professionalizing cadre of sociologists, ethnologists, and other social scientists, and, especially, government officials, both elected and appointed. The creation of the reservation system and the subsequent attempt to dissolve the reservations through the forced imposition of land allotments, the establishment of the system of boarding schools for Indian children, the abrogation of the treaty process, the admission of ten western states to the union between 1889 and 1912, and the judicial system's repeated denial of birthright citizenship to American Indians had placed the majority of Indian people in the position of legal wards of the federal government with very few means of influencing or even understanding the limitations and controls placed on their lives, much less changing them.[16] As Harvard law professor James B. Thayer noted in 1891, "He who tries to fix and express [the Indians'] legal status finds very soon that he is dealing chiefly with their political condition, so little of any legal status at all have Indians."[17] The combination of social and legal controls on the ability of Indian people to speak and act for themselves created a crisis of enormous proportions, a very real threat to the ability of Indian people to survive the pressures being brought to bear on them. The political and cultural manipulations of Indian people made increasingly necessary a public articulation of Indian perspectives and responses—that is, the creation of an Indian public opinion—as well as an Indian influence on the formation of state and federal policies.

It was within this context that what became the most important pan-Indian organization of the period, the Society of American Indians (SAI), was formed early in 1911. Six Indian representatives, meeting on April 3 in Columbus, Ohio, at the invitation of Fayette McKenzie, a white professor of economics and sociology at Ohio State University, constituted themselves as the executive committee of an organization they first considered calling the "Progressive Indian Association." (The six were Laura Cornelius [Kellogg], Oneida; Charles E. Dagenett, Peoria; Charles Eastman, Santee Sioux; Carlos Montezuma, Yavapai; Thomas L. Sloan, Omaha; and Henry Standing Bear, Lakota Sioux.) By early July of that year, the executive committee had sent a letter, issued on its own letterhead, to a list of potential members of the new organization. The letter asked, rhetorically, whether the recipient was content that the American Indian should continue to be "the creature of outside forces," and then supplied its own answer:

No! We earnestly believe the time has come when the American Indian should take the initiative in the struggle for his race betterment, and to answer in his own way some of the vital questions that confront him. . . . .
A great many problems have arisen out of the question of race adaptation

to new conditions. Mistaken work will continue unless the Indian expresses himself, for no one knows the heart of the Indian as the Indian himself. An organization that shall voice the best judgment of the Indian people, and that shall command the attention of the United States, has become a vital necessity. In no other way can we so effectively mould public opinion and bring about conditions for the good of the Indian race.[18]

There were many "outside forces" at work on Indian affairs by 1911, many non-Indian voices contributing to the discussions of Indian reform. At least twelve white organizations dedicated to Indian uplift were active by that date, the most important and visible of which were the Indian Rights Association, the Women's National Indian Association, and the Lake Mohonk Conference of Friends of the Indian.[19] In constituting their own reform organization with an Indian membership, the founders of the Society of American Indians were simultaneously joining and contesting the confident momentum of the swelling number of progressive reform groups that were focusing their attention on specific social problems, including the "Indian problem."

The energy with which turn-of-the-century American reformers set about improving the conditions of the country by healing its social ills was palpable and infectious. The journal *World's Work* dedicated its entire issue of July 1904 to a celebration of the encouraging effects of "uplift" it observed in practically every aspect of American life. The journal found "cheerful significance" in the fact that "our people are making remarkable social and intellectual and moral progress." The interested observer might "turn where he will—outside the slums and the little political rings—and he will find wholesome folk everywhere in the United States, living frankly, working cheerfully, full of ambition, lifting the level of life higher."[20] As Columbia University historian James Harvey Robinson put it only a bit less effusively in 1912: "Society is to-day engaged in a tremendous and unprecedented effort to better itself in manifold ways. Never has our knowledge of the world and of man been so great as it now is; never before has there been so much general good will and so much intelligent social activity as now prevails."[21] While there may have been a shared enthusiasm about social change and improvement, however, both the objects of progressive reform and the theoretical formulations of the reformers varied widely—so much so that recent historians have tended to concur that "progressivism as an ideology is nowhere to be found" and that the reform movements of the period represented "shifting, ideologically fluid, issue-based coalitions, all competing for the reshaping of American society."[22]

Still, historians agree that these reformers constituted, in general, a fairly homogeneous group: they were primarily white, middle-class Protestants (largely eastern), whose reformist ethos combined a vaguely Christian impulse toward charity with a belief, encouraged by a new confidence in the emerging social sciences, in the ability of social and cultural institutions, rightly constituted, to shape even the most "degraded" individuals into productive citizens. To take part in this reshaping process was to confirm one's confidence in the ultimate triumph of America's particular form of civil religion. Herbert Croly, one of the most prominent and articulate theorists of progressive social thought, wrote in 1909 that a complete faith "in the process of individual and social improvement" was "the deepest and most influential of American traditions. The better American has continually been seeking to 'uplift' himself, his neighbors, and his compatriots."[23] The work of uplift— whether pursued through primary schools, temperance societies, settlement houses, labor organizations, Christian missions, or manual training programs—produced and fostered a discourse shared among the reformers, one that named progress, social evolution, Christianity, civilization, and citizenship as the uncontested goals of liberal democracy in America.

The members of the Society of American Indians, in naming the uplift of Indian people as one of its goals, thus joined a discursive enterprise that was already working at full steam by 1911. In their original public statements, the SAI affirmed, even more overtly than most of the other reform groups, their confidence that the real work of uplift would be accomplished by "the natural laws of social evolution"; the specific task of the reformers was simply to remove the obstacles that stood in the way of the Indian's natural "advancement" in "enlightenment."[24] The SAI differed radically from the other groups dedicated to Indian reform, however, in their insistence, underscored by their policy of admitting only Indians to full membership (whites were invited to become associate members), that Indian people themselves were the ones best able to address, and resolve, the "Indian question." Their work, as well as their description of it, was a direct response to the paternalistic pronouncements of white reformers, whose rhetoric so often reduced all Indians to positions of either heedless self-destruction or helpless supplication. The statements of the Friends of the Indian, which met annually at Lake Mohonk, New York, to determine what to do about the Indians, are, for example, suffused with a typically self-congratulatory paternalism. The Friends proclaimed their determination to "make something out of [the Indian]" through their own good efforts, to effect the Indian's "redemption from heathenism and ignorance, his transformation from the condition of a savage nomad to that of an industrious American citizen." To transform the Indian was, as the Friends saw it, both the right and the duty of enlightened whites:

> With as much of kindness and patience as can find scope in general laws, we must break up the tribal mass, destroy the binding force of savage tribal custom, and bring families and individuals into the freer, fuller life where they shall be directly governed by our laws, and shall be in touch with all that is good in our life as a people.[25]

The Indian intellectuals of the SAI, in asserting their own agency, adopted and recirculated the established rhetoric, using it to revise their own positionality.[26] Their tactics inevitably call to mind the similar tactics of the American Negro Academy, founded in 1897, and one of its most prominent members, W. E. B. Du Bois. At its formation, the academy had announced its belief "that upon those of the race who have had the advantage of higher education and culture, rests the responsibility of taking concerted steps for the employment of these agencies to uplift the race to higher planes of thought and action." The organizer of the academy, Alexander Crummell, originally envisioned the process of uplift for African Americans as a matter of imitating the best of Anglo-Saxon culture. Du Bois quickly modified Crummell's frankly assimilationist position, emphasizing both the differences among races and the need for African Americans to define progress for themselves. In his now-famous address to the first meeting of the organization, Du Bois argued that "as a race we must strive by race organization, by race solidarity, by race unity to the realization of that broader humanity which freely recognizes differences in men, but sternly deprecates inequality in their opportunities of development."[27]

Both African Americans and Native Americans thus organized their own "uplift" organizations within a few years of each other, and articulated, largely in a received language, a broadly pluralist philosophy and a shared view that the responsibility for the uplift of a race belonged to the race. Although the two movements maintained a deliberate distance from each other, partly for reasons of "race solidarity" and partly for more complexly political reasons that I will address in chapter 2, their parallel beginnings help to illustrate how pervasive was the progressive reform ethos at the turn of the century, how widely shared were its basic theoretical precepts, how essential the leaders of both groups found it to establish both intellectual and administrative control over reform efforts that, in the hands of whites, largely elided the significant issue of race leadership, and how constrained all reformers were by a discourse that had become normative.[28]

The strategies of those involved in the two uplift movements were, in part, an attempt to bring the particulars of Indian and African American thought and experience into the larger American cultural arena, a space that was, by its nature, governed by assumptions taken to be universal. In his discussion of modern African American intellectuals, Ross Posnock notes that the early work of Du Bois was necessarily devoted to "creating a public sphere in which to be heard." According to Posnock, the logical way of proceeding for Du Bois, as a black man who needed to focus the attention of white elites on the needs of black people, was to maintain in his public statements "a dialectic between (unraced) universal and (raced) particular."[29] Posnock's formulation of Du Bois's public position offers a specific application of Edward Said's more general definition of the intellectual as one whose work illustrates "the interaction between universality and the local, the subjective, the here and now." In Said's terms, the intellectual is one who is acutely conscious of the need to articulate the continuities between the universal and the local and is capable of making such an articulation in a compelling way: "For the intellectual the task, I believe, is explicitly to universalize the crisis, to give greater human scope to what a particular race or nation suffered, to associate that experience with the sufferings of others."[30] My understanding of the role that Native intellectuals envisioned for themselves around the turn of the century is consistent with (and indebted to) the ways in which Said and Posnock describe the impulse and the method of the intellectual. The challenge for Native intellectuals, a dauntingly difficult challenge, was to define and represent the particularities of Native experience in ways that made them congenial with contemporary assumptions about universal values—that is, to articulate a specifically Native perspective on a set of universal principles to which Native people themselves could subscribe.

One of the most vocal and prolific advocates for Native rights in the period was Arthur C. Parker, scion of a distinguished Seneca family, active SAI member and editor of its *Quarterly Journal,* and for many years an archeologist with the State Museum of New York. In 1912, Parker published an article in the *Southern Workman* entitled "Progress for the Indian," in which he took up the major arguments about Indian citizenship then in circulation (which I discuss in chapter 2), all of which he characterized as extremist, discarding them in favor of a more moderate middle position. It would be politically and economically suicidal, Parker argued, for Indian people to follow too closely the advice of those who urged them to protect their cultural identity by refusing, on principle, to adjust their thinking or their traditional lifeways in response to the powerful hegemonies in place in the United States. On the other hand, it would be culturally suicidal for Indians to accept uncritically the argument that they must begin to think, act, and look like white people as completely as possible—and as quickly as possible. Parker urged instead a philosophy of "adjustment" to "modern conditions" that would allow Indian people to remain Indian, and to maintain a racial pride, while making the necessary provisions for their own physical and material well-being.

The essence of Parker's argument was that the Indian needed to cultivate both his Indianness and his humanity—his local and his cosmopolitan identities—not just for the purpose of making Indian people acceptable to white elites as potential citizens but also for the sheer sake of survival. Significantly, Parker's article said nothing about Indian rights and a great deal about the ability of Indian people to adjust to a set of imposed conditions. The Indian, he wrote, "will be preyed upon, be robbed and shifted about if he still persists in clinging to his own methods to the exclusion of all others. This will not be because he is an Indian but because civilization in its present phase is competitive and predatory." Parker thus acknowledged, through the terms of his own argument, that the survival of a generalized Indian identity as well as of individual Indian persons depended on the willingness and ability of Indians to perform their public roles on a universal stage according to a script they did not write themselves. Similarly, in cautiously staking out a middle ground, constructed by modifying and "adjusting" the more extreme arguments already in place, Parker's article acknowledged that Indian spokespersons could find entry into the conversation about their own futures only through a set of terms and conditions that had already been set.[31]

In many ways, the effort of Native Progressive Era intellectuals to insert Indian history and local Indian issues into a universal framework anticipated the kind of questions scholars of American Indian histories and cultures are still asking about the American public's resistance to taking American Indian intellectualism seriously. As Elizabeth Cook-Lynn has put it, "It is as though the American Indian has no intellectual voice with which to enter into America's important dialogues. The American Indian is not asked what he thinks we should do about Bosnia or Iraq. He is not asked to participate in Charlie Rose's interview program about books or politics or history." The work of the Indian progressives also anticipates the effort of some recent scholars (including Vizenor and Warrior) to broaden the categories of description and analysis commonly used in academic studies of the American Indian past. Melissa L. Meyer and Kerwin Lee Klein have questioned, for example, why so much recent scholarship on Native America has been set aside in the specially marked category of ethnohistory: "Why call the history of American Indians 'ethno-history' at all? Why not just 'history'?" Meyer and Klein argue that the nomenclature is an ill-disguised form of racial coding: " 'ethno-' history is red, 'social' history is black or white." Their call, like the call of the earlier intellectuals, is for a perspective on Native history that is more "cosmopolitan."[32]

These continuing, contemporary efforts to desegregate Native and white intellectual perspectives and give more public space to the Native perspective are clear reminders that the efforts of the SAI generation to address the problem of Indian exclusion from American public debates on social and political issues, especially on Indian issues, by no means solved that problem. The nature and the intransigency of the obstacles they faced became clearer to the members of that generation as they observed the results of their efforts. The enthusiasm with which the Native intellectuals prepared to enter the public debates was tempered in time by their experience of the entrenched paternalism of white elites, who refused to acknowledge the legitimacy of intellectual traditions other than their own, even when they were represented by individuals who could speak the same progressive, developmental language of reform as did the whites. The optimism expressed by Arthur Parker about the possibilities for Indian intellectuals to enter the debates *as* Indians, as long as they were canny about what the non-Indian public would demand of them, eventually flagged in the face of the federal government's continued refusal to grant Indian people—precisely *because* they were Indian people—a share in the rights and privileges of citizens. Intellectuals such as Parker also came to realize that maintaining Said's kind of interaction between the local and the universal or cosmopolitan in their roles as spokespersons was much more difficult to accomplish in fact than it was to endorse in theory. The problem for the Native intellectual was compounded by the sheer number and diversity of local situations and needs among the Indian population and by the urgency of those needs in many cases. No one person or organization could easily, perhaps even possibly, articulate a position that would provide a discursive map for all that Parker and the SAI hoped to accomplish: to engage with white elites on their terms and in their language; to "voice the best judgment of the Indian people"; to alter public opinion in ways that would work to "the good of the Indian race"; and, all the while, to represent, somehow, the many tribal groups and issue-oriented constituencies that made up that entity that over time seemed more and more fictitious, the "Indian race." By deliberately defining broad goals and focusing their rhetoric on universal ideals rather than local problems, the members of the SAI made it very difficult for the organization to find a way to channel its collective energy into the project of making specific changes.

In spite of these obstacles and in spite of what might seem in retrospect the overreaching of the SAI, it would be a serious misrepresentation to declare the organization a failure or to assume that the only reward for the activism of intellectuals in the period was frustration. As I argue at greater length in chapter 3, if some found their foray into national politics exhausting, others were energized and emboldened by the kind of intellectual ferment the SAI engendered as well as by the national publicity it accorded to its members and their concerns. Many moved on to other kinds of activity at the local or national level, taking with them the political lessons they had learned from their time in the SAI. In addition, the agendas and perspectives of the organization provided an important intellectual framework for some of the Native writers whose work was produced during the period, work that still needs to be read with an understanding of the issues with which the SAI wrestled as well as the political and cultural constraints that Native public intellectuals had to negotiate.

Those negotiations are the primary focus of this book. I wish to demonstrate, in particular, the ways in which Native intellectuals, in attempting to create a public, political space for themselves, deliberately adopted, manipulated, and transformed the means already available to them for addressing white audiences, particularly the means of performance. To that end, the chapters that follow examine the traditions of Native performance that conditioned the work of intellectuals and reformers; the variety of performative contexts within which Native intellectuals addressed white audiences; the racial theories that conditioned the discourse of Native intellectuals; the specific efforts of the Society of American Indians to wrest control of Indian performances out of the hands of managerial and paternalistic whites, especially through the dissemination of their own publications; and the productions of a few Native writers, whose work might best be understood as a performance based on a hidden transcript, the partial enactment of the contents of a closed book.

CHAPTER 1 A MIGHTY DRAMA
THE POLITICS OF PERFORMANCE

On February 6, 1904, the students at the primarily African American Hampton Institute in Virginia put on their annual commemoration of Indian Citizenship Day, timed to coincide with the anniversary of the signing of the General Allotment Act of 1887. The act (also known as the Dawes Act or Dawes Bill in acknowledgment of its sponsor, Senator Henry Dawes of Minnesota), had provided for the division of tribally held land—generally, reservation land—into individual parcels or allotments, to be distributed to enrolled members of each tribe under a twenty-five-year trust arrangement with the federal government. Allottees were not to be given legal title to their land until the expiration of the trust period. Under the original provisions of the act, which were still in effect in 1904, any Indian who accepted his or her allotment of land, even without the legal title to it, automatically became a U.S. citizen: hence the designation of the Dawes anniversary as the day for celebrating Indian citizenship.[1]

The allotment of Indians lands had been the pet project of many organizations dedicated to Indian reform, the Lake Mohonk Conference and the Indian Rights Association (IRA) primary among them, organizations that also supported the extension of government schools for Indian children. The two organizations had different motivations: the IRA saw land ownership and the conferral of citizenship as the surest means of protecting both Indian rights and some remnants of Indian land, while for the Lake Mohonkers the allotment of land and the education of children were twin pillars of the reformers' project of "civilizing" the Indian population as a first step in the process of full assimilation. Not surprisingly, the civilizing argument of the Mohonkers was reflected more clearly in the Citizenship Day celebrations, translating more easily as it did into the stuff of pageantry than the IRA's more practical concerns with legal and administrative matters.[2]

The observance of Indian Citizenship Day was mandated by the Commissioner of Indian Affairs, Thomas J. Morgan, in a set of instructions he sent to all superintendents of government-run Indian schools in December of 1889, his first year in the job. Commissioner Morgan was a former Baptist minister and professor of theology who had been a commander of African American troops in the Civil War. He was, in Frederick Hoxie's words, "captivated by the potential for moral uplift within the public schools and eager to focus their power on the job of 'civilizing' the Indian."[3] In addition to instructing the superintendents to fly the American flag at all times and to teach the students patriotic songs, Morgan specified that

> national holidays—Washington's birthday, Decoration Day, Fourth of July, Thanksgiving, and Christmas—should be observed with appropriate exercises in all Indian schools. It will also be well to observe the anniversary of the day upon which the "Dawes bill" for giving to Indians allotments of land in severalty became a law, viz, February 8, 1887, and to use that occasion to impress upon Indian youth the enlarged scope and opportunity given them by this law and the new obligations which it imposes.[4]

Although Hampton was a private school with a comparatively small contingent of Indian students among its mostly African American student body, it joined voluntarily in the observance of Indian Citizenship Day. (Hampton, in fact, had begun its observance even before Morgan sent his mandate to the government schools.) Hampton's magazine, the *Southern Workman,* boasted that at its celebrations "the whole school, and frequently visitors from Washington, the North, and the South, furnish a much interested audience. The observance of the day does much to increase the Indian youths' knowledge, and stimulate their appreciation, of the duties and privileges opening before them as American citizens." The passage of the Dawes Act, according to the *Southern Workman,* had been a "great event in Indian progress."

For the 1904 celebration of Citizenship Day, the Hampton chapel displayed the school motto, "Lifting As We Rise," along with pictures of Senator Dawes and the founder of the Hampton school, Gen. Samuel Chapman Armstrong, the son of missionaries to Hawaii and an active member of the Lake Mohonk Conference. As the Indian band played, the Indian students marched onto the platform en masse. The program for the event was extensive, including a reading of extracts from the Dawes Bill by an Indian student, a speech by another Indian student on "What the Dawes Bill Means to the Indian," a speech by an African American student on "Educational Growth of the Indian and the Negro," a choral presentation of "Indian melodies," a recitation from *Hiawatha,* and a rendering of the phrase "Lifting As We Rise" in seventeen Indian languages. These presentations were followed by three tableaux, performed by costumed Indian students, representing "The American Indian, A Host," "The Reservation Indian, A Ward," and "The Indian American, A Citizen." The exercises concluded with the singing of "My Country 'Tis of Thee," performed by a mixed group of Indian, African American, and white singers.[5] The program thus offered a combination of entertainment, dramatic spectacle, and instruction, all organized to reinforce a conception of uplift and racial progress that was both Hampton's raison d'être and the putative source of the allotment policy. The pageantry of the event also provided visual evidence, especially through the three tableaux, of the transformation of the Indians' status, from the original American Indians who were hosts to European settlers, through an intermediate stage of wardship and reservation dependence, and finally to the Indian Americans whose competency as citizens was evidenced by their very ability to perform convincingly, as disciplined orators, musicians, and actors, in the civic ritual of a commemorative, patriotic pageant.

Some version of the Hampton pageant must have taken place on many platforms around the country in that February, as there were at least 257 government Indian schools in operation by 1904. Ninety-one of these were reservation boarding schools, twenty-six were off-reservation boarding schools, and 140 were reservation day schools. The number of students in these schools approximated twenty-five thousand (these figures do not include the privately run Hampton or the forty-eight mission schools run by religious denominations).[6] Given Commissioner Morgan's instruction that all Indian schools under the jurisdiction of the federal government should commemorate Indian Citizenship Day, the month of February must have been the occasion for nearly 260 versions of the public performance at Hampton.

Although the Indian schools would have been the only ones to celebrate Indian Citizenship Day, they would have joined other American schools in marking national holidays—as Commissioner Morgan instructed them to do—with some kind of ritual or performance. These school observances drew on several practices that were already widespread in the public culture of the United States by 1904, including ritualized public affirmations of patriotism and national loyalty. The decade of the 1890s had seen the organization of a number of patriotic societies as well as a surge in public displays of patriotic and nationalistic fervor, partly in response to the dramatic increase in immigration to the country. The public schools responded to the intensification of "Americanist" sentiment with an increase in flag exercises and other displays of national allegiance. The school celebrations, including Hampton's, also reflected the increased interest in pageantry, especially historical pageantry, that characterized American public life in the late nineteenth and early twentieth centuries. As David Glassberg has demonstrated, although the pageantry of the early twentieth century was often used for the same purposes to which American pageantry had always been put, which included both popular entertainment and patriotic moralizing, the new, twentieth-century versions of pageantry added the element of reform, introduced through the influence of progressive movements in public recreation and the fine arts. The adoption of pageantry by progressive reformers meant, according to Glassberg, that the pageant became, within a relatively short time, "not only a new medium for patriotic, moral, and aesthetic education envisioned by genteel intellectuals, but also an instrument for the reconstruction of American society and culture using progressive ideals."[7] Among those who discovered the educational potential of pageantry in the early part of the century was W. E. B. Du Bois, whose "The People of Peoples and Their Gifts to Men" (later retitled "The Star of Ethiopia") was first staged in New York at the National Emancipation Exposition of 1913. Seeing his script performed before large, responsive audiences affirmed Du Bois's belief in the potential of pageantry as an important, accessible vehicle of education and uplift. "The Pageant is the thing," Du Bois concluded. "This is what the people want and long for. This is the gown and paraphernalia in which the message of education and reasonable race pride can deck itself."[8]

Because the costumed Indian fit so well into the stylized forms of historical representation for which pageantry was designed, the Indian became a thoroughly familiar figure in American pageantry of the period; most of the local historical pageants included at least some Indian scenes. Hampton's Citizenship Day production, however, differed from these local history pageants in two very significant ways: it represented the Indians as happily *joining* the march of American progressive civilization and participating in contemporary civic life, and it cast Indian students in the Indian roles. In local historical pageantry, the Indians were typically seen as receding into a mythic past to make way for the material realities of white progress, and the Indian roles were most often taken by white performers, frequently recruited from organizations that incorporated some aspects of Indian "lore," such as the Boy Scouts or the whites-only Improved Order of Red Men.[9] The St. Louis civic pageant of 1914, to take one example, used Indian figures (played by whites) in several scenes, beginning with the ancient Mound Builders and moving to a group of plains Indians, who were seen dancing, fighting with other tribes, and eventually reaching a peace agreement. A representative of the prehistoric

Mound Builders, designated as "The Prophet," mourned the disappearance of his people before the arrival of the white man, narrated the further decline of Indian civilization, and foretold the coming of a new white race:

Into the West our nations trooping slow,
And here our council places desolate.
The paleface rears in stone his mighty lodge,
And sets his town upon the crossing trails.

A group of Ojibwa performers from Minnesota had offered to take the Indian roles in the pageant, but—appropriately enough, given the pageant's focus on the replacement of Indian populations by white ones—the St. Louis Drama Association had declined the offer and chosen instead to use copper paint to turn local volunteers into pageant Indians.[10]

Some Indians did take part in the local history pageants, although their participation was more the exception than the rule. Students from the Carlisle Indian Industrial School, for example, played the roles of Indians in Philadelphia's Founders Week pageant in October 1908.[11] A few productions were even designed solely for Indian performers; among the most popular of these were the several dramatized versions of Longfellow's *Hiawatha*. As early as 1900, a Canadian entrepreneur, L. O. Armstrong, staged an outdoor performance of *Hiawatha* near the Garden River reserve in Ontario, in the Ojibwa language, using local Native actors. The play traveled to Chicago, New York, Philadelphia, Pittsburgh, and Detroit in 1903. In 1905 it went on a European tour; when the company ran out of funds and was stranded in London, the rights to the play were transferred to the Grand Rapids and Indiana Railway, which moved the production to a location near Petosky, Michigan. This *Hiawatha* continued to be performed each summer until 1914.[12] Armstrong also produced an Indian pageant for the Lake Champlain Tercentenary in 1909, again using Indian actors, this time from reservations in Quebec, Ontario, and New York. Hiawatha was once more the central figure in this pageant, although this time in a different incarnation. The program explained that the pageant depicted the "romantic wars" of the Iroquois and the "founding of their remarkable League by Hiawatha [as] told in Lighthall's recent romance 'The Master of Life' which Mr. Armstrong has used as the basis of the Pageant in leading us to the historic battle of Lake Champlain."[13] A group known as the Hiawatha Indian Company offered at least fifteen performances at midwestern Chautauquas during the 1912 season. The publicity for the group described them as "ten Ojibway Indians from Canada—part of the very band that originated the Hiawatha Play." Another version of the play, "Hiawatha: The Indian Passion Play," was presented in Middletown, Ohio. A 1913 souvenir program from that pageant noted that "each player is a full-blooded Indian, to whom the performance is as solemn as the Passion Play is to the peasant-actor of Oberammergau. The presentation may be classed as a Masque—the lines of the poem being declaimed or chanted while the players perform their parts, speaking and singing in their native tongue." The program also informed pageant-goers that a "four-reel photoplay" of the Hiawatha story was available for purchase. Jesse Cornplanter, the Seneca artist who worked with Arthur C. Parker and later with William F. Fenton in their ethnographic researches among the Seneca, traveled extensively with a Hiawatha pageant between 1912 and 1915. His group played venues in Alabama, Georgia, and Tennessee before ending up in Ohio. (Jesse's father, Edward, had earlier traveled as a performer in his own show, which was advertised as a "Double Show—Indian and Minstrel Concert.")[14]

The Hiawatha pageants were all designed to provide spectacular entertainment for large audiences; their outdoor settings allowed room for costumed Indian actors to dance, fight, run races, and even in some cases to make entrances and exits by canoe. They were therefore of a piece, conceptually if not ideologically, with the most popular, visible, and notorious of the staged Indian performances, the Wild West shows—a genre of performance that Charles Eastman described, approvingly, as "equestrian pageantry."[15] Buffalo Bill Cody's was the first major show of the kind—it opened in 1883—and it continued to be the most popular, although many smaller shows were soon organized to take advantage of the vogue created by Cody. (L. G. Moses's list of just the "larger and more successful" Wild West show organizations operating between 1898 and 1912 extends to twenty-five.[16]) Most of Cody's performers were recruited from Sioux reservations, and Cody took full advantage of the dramatic possibilities of recent Sioux history, especially the Sioux involvement in the battle of 1876 that resulted in the death of George Armstrong Custer. In 1885 Cody enlisted Sitting Bull, the fifty-one-year-old Hunkpapa Sioux leader, for his show, taking him on tour to more than forty cities in the United States and Canada in that year. Sitting Bull had toured the previous year with a small, eight-Indian show called "The Sitting Bull Combination" that had visited twenty-five cities. Although Sitting Bull toured for only one season with Buffalo Bill, his notoriety—based largely on the enticing but false rumor that he had killed Custer himself—was a major asset to Cody's enterprise.[17] In 1886, Cody staged his first indoor show, at Madison

Square Garden. Billed as the "The Drama of Civilization," the show ended with an enactment of the Custer fight, and from that point on, until the Cody show closed in 1913, a major battle scene provided the climactic moment for each staging.[18]

In his publicity for the show, Cody was careful to counter the charge that his productions were only spectacular entertainments, offering audiences none of the moral, patriotic, or aesthetic education more easily attributable to the historical pageants or the Hiawatha plays. Cody characterized his show as essentially a more dramatic form of pageantry, an enterprise meant primarily to educate audiences in the history of their country; if they were entertained at the same time, so much the better. The program for his 1895 tour called Cody a "progressive educator" and declared that the aim of the show was "to make the public acquainted with the manners and customs of the daily life of the dwellers in the far West of the United States, through the means of actual and realistic scenes from life." The audience was assured that "the performance, while in no wise partaking of the nature of a 'circus,' will be at once new, startling, and instructive." When Cody died, he was eulogized by a writer for the *Outlook* who called Cody's show "a university, a traveling course in the history and social life of the United States at one of its most interesting eras. Buffalo Bill helped to lay the foundations for the civilization of our modern West."[19]

At the time Sitting Bull visited Philadelphia on his original tour with The Sitting Bull Combination, the young Luther Standing Bear was living in the city, working in John Wanamaker's department store. Standing Bear had been a student at the Carlisle Indian School; when John Wanamaker asked the founder and director of the school, Richard Henry Pratt, to send him two Indian boys to work in his Philadelphia department store, Standing Bear was Pratt's first choice. For both Wanamaker and Pratt, the employment of a reservation boy who had been schooled at Carlisle was an opportunity to demonstrate to the public and to other Indian students the success of Pratt's methods of training the students for gainful employment and eventual assimilation; the demonstration would be especially effective if the boy was one of the "wild" Sioux. When Sitting Bull and his entourage appeared in Philadelphia, Standing Bear attended the show and was stunned to hear Sitting Bull introduced as the man who had killed Custer, a claim Standing Bear knew to be false. Sitting Bull then gave a speech, in Lakota, without an interpreter. What Sitting Bull spoke about, according to Standing Bear, was the end of his fighting days and his plans to visit Washington to shake the president's hand. The white man in charge of the show, however, gave a very different account, explaining to the audience that the speech was all about Custer and the battle of the Little Big Horn. In writing about his experiences years later, Standing Bear expressed the outrage he was too young to feel at the time:

> As I sit and think about that incident, I wonder who that crooked white man was, and what sort of Indian agent it could have been who would let these Indians leave the reservation without even an interpreter, giving them the idea they were going to Washington, and then cart them around to different Eastern cities to make money off them by advertising that Sitting Bull was the Indian who slew General Custer! Of course at that time I was too young to realize the seriousness of it all.[20]

Standing Bear's narrative acknowledges Sitting Bull's role as a show Indian who was exhibited as a curiosity and used to make a profit. The narrative is less forthright, however, about the way in which the young Standing Bear himself had, in the hands of Wanamaker and Pratt, become a show Indian of a different sort, sent out in this case to fulfill, in Standing Bear's words, "all the hopes of my school and race" by becoming a successful worker.[21] Pratt's Carlisle students were frequently presented to the public—after having been carefully prepared—as advertisements for the success of the Carlisle method. (The cornerstone of that method was the separation of Indian children from their families and their education in boarding schools far from the reservations.) Standing Bear notes, for example, that while he was at Carlisle, "Captain Pratt was always very proud to 'show us off' and let the white people see how we were progressing." Pratt ran summer camps for any of his students who were not placed in jobs over the vacation period. The camp children were prepared for display: "Many white people called at our camp, at Captain Pratt's invitation," Standing Bear recalled, "to see how we were getting along. They were quite surprised to see how we were acquiring the white man's ways."[22] Standing Bear also traveled to New York with the Carlisle brass band in May 1883 to play for the opening of the Brooklyn Bridge.

Pratt generally welcomed, even sought, such opportunities to display his Indian students as a way of touting the civilizing effects of his educational methods. In 1892, he took more than three hundred Carlisle students to New York and Chicago to march in Columbus Day parades. In New York, the students carried a banner reading "Into Civilization and Citizenship"; in Chicago, where the celebration anticipated the opening of the World's Columbian Exposition, the students marched in platoons, each representing some department of the school.[23] Pratt detested the Wild West shows, not only because they constructed and celebrated a version of the old, "wild" Indian life but also because, in his view, they degraded the Indian performers; he saw the restrained and disciplined performances of his Carlisle students as a corrective to the noisy paint-and-feather simulations of Indian warfare. With each appearance of the Carlisle students, he insisted, "the cause of Indian education and civilization and public confidence therein went forward at a rapid pace."[24]

Although this kind of public performance was an essential part of the Carlisle experience, students at other Indian schools, including Hampton, were also conscious of being used for display purposes, some expressing more discomfort in the role than did Luther Standing Bear. In 1880, Booker T. Washington, who was then in charge of the Indian students at Hampton, wrote a column for the school newspaper describing the female students' frustration at being constantly on show:

> There have been a great many excursionists here this summer and of course all of them had to see the Indians. At first the girls did not mind them very much; but they came in such bodies, crowded around them in such numbers and asked so many absurd questions that they soon got tired and would hide when they heard them coming.[25]

Daniel La France (Mohawk), writing about his experience at an unnamed school in the late 1890s, described himself as one of the "show Indians" of the school: "The reason why I and others like me were kept at the school was that we served as show scholars. . . . I was good for various show purposes. I could sing and play a musical instrument, and I wrote essays which were thought to be very good." At La France's school, according to his testimony, it was the display that mattered: "Boys who had been inmates of the school for eight years were shown to visitors as results of two years' tuition, and shoes and other articles bought in Philadelphia stores were hung up on the walls at public exhibition or concert and exhibited as the work of us boys."[26]

Luther Standing Bear continued his performing life after he left Carlisle. He joined Cody's Wild West Show in 1898 as an interpreter and performer, traveling to Europe with Cody and then helping to recruit other Sioux for a subsequent tour. Standing Bear's wife and child accompanied him on the 1898 tour, and a second child was born while the company was in Birmingham, England. At Cody's request, Standing Bear's wife and infant child (who was given the name Alexandra Birmingham Cody Standing Bear) were displayed as part of a sideshow; his young son, dressed in buckskin costume and wearing paint, collected money from customers who came to view the Indian woman and child. After he left Cody's show, Standing Bear joined another show appearing at the Hippodrome in New York—for which Standing Bear's brother Henry had recruited the Indian performers. Luther Standing Bear remained with the New York show for six months. He then stayed in New York after the other performers went home, appearing in theaters and sideshows and giving lectures.

Standing Bear does not address directly the argument of Pratt and others that the "show Indians" were being exploited and demeaned, but he does express his admiration for Cody and notes that being a performer gave him a chance to travel, to be independent, and to escape the demeaning life of the reservation Indian: "With all my education and travels, I discovered that as long as I was on the reservation I was only a helpless Indian, and was not considered any better than any of the uneducated Indians—that is, according to the views of the white agent in charge of the reservation."[27] His preference for the life of the show Indian over that of the at-home reservation Indian was apparently shared by many of his coevals; by 1924, the recruiting of Indian performers had become so intense that the Commissioner of Indian Affairs was led to remark that "if sanction were given to all the requests received for so-called Indian pageantry lasting several weeks, large numbers of the Indians would be on the road much of their time with little at home of any value when they returned."[28]

Many of the Wild West shows, including Cody's, were held in conjunction with fairs, circuses, and expositions, including the large international expositions. In addition to their appearance at the 1893 Chicago Columbian Exposition, where their show was seen by over two million people, Cody's troupe also performed at the Atlanta Cotton States and International Exposition in 1895, while other outfits provided the Wild West entertainment at the Trans-Mississippi and International Exposition in Omaha in 1898 and the Pan-American Exposition in Buffalo in 1901. At the Atlanta exposition, an Indian village was set up on the midway; many of the occupants of the village were Sioux who had been involved in the Ghost Dance movement and the subsequent conflicts with United States troops that had culminated in the Wounded Knee massacre, just five years earlier. (Among those on display were a woman and her child who were both identified as having been wounded by the gunfire at Wounded Knee.) The Omaha exposition included a procession of 150 Indians carrying "scalps"—actually bits of flesh and hair from a slaughtered steer—and a sham battle between Indians and whites organized by the Improved Order of Red Men, which involved over seven hundred Indian and white participants. The Omaha conflict, unlike Cody's grand finale, which had the Indians defeating Custer's soldiers, ended with the defeat of the Indians and their removal to a reservation by U.S. Army troops. (Richard Pratt was incensed to discover that a number of former Carlisle students had taken part, in Omaha, in what Pratt called "a Wild West Show of the most degenerate sort."[29]) The fair in Buffalo also offered sham battles, as well as an exhibition of living Indians, including Geronimo, probably the most famous show Indian of the time. Geronimo was again on exhibit at the Louisiana Purchase Exposition in St. Louis in 1904, along with two other well-known Indians, Chief Joseph and Quanah Parker. At the Panama-California Exposition held in San Diego in 1915–16, fairgoers were given the chance to dress in Indian costumes and dance something called the Indian Rag. They could also visit a Painted Desert exhibit, including several pueblos constructed for the occasion.[30]

As in the case of the Chicago exposition, most of these fairs also included, in addition to the spectacles and entertainments, very different Indian displays and performances that were more clearly calculated to contribute to the didactic and celebratory design of the fair as a whole. The Omaha fair, for example, included a fifty-acre "Indian Congress" offering exhibits of traditional houses, Indian dancing, and enactments of ceremonies. Perhaps the most elaborate of the Indian educational exhibits, and the one with the most egregiously ideological purpose, was mounted at the 1904 Louisiana Purchase Exposition. To prepare its readers for the Indian exhibits at the St. Louis fair, *World's Work,* in its May 1904 issue, carried an article by Charles M. Harvey entitled "The Last Race Rally of Indians." The opening of the article announced prophetically that "at the St. Louis Fair the American Indian will make a last spectacular rally as a distinct race." The article concluded with a more specific pronouncement about the implications of the St. Louis exhibits: "The Indian as an Indian is doomed by the law of the survival of the fittest. The Indian is being evolved into a civilized man. Under our eyes is being performed a mighty drama in the transformation of a race."[31] (Harvey was fond of sounding—quite cheerfully—the death knell for the Indians. In a 1906 article in the *Atlantic Monthly,* he declared that granting citizenship to the members of the Five Civilized Tribes of Indian Territory would close "the final chapter in the Indian's annals as a distinct race." Citizenship would provide an appropriate closure to the work begun with the allotting of tribal land: "That work has been grandly finished. . . . The epic of the American Indian has closed."[32]) The central feature of the St. Louis exhibits was, as it had been at Chicago in 1893, an Indian schoolhouse in which students of varying ages demonstrated their "civilized" skills. In St. Louis, however, the ideological work of the school was given a more theatrically symbolic treatment than it had been in Chicago. This time, the Indian school was part of a larger ethnological exhibit, labeled the "Congress of Races." The exhibit was situated on a hill, with the Indian school occupying the top of the hill; along the slope leading up to the school were arranged representatives of various "primitive" groups: Ainu from Japan, Patagonians, Pygmies, Cocopa Indians from Mexico.

The visual narrative of the exhibit confirmed the possibility of movement upward from savagery to civilization, through the agency of the white man's education. The organizer of the exhibit, the Smithsonian's W. J. McGee, explained that the arrangement of the Congress of Races "embodies the experience of the United States Indian Office, and especially of Indian education; and it is the aim to render it at once a practical illustration of the white man's burden and a witness to the normal course of human progress — which is from ignorance toward knowledge, and from helplessness toward competence." The indoor portion of the ethnological exhibit, McGee explained, relied on the evidence of relics to establish the earliest stages of human evolution.

> But the outdoor exhibit, beginning at the foot of a sloping hill, where the bearded men and the tattooed women of the Ainu sit outside their thatchwork huts and carve bits of wood into patterns, employing their toes as well as their hands, and ending with the Government Indian school, at the top of the hill, where Sioux and Arapaho and Oneida attend kindergarten, primary, and grammar classes, and build things so fitted to modern needs as farm-wagons — this exhibit tells two living stories. It presents the race narrative of odd peoples who mark time while the world advances, and of savages made, by American methods, into civilized workers.

The Indian school was surrounded by representatives of a number of American Indian tribes, all established in "typical" tribal dwellings. McGee had a supply of epithets ready at hand to describe his collection of tribal types:

> First comes the village of the Sioux . . . , people of magnificent physique and of minds amenable to instruction. The tough and hardy Apache come next, and then the gentle Pueblo folk, busy molding pottery. A Wichita

group, dwelling in grass huts, are next to the brilliantly clothed Pawnee braves, endlessly giving a war-dance to the sound of cacophonous drums in the faintly smoky interior of the commodious lodge. . . . The dance-loving Cheyennes come next, and then the Navajo, weaving their gorgeous blankets and cutting ornaments out of silver money. Then there are . . . the intelligent Chippewa quilt-workers, who match the Sioux for quickness in learning.

Each evening during the exposition, the United States Government Official World's Fair Indian Band, a thirty-five member group from the Chilocco Indian School in Oklahoma, played "The Star-Spangled Banner" outside the model school while uniformed students stood at attention and saluted. McGee found the entire ensemble, the visual representation of Harvey's "mighty drama" of transformation, successful in achieving its intended purpose—to show that "a race which cannot of itself make the necessary strides to civilization may be helped" and that part of the development of an already civilized people is "the growth of an altruism and a sense of justice that prescribe the giving of such help."[33]

Even after the decline of the Wild West shows and the Indian exhibitions at the large expositions, Indian performances and pageantry, on a generally smaller scale, continued to be popular. In 1923, to take just one example, Chicago hosted a three-day encampment of Indians of several tribes. After a welcome by the Daughters of the American Revolution and the Daughters of 1812, the Indians retired to a forest preserve and set up camp. The *Chicago Daily News* reported that here the "copper-colored visitors" put on their buckskins, feathers, and beaded moccasins to "present primitive life and customs in the tepee and around the council fire." The performances were facilitated by a group of one hundred Boy Scouts who acted as messengers and guides for the occasion.[34]

In addition to these more spectacular exhibitions, many individual Indians took to the stage to give performances or lectures, offering audiences a spectacle of a different sort—the educated, articulate Indian. Pauline Johnson, who was billed as the "Mohawk Princess," toured in Canada and the United States from 1892 until 1909, with one tour to England in 1894, performing her own poetry. Johnson wore a fringed buckskin dress for the Indian portion of her performance and an evening gown for the rest.[35] Luther Standing Bear lectured after leaving Cody's Wild West Show and before moving to California to become a film actor. Charles Eastman, who had a varied career as a physician, employee of the Bureau of Indian Affairs (or Indian Service, as the BIA was often referred to during this period), representative of the YMCA, and writer, spent many of the later years of his life on the lecture circuit. His availability as a lecturer was promoted in advertisements picturing Eastman in full Sioux regalia and promising that "Dr. Eastman will appear upon the platform, when especially invited to do so, in the full-dress costume of a Sioux chief, beautifully made in the old style of beaded, Indian-tanned deerskin, with war-bonnet of eagle feathers." The advertisements also promised that Eastman, in his lectures, would be "setting forth in a fashion as convincing as it is picturesque THE TRUTH about the much misunderstood red man." Although these promotions for Eastman's lectures are not dated, they appear to have been circulated about 1909; by this time, according to the promotional literature, Eastman had already appeared in "nearly a hundred different towns and cities in New England alone."[36] Eastman's daughter, Irene, also took to the platform, using the stage name "Taluta" and offering an evening of "American Indian Melodies by an American Indian Maiden."

One of the more curious Indian lecturers of the period was Joseph K. Griffis, who made his public appearances using the name "Tahan" or sometimes "Tahan the White Savage." Griffis, who published his autobiography in 1915, claimed to have been born in Texas, the son of an Osage mother and a peripatetic white mountain man and government scout known only as California Joe. When he was two years old, according to Griffis, his mother was killed in a Kiowa and Comanche raid; he was taken captive and raised to become a Kiowa warrior. His biography describes, in dramatic detail, his participation in a series of raids and battles and his capture by a group of soldiers who were part of Custer's command. He was then sent back to white relatives in Texas but soon ran away from them and rejoined the Kiowa. He eventually drifted east, was taken in by the Salvation Army and converted to Christianity, and became a Presbyterian minister and frequent lecturer on the Chautauqua circuit. His autobiography, *Tahan: Out of Savagery into Civilization,* includes a preface by Arthur C. Parker, who was at that point secretary-treasurer of the Society of American Indians and the editor of its journal. Parker's preface vouched for the authenticity of the life story, calling Griffis

a man who has passed through a series of transitions that have led him up from savagery, through the experiences of an Indian warrior, a medicine man, an outlaw, a scout, a deserter under sentence of death, a tramp, a Salvation Army captain, a successful evangelist and a clergyman, to the state of broad culture that fits him for his association and friendship with scientists, statesmen and leaders of world-thought. . . . I hope every sociologist, every ethnologist, every friend of man, every lover of the strangeness of real life, will read this life story of Tahan, for beyond the value of his tale, there is a potency in his message that is good for every man.[37]

As a "progressive Indian," an active advocate of Indian uplift and reform, Parker was willing and perhaps even eager to see in the life of Griffis an example of the ability of the individual to transcend environment and training and move in new directions of his own choosing—to accomplish, that is, a version of the progression "out of savagery and into civilization" proclaimed by the subtitle of the autobiography. Others who were not so invested in the pattern represented by Griffis's stories, however, were not so easily persuaded by them. In a 1930 issue of the *Chronicles of Oklahoma,* Dan W. Peery described his attempts to confirm the identity of Tahan and the veracity of his claims. Peery was not able either to refute or to confirm Griffis' story, but he was clearly less sanguine than Parker had been about its accuracy. Peery concluded his article by saying to his readers that "I will leave it to you as to whether J. K. Griffis is the real 'Tahan,' the Kiowa captive, or, if this be but a romantic story that Rev. J. K. Griffis employed to entertain the people of the East for so many years."[38]

Griffis entertained easterners by lecturing in Indian costume, including a full feathered headdress, booking his tours through a Lyceum bureau and then joining the Chautauqua circuit. (His lecture topics included "Things I Saw and Did as a Savage," "The Tragedy of the Red Race," and "Up from Savagery.") Pauline Johnson also spent the 1907 season on the Chautauqua circuit, traveling for part of the time with William Jennings Bryan. Among others making Chautauqua appearances between 1908 and 1917 were "Shungopavi," identified as a "full blood Moqui Indian, a descendant of the Cliff Dwellers," who offered audiences "an evening devoted to the history and legends of his race and native Indian Magic, which is most mystifying," and "Wa-Tah-Wa-So, Indian mezzo-soprano," described as a genuine "Penobscot princess" who "delineates the pure Indian songs, folk-tales and legends only." The Hiawatha Indian Company also toured the Chautauqua circuit, providing an afternoon program of tableaux of Indian life and an evening performance of *Hiawatha.* Chautauquas often featured Indian programs as part of their children's entertainments, which generally involved having the children "play Indian" by dressing in feathers and paint and dancing to homemade drums. Although the Chautauquas did not make a significant effort to recruit many Native performers, evidently to avoid the association of Chautauquas with Wild West shows, Arthur Parker was consulted, in 1916, by a Chautauqua booking agency looking for potential Indian lecturers. Among the names Parker sent were those of Charles Eastman and Gertrude Bonnin.[39]

Joseph Griffis and Arthur Parker corresponded in late 1911 and early 1912 about the importance of Griffis's public appearances. Parker encouraged Griffis to use the opportunity of his tours to stir up interest, especially among his white contacts, in the newly formed Society of American Indians. Admonishing Griffis that "we must be circumspect and move cautiously if we are to win confidence," Parker suggested that Griffis "put it up to the whites and to the Indians that it will be considered an honor to be a member of the Society of American Indians and a badge of aristocracy." He then offered Griffis a sketch of his own philosophy: "Manitou bless you in your work of Indianizing the white man. The Indian, no, does not need to be white washed or whitemanized. He needs an opportunity to develop along his own lines of individuality so far as these are consistent with modern environment. And remember we are not the bleached out devitalized enervated de-Indianized Indian or the new Indian but the same old Indian adjusted to modern environment." Griffis wrote back to Parker early in January 1912, expressing his agreement that those in the SAI needed to "boost and do our best just now."[40]

Griffis did include an endorsement of the SAI in his 1915 book, as well as a brief replication of the philosophy articulated by Parker: "The Indian," Griffis wrote, "needs the opportunity to develop himself according to the laws of evolution; he needs the chance to fit into the trend of modern progress; but he cannot have this opportunity while confined in a prison called a reservation." Griffis went on to describe the purpose of the SAI, however, in language that, while it might well have appealed to white readers of his book, would not have accorded exactly with the more careful formulations published by the SAI. The society, Griffis wrote, "recognizes the inevitable—the assimilation of the Red Man with the conquering Caucasian race, and its purpose is to break down every barrier in his progress toward civilization."[41] Terms like *assimilation* and *conquering* are ubiquitous in white statements about the "Indian question" in the period, but they are precisely the kinds of terms that Parker and others in the SAI wished—cautiously and with circumspection—to modify or even eliminate from the discourse, preferring language that avoided any implications of racial hierarchies or of forced and inevitable assimilation.

The various kinds of performances in which Indian people participated at the end of the nineteenth century and in the early years of the twentieth provided one of the few means of contact between Indians and the general public, especially in the East. Those performances tended to display Indians in one of two ways: as the remnant of a "vanishing race" that had once flourished in the West and had gone down to tragic and inevitable defeat at the hands of the more powerful whites, or as examples of the stunning transformation of former primitives—who had only murderous intentions toward whites—into assimilated sophisticates whose acquired social skills might allow them to pass for white or at least to pass *among* whites. (The subtitle of Griffis's book, *Out of Savagery into Civilization,* and the title of one of Charles Eastman's books, *From the Deep Woods to Civilization,* specifically emphasized the second of these aspects of Indian performance, as did the advertisements for Eastman's lectures. One of his fliers quoted the *Boston Post* as declaring: "If it were not for his bronzed features, one would take Dr. Eastman for the typical, hospitable New Englander."[42])

One of the most remarkably elaborate series of Indian performances of the period was designed to combine these two aspects of the Indian performance (vanishing and assimilating) in a new way, by providing the public with a view into the heart of the "mighty drama" that Charles M. Harvey had defined: the "primitive" Indian in the very process of transformation into the assimilated citizen. These performances were sponsored by Rodman Wanamaker, son of the founder of the Philadelphia department store empire (who had hired Luther Standing Bear when he was a Carlisle student), and engineered by his employee, Joseph Kossuth Dixon, a former Baptist minister who had joined what was then called the "education bureau" of the Wanamaker department stores. Their collaboration resulted in three well-publicized "expeditions" to Indian reservations around the country, a collection of thousands of still photographs and literally miles of film, several print publications, a number of public ceremonies, and considerable publicity for both Wanamaker and Dixon.

The collaboration began with Dixon's first trip to the West, in 1908, to the Crow Reservation in Montana. This trip, like the two subsequent ones, was funded by Wanamaker. Dixon's primary objective on the first trip was to take as many pictures of Indians as he could, for purposes that, Dixon insisted, were both educational and patriotic: "Mr. Rodman Wanamaker," he explained, "is a high priest of great ideas, and he conceived the patriotic and educational idea of perpetuating the memory of the North American Indian

1. Joseph Dixon's photograph of two unidentified Indians, dressed for the camera, examining a roll of exposed film. (Courtesy of the Prints and Photographs Division of the Library of Congress.)

and of preserving for history the record, in motion, and on the photographic plate, of the manners and customs of a vanishing race."[43] Dixon and his entourage—which included three photographers, one of them his son—camped on the Little Big Horn River and began taking pictures. In addition to fifteen hundred still negatives, Dixon also produced a film version of *Hiawatha,* with local Crow Indians playing all the (Iroquois) roles; Dixon subsequently used his photography as the basis for a lecture on *Hiawatha* that he delivered, according to his own account, 311 times in Wanamaker's auditoriums in Philadelphia and New York.[44] He also published a booklet, the *Wanamaker Primer on the North American Indian,* to accompany the lectures and the film. The booklet contains a selection of Dixon's photographs and a rather randomly pieced-together text that includes sections on "The Indian's Yesterday," "The Indian's Today," "The Indian's

Tomorrow," and "The Wanamaker Expedition," as well as a synoptic outline of *Hiawatha*.

The section on the expedition begins with Dixon's lengthy and effusive rationale for the project as a whole:

> Because the Indian is fast moving toward his last frontier; because the nations are looking at the sunset of a dying race; because the Indian was the first American; because of the abiding interest attached to the Red man's life and career, his manners and customs; because of the fact that he is a mystery and a puzzle; because men of letters and art have delved into the ethnology of the Indian; because the platforms of the Wanamaker Auditoriums in New York and Philadelphia have for their purpose the educational uplift and stimulus of the community; and because the rising generation needs to know more about the early history of our great country—an expedition was planned during last summer to study the North American Indian on his own ground, in his own home, and in a manner that would compel a true photographic, geographic, historic and ethnic record.[45]

Dixon emphasizes here, as he does in all of his published references to any of the three expeditions, the educational and philanthropic purpose behind Wanamaker's sponsorship and Dixon's productions.[46] This emphasis seems calculated to deflect the criticism—which was quickly directed at Wanamaker and Dixon from several quarters, including the Society of American Indians and the Indian Rights Association—that the real purpose of the project was to provide advertising for Wanamaker's stores. The *Primer* also emphasizes the idea that was to be the sentimental and oft-repeated theme of all of Dixon's Indian work for Wanamaker: the American Indians are a vanishing race. If the American public needed to be educated about the Indians, in Dixon's view, then most of what they needed to know was conveyed through the trajectory of the pathetic story of Longfellow's *Hiawatha*, a story confirming that "the day will soon dawn when the last real North American Indian will be folded in his blanket and laid amid the sighing branches of the pines upon some lonely and desolate hill crest, whose only dirge will be the liquid notes of the meadow-lark." Given this sad inevitability, according to Dixon, "Our only hope, if we wish to keep the Indian, is to carve a statue of him in stone or mould his figure in bronze."[47]

Dixon's seemingly gratuitous mention of a memorial statue was actually a calculated means of promoting a scheme that was to become closely associated with his expeditions. The possibility of a grand memorial to the

American Indian was first raised in public by Buffalo Bill, at a testimonial dinner given for him by Wanamaker in May 1909. Cody suggested New York Harbor as the site for the memorial, and Wanamaker (and Dixon) immediately seized on the idea. Dixon had just come back from his second expedition, on which he had returned to the Little Big Horn with his cameras, this time for the express purpose of staging what he called the "Last Great Indian Council," a performance designed to reinforce Dixon's proclamation that the "real" Indian was vanishing quickly; Indian life and thought needed to be recorded immediately, according to Dixon, by someone with the skill, sympathetic understanding, and organizational savvy of a Dixon—and the money of a Wanamaker. With help from the BIA and reservation agents, Dixon had assembled twenty-one older Indian men from eleven western tribes (seven of the men were Crow), designating them all by the title of "chief" or "head chief" and claiming, with a degree of hyperbole remarkable even for the blustering impresario, that they came from "nearly every Indian tribe in the United States." With the cameras rolling and interpreters present, Dixon prompted the men to talk about their childhoods and about the greatest events in their lives. Their speeches—as recorded by Dixon—were published in his 1913 book, *The Vanishing Race: The Last Great Indian Council.* The book also contains a preface by Rodman Wanamaker, many of Dixon's photographs, and a great deal of Dixon's extremely florid prose. Because the Indians he assembled were persuaded to "pull in twain the veil of [their] superstitious and unexplained reserve" and speak openly, Dixon claims, his book accomplishes what no one else had been able to do; it reveals "what the Indian thinks and how he feels." Therefore, "all future students and historians, all ethnological researches must turn to the pictures now made and the pages now written for the study of a great race." Having established himself as the ultimate authority on "the Indian," Dixon could make his pitch: "The original Americans *Deserve a Monument.* They have moved majestically down the pathway of the ages, but it culminates in the dead march of Saul."[48]

The gathering of tribal elders on the Little Big Horn was carefully orchestrated by Dixon, and his voice dominates and shapes the material in his book. Both the council and the book are dramatic performances staged for a white audience that is encouraged to respond appropriately to the "epic of sorrow" that Dixon records in his text and photographs. The hand of Dixon is not light. The final photograph in the book, for example, is of four riderless horses. The caption for the photograph is "The Empty Saddle," and the adjacent text vies with the photograph for bathetic overstatement: "Ninety millions, with suffused eyes, watch this vanishing remnant of a race, whose regnant majesty inspires at the very moment it succumbs to the iconoclasm of civilization. It is the imposing triumph of solitary grandeur sweeping beyond the reach of militant crimes, their muffled footfalls reaching beyond the margin of an echo."[49]

Interestingly, the speeches of the assembled Indians, as recorded (whether reliably or not is difficult to determine), are often at odds with Dixon's own effusions and pronouncements. The men speak of their age and the prospect of their deaths, and of significant changes in their lives, but they don't speak of themselves as part of a "vanishing race"; in fact, they are more inclined to speak of the futures of their children and grandchildren and, at times, of pressing practical matters requiring their attention. Most note their pleasure in meeting men from other tribes, some of whose names they already knew well, and they acknowledge that they are not likely to meet together again. But no one seems much inclined to *vanish,* and their speeches about practical matters often strike a discordant note in an otherwise lugubrious text. Several speak of reservations and allotments, of Christianity, or of the education of their children. The men mention such things as the problem of getting adequate money for leased land, their distaste for the new kinds of food they have been forced to eat, and the frustrating confinement of farming life on reservation land. A few speak of more serious personal losses. Runs-the-Enemy, a Teton Sioux, comments that he sent all of his seven children to boarding school at the insistence of government agents, and all seven died of consumption. White Horse, a Yankton Sioux, tells a similar story about sending his children to Hampton Institute; all of them returned home with consumption, and all of them died. Apparently, none of these matters were of much concern to the rhapsodizing Dixon.[50]

The parting speech of an Umatilla man whom Dixon calls Chief Tin-Tin-Meet-Sa is suggestive of the shape and the generally hospitable and complimentary tone of many of the recorded speeches:

My idea of this meeting is that we are doing a great thing. I am of old age and I feel strange to these people whom I have met here at this place for the first time. . . . The man who was sent here to do this work has been very kind to the Indians and is a fit man to do this kind of work. The work he is doing is one of the greatest works that has ever been done. The record made here will not perish. . . . I have no hard feelings toward any one in this camp, and I am only worrying about my hay at home.[51]

Running Bird, a Kiowa, speaks somewhat less formulaically:

I am sixty years old, and when I came to this ground it was ground I had never seen before in my life. I met the chiefs whom I had never seen before. I had heard of them but had not seen them. I was very glad to come here and see the old-time tepees, the kind of tepees our fathers used to live in. I grew up to manhood myself in this kind of a tepee, and I had good health. Now when they give us a house to live in I am not healthy at all. I am getting old now, and am getting up in years, and all I wish now at the present time is that my children shall grow up industrious and work, because they cannot get honour in the war as I used to get it—they can only get honour now by working hard. I can only teach my children that the way to get honour is to go to work and be good men and women. These impressions have been strengthened by this council. I shall go home and tell the other Indians and our agent about the council, for the meeting of the chiefs will always live in my memory.[52]

Undeterred by the incompatibility of these politely ceremonious speeches with his own determination to give the gathering a tragic finality, Dixon surrounds them with the elements of his requiem for the vanishing American Indian—and Dixon, of course, has the last word.

After the 1909 expedition, Dixon devoted much of his energy to promoting the plan for an Indian statue in New York Harbor. He appeared before a House of Representatives committee in 1911 to urge congressional support for the project, and as he worked to sell the plan, he also worked to enlarge it. His idea now included a vast museum, located in the base of the statue, that would house—among other things—his own photographs. The statue itself was to be a sixty-foot-tall bronze figure, facing out to sea, extending his hand in a gesture of welcome. One of the sources from which Dixon sought support for the project was the Improved Order of Red Men, a fraternal organization that incorporated its own highly romanticized version of Indian ceremonialism while specifically excluding Indian members.[53] The Red Men were an appropriate group for Dixon to enlist, given their shared conviction that Indians in general were a moribund group, useful primarily as a source of symbols and tropes that could be manipulated in the service of a particular kind of American patriotism. The official history of the Red Men makes clear their position:

When the Indian has disappeared forever from the hills and the valleys, the forest and the stream, then the paleface who occupies his wigwam, who

2. *Drawing of the proposed Memorial to the North American Indian planned for the Fort Wadsworth site. (Courtesy of the William Hammond Mathers Museum, Indiana University.)*

owns the land where once he trailed, will look upon the skins and scalps which long before were brought home from the hunt or from the warpath, will take down the totem by which the primitive Red Man distinguished his friend from his foe, and from them teach object-lessons of the history of his country, and of Freedom, Friendship, and Charity to the coming young American.[54]

For Dixon and the Improved Order of Red Men, the Indian memorial had a funereal significance; it bid farewell to Indian people and buried contemporary Indian issues under a blanket of sentimental discourse and tons of metal and stone.

Dixon lobbied for two years before the use of public land for the statue was authorized by Congress and a design for the memorial was produced. The official groundbreaking took place on Washington's Birthday, 1913, at Fort Wadsworth on Staten Island. The ceremonies on the occasion, which were well covered by the press and widely reported, gave Dixon an unparalleled opportunity to display his showmanship. Dixon had arranged for a group of Indian men to participate in the ceremony, many of them the same men who had been part of the 1909 "last council."[55] The *New York Times* identified the men as chiefs, "old men of the purest blood"; they were, according to the *Times,* "resplendent in the feathers and buckskin and beads of their tribal dress, and the paint gleamed from their high cheek bones." President Taft attended the ceremony and gave a brief, remarkably triumphalist speech, endorsing "this monument to the red man, recalling his noble qualities, of which he had many, and perpetuating the memory of the succession from the red to the white race in the ownership and control of this Western Hemisphere." Taft was then joined by one of the attending Indians, a Cheyenne named Wooden Leg, in performing the groundbreaking—Taft using a shovel and Wooden Leg using the bone of a buffalo. The group of Indians next joined in a choreographed raising of the American flag while the U.S. Army band played "the Indian requiem, the 'Vanishing Race,' composed by Dr. Irving J. Morgan." The culminating event of the ceremony was the public introduction of the new Indian-head nickels, a bagful of which were distributed on the spot by George Frederick Kunz, president of the American Scenic and Historical Preservation Society. The *Times* report on the ceremonies included the laconic observation that "if any of [the Indians] felt something of the irony of their invitation to the inauguration of their memorial as a race no gleam of such feeling showed in the shrewd old faces."[56]

Prior to the ceremony, according to the *Times,* the group of Indians took a short trip, in full regalia, on the Sixth Avenue train and "in their exuberance treated themselves at the station to a little dance. The effect of the war cries and the waving tomahawks was too much for the nerves of several women who chanced to be on the platform at the time and they retreated in panic." On the Monday following the Saturday ceremony, the group was taken on a tour of sites in New York, including the American Museum of Natural History and the Bronx Zoo, before heading off to Philadelphia to be entertained by Rodman Wanamaker.[57]

The most elaborate and extended Indian performance staged by Dixon took the form of yet another expedition, the longest of the three, which Dixon declared to be an "Expedition of Citizenship" and which he specifically linked to the Fort Wadsworth memorial. In a report he prepared for the Commissioner of Indian Affairs, Dixon set out the purpose of his third trip to Indian country: "These Red Men are to be harmonized, unified, uplifted, and are to have a share themselves in the great Memorial that is to stand, a lonely, lofty figure, where the sea will forever moan a dirge for a vanished race." Without explaining why the Indians might wish to memorialize their own passing, or how the contradictions inherent in the project of preparing a vanishing race for citizenship might be reconciled, Dixon declared that "the paramount idea" of the expedition was "to instil [*sic*] into the Indian mind an ideal of patriotism that would lead him to aspire to citizenship; for the Red Man needs ideals as well as the White Man."[58] The rhetoric that Dixon marshaled so clumsily in describing his exploits drew on both the popular trope of the vanishing Indian—the trope that the Wild West shows had worked so successfully in their extravaganzas—as well as the language of the civilizing white reformers who were addressing themselves to "the Indian question." In Dixon's hands, however, the two formulations stood only in confused relation to each other. Their purpose was simply to establish a lyrical discursive frame, with the widest possible appeal, for the staging of grand performances.

Having secured various official endorsements, Dixon set off on his third tour, in June 1913. This time he took with him three photographers (including his son Rollin), a stenographer, and Maj. James McLaughlin, a veteran inspector for the Interior Department, who had spent many years as agent at the Standing Rock (Sioux) Reservation in North Dakota. Dixon also took along phonograph recordings of brief speeches by President Woodrow Wilson, Secretary of Interior Franklin K. Lane, and acting Commissioner of Indian Affairs Franklin Abbott. The group spent six months visiting at least eighty-nine Indian reservations and covering more than twenty thousand miles.[59] The protocol for each reservation visit was essentially the same. The reservation agent, who had assembled as many of the local Indians as possible, offered a welcome and introductions. Dixon then played the recorded speeches, which included these remarks from President Wilson: "The Great White Father now calls you his 'Brothers,' not his 'Children.' Because you have shown in your education and in your settled ways of life, staunch, manly, worthy qualities of sound character, the nation is about to give you distinguished recognition through the erection of a monument in honor of the Indian people, in the Harbor of New York."[60] The flag that had been hoisted at Fort Wadsworth, and which was carried from one reservation to the next by Dixon, was then raised by selected Indian attendees. Dixon instructed the Indians on the meaning of the flag and the ceremony and presented the group with their own flag, which was also hoisted. Dixon's speeches were characteristically patronizing and oblique. At Standing Rock, for example, Dixon dedicated the flag "to the North American Indian. I dedicate the Stars and Stripes, the Red, White, and Blue, to justice and fair play to the Indian. And I dedicate you Indians to loyalty to this flag, and I pray you to translate your loyalty into a faithful following of the guidance of your superintendent, into better homes and better farms and better schools, and I pray you to be loyal to every fold of it." At Neah Bay, Washington, Dixon admonished the assembled Indians to "translate your patriotism into smiles. Go up and down the walks of life as though the sun were shining in your soul as it tries to shine through those clouds. . . . Be the happiest Indians in the United States." To conclude each ceremony, all of the Indians present were asked to sign a "declaration of allegiance" to the United States.[61]

Dixon declared in his report following the tour that he had been responsible for giving "to every tribe an American flag, which the Indians have raised, for the first time, over their homes, and which they now cherish as their greatest possession." (Others were quick to point out that there were American flags already flying on most reservations well before Dixon arrived, but his rhetorical flourishes never seemed susceptible to taming by fact.) The results of his traveling performances, Dixon claimed, had been nothing less than revolutionary:

The influence of the flag has prepared the Red Man to unite with the White Man in a common purpose, common aims, common aspirations. . . . He realizes now, for the first time, that the white man is sincere in his friendship and spirit of brotherhood, and thus the Expedition has changed the destiny of a whole race.[62]

Major McLaughlin, who made the tour with Dixon, also filed a report; his was much longer and fuller, and his sense of what was accomplished differed markedly from Dixon's assertion that the destiny of American Indians had been forever changed—an assertion that McLaughlin called a "monstrous absurdity." The expedition actually had no beneficial effects whatsoever, McLaughlin reported, although it had probably done no damage, either; the most McLaughlin found himself able to say about the effect of the expedition was that it had been "harmless." McLaughlin had been chagrined to discover that the primary purpose of the expedition seemed to be the securing of a good collection of photographs and that, at every stop, "each point in the ceremony was the subject of much arrangement and re-arrangement by Dr. Dixon and the two photographers." Dixon was careful, he reports, to put Indians wearing tribal regalia in the center of the photographs and relegate those in ordinary street clothes to the background. The exasperated McLaughlin declared the whole enterprise a "press-agent stunt for the benefit of the names of Dr. Dixon and Mr. Wanamaker."[63]

THE FLAG IS MORE THAN A PIECE OF COLORED BUNTING. THE RED STRIPE IN ITS FOLDS IS SYMBOLIZED BY THE RED BLOOD IN YOUR VEINS AND MINE, BY THE RED GLOW IN THE SUNSET, BY THE RED IN YOUR CEREMONIAL PIPE.

THE WHITE STRIPE FINDS A SYMBOL IN THE WHITE CLOUD THAT FLOATS IN THE SKY, IN THE WHITE SNOW THAT DRIFTS ACROSS THE PLAINS, IN THE PUREST THOUGHT THAT GOES FROM YOUR HEART TO THE GREAT MYSTERY.

THE FIELD OF BLUE WITH THE WHITE STARS YOU MAY SEE EVERY CLEAR NIGHT AS YOU LOOK INTO THE GREAT DOME ABOVE YOUR HEADS.

IT IS THE ONLY FLAG IN THE WORLD THAT TAKES HEAVEN AND EARTH AND MAN TO SYMBOLIZE. THIS MAKES OUT OF IT AN ETER-NAL FLAG, AND WE OUGHT TO BE ETERNALLY LOYAL TO IT.

WE THEREFORE DEDICATE THE AMERICAN FLAG TO JUSTICE, MERCY AND FAIR PLAY TO THE NORTH AMERICAN INDIAN.

3. Montage created by Joseph Dixon's son Rollin. The image, from the 1913 Wanamaker expedition, combines a copy of the flag dedication composed by Dixon with a photograph of Dixon directing the arrangement of a group of unidentified Indians, with flag, for the camera. (Courtesy of the Prints and Photographs Division of the Library of Congress.)

McLaughlin also reported (as Dixon did not) on the misrepresentations of the expedition, its misfires, and even its comic aspects. He noted that in several places the Indians attended the ceremony assuming that its purpose was to confer citizenship on them, on the spot. Others held back from signing the "declaration of allegiance" because they were suspicious of its implications. In some cases very few Indians turned out for the ceremony and in others the Indians who did come grew impatient with delays and walked away. Often, the Indians who participated in the ceremony used the occasion to raise issues of immediate concern to them—water and timber rights, taxation, allotments, land prices—that Dixon had no interest at all in discussing and therefore ignored.[64] At the Kiowa agency, a rainstorm resulted in a comically rearranged conclusion to the ceremony that must have been galling to Dixon: "A downpour of rain cut the ceremony short," McLaughlin reported, "and the address of Delos K. Lone Wolf was delivered by him to myself and Dr. Dixon after we had retreated to shelter, and the Indians had dispersed."[65]

McLaughlin was not the only one who reacted with outrage to Dixon's performances. Matthew K. Sniffen, at that time the secretary of the Indian Rights Association, wrote to Arthur C. Parker in February of 1913, in response to the groundbreaking for the New York statue, to convey his nervousness about the efforts of Dixon and "the Wanamaker people" to organize the National Indian Memorial Association. "I feel that we ought to watch the progress of these fakirs," Sniffen wrote, "and get all the definite information regarding them that is possible." John Oskison, an editor at *Collier's* and an active (Cherokee) member of the SAI, wrote in March to another active member, Carlos Montezuma, to register his outrage at Dixon's manipulations. Dixon had brought in "a bunch of fullbloods," Oskison fumed, who were "stuck on the roof of the McAlpin hotel to live in tipis and furnish copy for the hotel's press agent. A rotten episode."[66] Sniffen wrote to Parker again in May, this time to express his dismay at the news of the third "junket" Dixon was planning. "Just think of his proposed trip of 23,000 miles, his private car, etc. etc.! And what will it accomplish, aside from the advertising features? It is enough to make angels weep!"[67] Sniffen's outrage led him to publish a pamphlet, under the imprint of the Indian Rights Association, in which he denounced the "absurd and extravagant claims" made by Dixon, comparing Dixon's efforts unfavorably to the "thorough work" being done by another photographer, Edward S. Curtis. Sniffen addressed several of Dixon's most egregious errors of fact or judgment, refuting them in some detail, and citing with approval an article from the school paper of the Chilocco Indian School which called Dixon's whole project "a spectacular exhibit." The Indian agents who were directed to cooperate with Dixon, Sniffen noted, "for the most part, regarded the affair as a huge joke."[68]

Arthur Parker took up the matter of the proposed memorial statue in the first issue of the new *Quarterly Journal of the Society of American Indians,* of which he was the editor. That inaugural issue came out in April 1913, only two months after the groundbreaking ceremonies for the statue. Parker went straight to the point: "The irony of building a gigantic statue to a race of men who have been so grossly injured by the evils of civilization can not but be apparent to those who think even superficially."[69] In the fourth issue of the journal, published at the end of that year, Parker offered an editorial comment on the "Citizenship Expedition," calling the whole project "a flagrant insult to the United States authorities and an insult to the Indian, all for the benefit of Wanamaker advertising. We suppose now that the Tobacco Trust will start 'The Dukes Mixture Expedition of Christianity to the Indian,' and present a Bible to every tribe on the assumption that missionaries and educators have not done their duty or that Indians are not Christians." Parker returned to the subject in a subsequent issue, this time noting that "neither progressive nor representative Indians had anything to do with the expedition ceremonies. It must have been a trying time for [Dixon], for the Indians were suspicious and balked again and again."[70]

In spite of protests like these from individuals directly involved in Indian reform, both the citizenship expedition and the memorial project continued to get good press, and Dixon continued to exploit his opportunities. Hampton's *Southern Workman* published a positive editorial comment on the Ft. Wadsworth ceremonies in its April 1913 issue. Noting first the "picturesque elements" of the occasion, provided largely by the "vanishing types of the race" in their regalia, the editorial went on to emphasize the "particularly touching and pathetic" speeches of the Indians, who were acknowledging that "the old trails are lost and the old order of things has passed away."[71] Later that year, the *Southern Workman* commented on the Expedition of Citizenship, which was then in progress. In keeping with Hampton's strong emphasis on assimilation and civic responsibility, the editorial writer applauded the patriotic goals of the project:

> The purpose of the expedition . . . is to emphasize to the Indian his responsibility to the whole country and to arouse his patriotism by making him feel that he is a part of the nation. The idea is a good one and it is to be

hoped that the mission will succeed in turning the thoughts of the Indian
. . . to the nation at large with the destinies of which his fortunes and his
race are inevitably interwoven.[72]

The *Chicago Evening Post* reported on the return of the Expedition of Citizenship to Philadelphia, quoting without demur Dixon's extraordinary claim that
the tour had "changed the destiny of the Indian race" and that, as a result of
his efforts, "in the future . . . the red man will welcome the just advance of
the white man."[73]

Dixon took his photographs and his showmanship to the opening of the
New York Commercial Tercentenary Exposition at the Grand Central Palace
in March 1914. For this extravaganza, he constructed a model Indian village
adjacent to a model of the Woolworth Building; an arcade leading to the
models was lined with his Indian photographs. To launch the exposition,
Dixon arranged to have one Indian step out of the model tepee and strike the
pose of the proposed memorial statue, fingers of one hand pointing upward.
At the same moment, the lights flashed on in the model of the Woolworth
Building. The *New York Times* described the rest of the ceremony:

> The Indian's sign was a message of peace to all the world, and the wireless
> instrument caught it up, flashed it out in code to a receiving station across
> the long floor space, and to a sending station on the roof, which wafted it
> out to space in general. As the wireless instrument spluttered the Indian
> Chief picked up a blanket and waved it according to a code system so that
> Chief Corn Planter, who was far down the corridors, caught the signal and
> replied to it. Then twenty Indians, surrounded by what looked like
> primeval forests leading directly into the old-time Park Row, began a
> dance of peace.[74]

The gate money taken in at these opening night exercises was dedicated to the
fund for the Fort Wadsworth memorial.

The memorial was never built, however, largely because Dixon was never
able to raise sufficient funds, although he continued to campaign for his pet
project and to enlist others in the effort. He took his collection of photographs to the Panama-Pacific Exposition in San Diego in 1915, where copies
of the pictures were for sale and where Dixon lectured on his expeditions
three times a day. In 1916, two Oklahoma Indian women, Irene C. Beaulieu
and Kathleen Woodward, published an anthology to which they gave the title
Tributes to a Vanishing Race. The collection contains their own poetic contri-

butions (signed with the names "Wenonah" and "To-Wam-Pah") as well as selections on Indian themes from Whittier, Freneau, Bryant, Longfellow, and other recognizable literary figures, extracts from contemporary magazine articles, and a few folkloric tribal stories. The book begins with a poetic prelude by "A Paleface" that admonishes the reader to "be glad these tales are written / And that the race, tho' dying, has given / Us such sturdy men and women, / And such brilliant minds in them." The final entry in the book—unsigned, although in an overblown prose style that strongly suggests it came from the pen of Dixon—is a pitch for the Fort Wadsworth memorial, which, according to the author, "has been called by the press of the entire country, the greatest single idea in many years."[75]

The long campaign of Wanamaker and Dixon to declare the American Indians moribund and then to memorialize them, a campaign that progressed through a series of elaborately staged performances, had its effect on public perceptions, even if it produced few tangible results—and certainly no discernible benefits for Indian people themselves. Wanamaker was awarded a grand prize at the Panama-Pacific Exposition for his "uplift" work among Indians, and his entry in the *National Cyclopaedia of American Biography* credits him with initiating a movement to reorganize the administration of Indian affairs as well as a movement to grant citizenship to all Indians—both of which were issues that had been the subject of lobbying and debate long before Dixon and Wanamaker publicly supported them.[76]

One of Dixon's ideas for an Indian spectacle seems to have been adopted—or perhaps stolen—by the Denver Convention Association, which planned its own "last great council of Red Men" for 1915. Denver invited the rest of the world to come and see its spectacular pageant:

All ye Nations, Come! Behold it!
Soon the Whole Wide World Will Tell
Of the White Man's Western Triumph,
And the Red Man's Grand Farewell. . . .
Come ye Nations, To the Red Rocks!
To the Playground of the Sky!
Come! Come up, to Colorado!
Here [*sic*] the Red Man—Say—GOOD BYE.

The Denver Convention Association sent a special invitation to the Society of American Indians, urging the SAI to hold its annual convention in Denver at the time of the pageant so that SAI members could attend "the Last

Farewell Meeting of the Only Real, True American—THE NORTH AMERICAN INDIAN."[77] Arthur Parker responded to the invitation, explaining diplomatically that the aims of the Society of American Indians were completely incompatible with Denver's plan to celebrate the triumph of the white man and say a spectacular farewell to the red man. Denver persisted; Parker was answered by J. B. Maling, "director of exploitation" for the Colorado Publicity League, who protested (in spite of his title) that the desire of the planners of the Denver "last great council" was not to "exploit the Indian for profit, but rather to do him the justice of showing all that he was when living his life in ways of his own seeking." In a bit of rhetorical backpedaling that lacked both logic and persuasiveness, Maling declared that the last great council meant "not a final farewell to the American Indian as a citizen and as an individual, but a farewell to all that has hampered and held him back." At the same time, Maling continued, the Denver organizers believed that "it will be best to present something of a spectacular nature that will have an influence in drawing the people to this grand council." Maling suggested, tentatively and unimaginatively, that a reenactment of the battle of the Little Big Horn might be just the thing.[78]

Parker also had a letter of invitation from the governor of Colorado, Elias M. Ammons, again extending the invitation for the SAI to meet at the time of the last great council. The response of an apparently exasperated Parker to Ammons was straightforward. He pointed out, first, that Wanamaker was already showing the Dixon films of a "last grand council," made two years previously. He then gave the governor a brief lesson in SAI politics:

As the *coming race,* not the vanishing one, we however feel that our men and women who have risen through the old and have come into and adjusted themselves to the new culture, are Indians still, in blood, in loyalty, and in ability to make the country wonder even yet what the red skins are going to do next. To me the last grand council seems an event far in the misty future; meanwhile we are sending our citizen fellows to congress as senators and representatives, to state legislatures, putting them on the legal bench, filling county and state offices with them, graduating them as doctors, lawyers, clergymen of all creeds, scientific men, and we are moulding the sentiment of the country by members of our race who are newspaper men and editors. We are red men still, even though we have plucked the feathers from our war bonnets and are using them for pens. The battle scene has shifted and the contest becomes one of brain and wit. . . . Can

Colorado boost a conference of men with such ideas? We should like to test her by a Conference in 1913, just to get acquainted for a serious consideration for 1915.[79]

The SAI did hold its 1913 conference in Denver, despite the outraged protests of some members, including Richard Pratt, who warned Parker that the SAI was being used by Denver to promote "the greatest Wild West Show ever witnessed" and threatening not only to resign from his associate membership in the society but to write to two thousand former Carlisle students encouraging them to have nothing more to do with the SAI.[80] Pratt also wrote to Dennison Wheelock, an Oneida attorney, graduate of Carlisle, and one of the founding members of the SAI, repeating his warnings about the dangers of cooperating with the Denver boosters: "Denver is not particularly interested in Indians that are progressive and reaching out into our American civilization as the only promising outlet for their future. It will emphasize Indianism most emphatically. I therefore find it utterly impossible to sympathize in any way with the performance."[81] When the SAI decided to meet in Denver anyway, Pratt followed through on his threat and resigned from the society despite Parker's efforts to keep his name on the rolls. At the Denver meeting, Chauncey Yellow Robe, a Sioux product of Pratt's Carlisle education who was perhaps standing in for the absent Pratt, gave a brief address on the subject of "The Indian and the Wild West Show" in which he declared the shows "degrading, demoralizing and degenerating." Yellow Robe linked the Wild West shows to other contemporary representations of the Indian, including Dixon's: "He is exhibited as a savage in every motion picture theatre in the country. We see the Indian, in his full native costume, stamped on the five-dollar bills as a reminder of his savagery. We see a monument of the Indian in New York harbor as a memorial of his vanishing race. The Indian wants no such memorial monument, for he is not yet dead." Perhaps because of the protests of Pratt, Yellow Robe, and others, the SAI did not return to Denver in 1915.[82]

The controversy stirred up by Denver's wooing of the SAI suggests some of the complications in the attitudes of the organization and its membership toward the idea of Indian participation in public performances and exhibitions. The distaste of Pratt and Yellow Robe for Wild West shows was widely shared among those who spoke out on issues of Indian reform—but not, apparently, by those who actually participated in the shows, like Luther Standing Bear. (Perhaps significantly, Standing Bear was never active in the SAI, although his brother Henry was a founding member.) The extravagant performances put on by Wanamaker and Dixon, as we have seen, also elicited contempt from many educated and professional Indians, while the reservation Indians who constituted the audiences for these performances seemed, for the most part, to view them with bemusement, confusion, or indifference. Arthur C. Parker spoke out strongly against the Wild West shows, for reasons that had little to do with the well-being of the Indian performers—who evidently enjoyed performing, on the whole—and very much to do with pleasing the right audience, especially the white reformers. The Indians in the shows, Parker told the Buffalo Historical Society, "misrepresent their people, libel the work of patient teachers and devoted missionaries, and defraud the public. . . . This causes the utmost humiliation to the better class of Indians and brings despair into the hearts of missionaries and teachers." Parker made it clear that he was not speaking just for himself: "It is in behalf of the teacher, the uplifter and in behalf of the great class of decent Indians that I register this protest."[83]

Richard Pratt had used language similar to Parker's when he wrote in 1908 that the effect of Indian participation in Wild West shows was "to bring discredit upon the educated Indian and degrade and deceive the public mind in regard to Indians generally."[84] Parker and Pratt were both vehement in their opposition to the Wild West shows, assuming the audience would too easily equate the Indian performers with their performances as terrifying feathered warriors. Neither, however, was opposed to other kinds of public performances by Indians, even some costumed performances. Pratt, as we have seen, put his students on public parade as often as possible, and Parker's SAI typically incorporated forms of pageantry and costumed performance into those parts of its annual meeting that were open to the public.

At its very first meeting, in 1911, the SAI offered a concert of Indian music for which it charged admission as a means of defraying the costs of the convention. (The concert drew a crowd of fifteen hundred people and raised seven hundred dollars for the SAI.) The program included songs by the Carlisle quartet and a series of solos by various Indian performers, who appeared in borrowed native costumes. According to the *Ohio State Journal*, a delay in the arrival of the costumes, which were being shipped in, caused some initial concern to the concert organizers because, according to the *Journal*, "blankets and feathers, they know, will add to the attractiveness of the concert." The *Journal* also reported (presumably reliably) that the delegates to the meeting were taken to visit one of the prehistoric mounds outside Columbus. "Before leaving the Indians gathered on top of the mound and sang 'America,' and following that the younger Indians gave an impromptu war dance on the same elevation."[85] Prior to the 1912 meeting in Columbus, Arthur Parker was consulted by Caroline Andrus, then an employee at Hampton Institute, who was planning to send four Hampton boys—two Chippewa and two Cherokee—to perform songs and tribal dances at the convention. Andrus wondered whether Parker thought the boys should appear in tribal costume, and whether "these songs and dances will reflect discredit on Hampton, or lead people to suppose we stand too much for the old customs?" Parker wrote back giving his full endorsement to the costumed performances and adding that "the people of the city are looking forward with especial interest to these interesting numbers."[86] At the 1918 meeting in Pierre, South Dakota, the Friday night entertainment included the reading of the "Eulogy of Sitting Bill" by Gertrude Bonnin, who appeared, as she often did, in full regalia.

The SAI even staged its own full-costume Indian pageant, "The Conspiracy of Pontiac," written by Charles Eastman, at its 1919 meeting in Minneapolis. According to a local newspaper, the pageant depicted "the coming of the French and the English to the colonial frontiers, the plots and counterplots, the uprising under Pontiac against the English, and the chief's betrayal."[87] Eastman and his wife, Elaine Goodale Eastman, were at the time running an Indian-themed summer camp for young women in New Hampshire. The Pontiac pageant was developed and first performed at the camp, with the campers—students from Wellesley, Vassar, and Smith—taking the roles.[88] In Minneapolis, where the pageant was open to the public for a small admission fee, Eastman was able to put together an Indian cast; Eastman played the role of Pontiac and other delegates to the convention, including Gertrude Bonnin and Carlos Montezuma, took the other Indian roles. Eastman noted to the *Minneapolis Journal* that the cast members had all brought their own costumes with them to Minneapolis. Because the pageant had to be performed indoors, the script was cut and the horses and canoes used in the summer camp production had to be omitted. The action of the pageant was presented in pantomime, with a narrator providing a synopsis of each scene.

Eastman was especially interested in the reception of his pageant in Minneapolis since the businessmen of that city were looking for a performance to become the centerpiece of a planned annual carnival with an Indian theme, and "The Conspiracy of Pontiac" was a likely prospect. Officers of the local Civic and Commerce Association attended the pageant to see whether a version of Eastman's script, performed outdoors, could fill the bill. The *Journal* sketched out the planners' vision for a carnival that would rival the Mardi Gras in New Orleans:

> Plans discussed by Minneapolis businessmen contemplate the co-operation of the entire city in a week of merrymaking, arranged as the largest "powwow" ever seen in the northwest.... Clubs, named for Indian tribes, are being discussed to keep the carnival spirit at top pitch with sun dances, barbecues, and frolicking in costume to the music of tomtoms. If plans materialize, Minneapolis in future will devote one week of every August to the frolics of white youths and maidens—and their parents—masquerading in fringe, beads and war paint.

Eastman was initially enthusiastic about the possibility of making his pageant an annual event in Minneapolis; he declared Minneapolis not only to be "the Paris of Indian costuming," according to the *Journal,* but also to have the appropriate kind of natural settings for staging an outdoor pageant. His conception of the production clearly differed significantly from the frolicking envisioned by the Civic and Commerce Association. Eastman saw the project as an Indian undertaking with possibilities for educating a white audience rather than inviting them to play Indian, anticipating that he could produce three hundred Indians to take part in a pageant and promising that "in such a production they could show true Indian life, and the many phases of it the white man never sees."[89] Eastman wanted a historical pageant, but because Minneapolis insisted on a carnival with tom-toms and war paint, nothing ever came of the proposed project.

The men and women who performed in costume in "The Conspiracy of Pontiac" were also delegates to a conference at which a number of significant political and social issues were discussed: the need to secure birthright citizenship for all Indians, the abuses of the Bureau of Indian Affairs, and the poor sanitary and health conditions on reservations, among others. The conference adopted a resolution calling for the abolition of the Indian Bureau and appointing a committee of five attorneys, all Indians, to present their resolution to Congress.[90] Speakers at the conference emphasized the need to, as one of them put it, "enlighten the American public as to the true status of the Indian" as a disenfranchised ward of the government. Carlos Montezuma, the Chicago physician who played the role of a medicine man in the Pontiac pageant, argued in an impassioned speech to the conference that "only through action of Congress can Indians get justice, and Congress will only act when public sentiment compels it." Gertrude Bonnin urged delegates to speak out confidently on issues that concerned them: "We are rational human beings. Shall we think or shall somebody think for us?"[91] For these delegates, the reform agendas of the association seemed not to be in conflict, in any way, with the presentation of a historical pageant using costumed Indian performers. In fact, the performance was, for them, consistent with their emphasis on the need to change the way the public thought about Indians. The pageant, like the delegation of Indian attorneys, was a way of communicating with the public and educating them, not only about needed reforms but also about the ability of Indian people to represent themselves and to perform their own history—to show "true Indian life," in Eastman's words—and to participate in established American forms of ritualized representation.

When Fayette McKenzie first proposed the idea of an association of progressive Indians—which eventually became the SAI—he stated his belief that "the chief reason we continue to have an Indian problem is because the public generally does not believe that the Indian is capable of education, culture, or high morality."[92] A performance such as "The Conspiracy of Pontiac" was a means of demonstrating several things to the public: the performers' perspective on their own history; their capability (as McKenzie would have it) for understanding and exploiting the educational and cultural resources of the pageant form; and their possession of the kind of self-awareness necessary for successfully ritualized self-representation. Of course, the spectacular elements of the public performance also had their uses. The costuming was a surefire draw, a way of attracting and keeping the attention of an otherwise inattentive public that had much to learn and whose attention was necessary if essential reforms were to be made. As Du Bois had said of his "Star of Ethiopia," pageantry provided the "paraphernalia" in which an important message about race, progress, and pride could "deck itself."

N. Scott Momaday opens his 1969 book, *The Way to Rainy Mountain,* with a compact, one-paragraph sketch of the history of the Kiowa people, noting their migration from the northern mountains to the central plains, their adoption of the Sun Dance, and their eventual military defeat by United States troops in the 1870s. The sketch moves almost laconically through its brief notations of struggle and decline; the plains culture of the Kiowa, Momaday writes, "withered and died like grass that is burned in the prairie wind." Having set down this condensed history, with all its submerged complexities and implications, Momaday then makes a sudden shift in the trajectory of his narrative. "But these are idle recollections," he concludes, "the mean and ordinary agonies of human history. The interim was a time of great adventure and nobility and fulfillment." By describing the historical moment of the Kiowa's defeat as "a day like destiny," Momaday seems to deliberately forestall a politicized or polemical or even fully historicized reading of the Kiowa story; in this representation, the Kiowa succumbed to a vague universal destiny rather than to decisions made by specific human actors with aggression and domination on their minds. With this prologue as an interpretive frame for the reader, Momaday goes on in the rest of the text to relate, often in minute detail, specific events in the history of the Kiowa people and of his Kiowa family in particular, setting these local details within the context of the larger "human history" to which he has assigned them.[1]

Momaday's turn to the universal in this text—his locating of the specific details of Kiowa history within a very generalized universal narrative—can seem surprising and even problematic to the reader. To acknowledge the deliberate suppression of the Kiowa by whites with superior firepower and then to dismiss the suppression as an "ordinary" part of "human history" might seem an odd tactic, especially to the modern reader who has become accustomed to seeing appeals to the universal as efforts to occlude parts of the historical record or to privilege one ideological narrative over others by declaring it to be the universal story. The reasons for Momaday's move can become clearer if we recognize its genealogical relationship to the rhetorical tactics of earlier Indian intellectuals, including those within the Society of American Indians, who made their own calculated turns to the universal in their public statements. The SAI declared in 1913, for example, in the second issue of its new journal, that its objective was to bring Indian people into better alignment with universal movements and patterns: the society aimed to "promote and co-operate with all efforts looking to the advancement of the Indian in enlightenment which leaves him free as a man to develop according to the natural laws of social evolution" and to "direct its energies exclusively to general principles and universal interests."[2] For the SAI spokespersons, these references to the universal and to natural laws drew on a developmental discourse that would have been quite familiar to their contemporaries.

The SAI's appeal to the universal was part of a deliberate political strategy that focused on the possibilities of the future as intently as Momaday's text focuses on the determinations of the past. Whereas *The Way to Rainy Mountain* envisions human history as a series of generalized agonies, an endless and inevitable rising and falling of entire nations and peoples, the SAI rhetoric reflects the progressive optimism (and the progressive rhetoric) of its time, locating in the patterns of history not the repeated failures of *nations* but the "advancement" in "enlightenment" of those *individuals* who are not prevented, by artificial interventions and obstructions, from evolving according to the universal laws of nature. The positions of both Momaday and the SAI can be understood as responses to the cultural politics of their respective times. The position Momaday takes in the late 1960s provides a rhetorical means of lifting the Kiowa out of the category of special victims of white American imperialism, already consigned to the margins of American history before the end of the nineteenth century and available for twentieth-century condescension or nostalgia or pity. In one paragraph, Momaday restores the Kiowa to a shared world or human history. The language of the SAI, addressed to the cultural politics of a different time, works against those theories of the early twentieth century that rejected the notion of a common human history and experience in favor of a hierarchized and racialized vision of history. Their rhetoric specifically countered the racial determinism of those like Joseph K. Dixon who insisted on seeing all Indians as doomed to be written out of universal human history *because* of their race, which made them unfit to compete successfully with the naturally stronger whites. For these racial determinists, the whole of the "Indian problem" was traceable to the racialized Indian body itself. For them, therefore, Indian history had become a subject only for epics and elegies, a more or less pathetic interlude in the universal story of human progress. The SAI rhetoric clearly places the problem outside the Indian body, in those imposed constraints that limit the Indian person's freedom to develop "according to the natural laws of social evolution." Merging Indian history and human history in its public, theoretical statements was, for the SAI, a first step toward legitimizing its claims to a full share in the practical benefits of full citizenship and social equality.

In his work on black uplift, Kevin Gaines has cast a very skeptical eye on the discourse of universalism that characterized the post-Reconstruction reform efforts of African American activists. Gaines has argued insistently that the uplift ideology sanctioned by educated African Americans was grounded in a specious universalism that, on the pretext of dismantling hierarchies based on race, actually worked to reinforce an existing structure of power relations that was in fact thoroughly racist. Black intellectuals and reformers, according to Gaines's argument,

> sought to refute the view that African Americans were biologically inferior and unassimilable by incorporating "the race" into ostensibly universal but deeply racialized ideological categories of Western progress and civilization. Generally, Black elites claimed class distinctions, indeed, the very existence of a "better class" of Blacks, as evidence of what they called race progress. Black middle-class ideology cannot be isolated from dominant modes of knowledge and power relations structured by race and racism.

The universalist discourse, in Gaines's view, simply replaced race distinctions with class distinctions, making citizenship a bourgeois privilege belonging to those who could claim "a normative, often unenunciated whiteness." For Gaines, the ideology of black uplift was, in the end, only a rhetorically disguised form of accommodation to an intransigent white supremacy.[3]

Gaines's argument has been countered by Ross Posnock's reassessment of the uses of universalist discourse by black intellectuals. While Posnock acknowledges the misuses to which "color-blind ideals" can and have been put, he also argues that the turn to the universal was historically necessary as a means for black intellectuals to enter the political public sphere—against the opposition of those who would reserve the public sphere for white elites. The use of a cosmopolitan, deracialized, universalist discourse by black intellectuals was, in Posnock's view, a useful and successful means of contesting the status quo of white supremacy. The radical distrust of universalism, he argues, is a recent phenomenon, the result of politically conservative abuses of the concept on the one hand and, on the other, the emergence of identity politics (often race-based). "To recover the intellectual," Posnock concludes, "is to recover a cosmopolitan universalism that has been held under suspicion during the reign of postmodernism" but that was crucial to the thinking and the strategies of W. E. B. Du Bois and other black intellectuals a hundred years ago.[4]

The histories of black uplift and Indian uplift are distinctive, with fewer similarities than one might at first assume. However, examining the positions taken by Gaines and Posnock on the issue of black uplift can be instructive for understanding the universalist rhetoric of the SAI and the intellectuals associated with it. Posnock's model works most usefully and persuasively as an approach to understanding the perspectives of those Indian intellectuals who were roughly contemporary with Du Bois, especially when one factors in one of the most crucial differences between discussions of the "Indian question" and discussions of the "Negro question" at the time: the prevalence of the myth of the vanishing Indian. The popularity of this myth gave particular urgency to the universalist rhetoric of Indian intellectuals. In making their claims to a share in a universal human history, the SAI intellectuals were intervening in and attempting to reshape an ongoing debate among white intellectuals, reformers, and writers about a very basic question: whether American Indians, as a generic category of people, were truly a "vanishing race" and thus could expect no share in the nation's (or the world's) future, or whether they were, on the other hand, intellectually, psychologically, and morally fit to survive in a changing America and contribute to the economic and civic culture of the country.

Sherman Coolidge (Arapaho), an Episcopal minister, founding member of the SAI and its first president, contributed an essay to the society's journal in 1914 in which he provided a cautiously constructed rationale for the existence of the organization:

> The existence of the Society of American Indians means that the hour has struck when the best educated and most cultured of the race should come together to voice the common demands, to interpret correctly the Indian's heart, and to contribute in a more united way their influence and exertion with the rest of the citizens of the United States in all lines of progress and reform, for the welfare of the Indian race in particular, and all humanity in general.[5]

Coolidge's sentence is loaded with reformist buzzwords, and it responds, delicately, to some of the pressures on the SAI that will be discussed more specifically in chapter 3. What is important to note at this point is Coolidge's rhetorical conflation of three things: the needs of Indians, the interests of the nation, and the welfare of all humanity. Making those connections was a strategic move, a means of claiming a space on the public platform where the "best educated" and "most cultured" of the non-Indian population were already well established and having plenty to say about the Indians' future.

The white Indian-reform organizations that claimed a space on the public platform were largely committed to the project of "saving" the Indians through enforced assimilation. Although the various groups were not in complete agreement about their methods, they did agree that Indian people needed to be, and could be, "uplifted" to prepare them for assimilation. Not everyone, of course, shared these reformers' comparatively optimistic vision; many who commented publicly on Indian affairs saw the question of the Indians' future as already definitively settled. The anonymous author of an article published in the *Forum* in 1903, for example, declared of the American Indian that "the hour of his elimination is at hand." The "minor tribes" of the country, the author announced, were already clearly moribund and "must be classed among the melancholy human relics left over from a barbaric age." A 1909 issue of the *Atlantic Monthly* carried an article by Kelly Miller, the Howard University sociologist and prolific writer on race, civil rights, and African American education, in which Miller identified the American Indians as one of the "weaker races" that had, for all practical purposes, already succumbed to their grim fate:

> The red and brown races have faded before the march of civilization as a flower before the chilling breath of autumn. The Australian has gone; the red Indian has been dispatched to his happy hunting-ground in the sky; many of the scattered fragments of the isles of the sea have vanished away, while others are waiting gloomily in the valley of the shadow of death. These people have perished and are perishing not so much by force and violence, as because they were not able to adjust themselves to the swift and sudden changes which an encroaching civilization imposed.

In 1918, Franz Boas wrote in the *World Forum* that, because of the rate of intermarriage among white men and Indian women, "the male line of the Indian is bound to disappear while the female line of the Indian will gradually merge in the whites." For Boas, this trend meant the erasure, regrettable but inevitable, of cultural distinctiveness for American Indians. "Much as we may regret the extinction of the cultural achievements of the Indian race," Boas wrote, "there is no great hope that these can be preserved for any length of time; and the best we can do is to learn whatever we can from the Indian and to preserve it in our own way."[6]

In spite of significant tonal differences and ideological purposes, the statements of Miller and Boas have something in common with the position of the eugenicist Seth K. Humphrey, who cheerfully assured his readers that they needn't worry about the Indian:

> He bids fair to become in time an attenuated infusion in the white blood of the nation—the more attenuated the better, for despite his good qualities the Indian had little in his inheritance to benefit the Aryan stock, and much to encumber it. We are to be mercifully spared at least one source of racial impoverishment by the fading away of the American Indian.[7]

Humphrey was an unabashed white supremacist, and in that sense he was ideologically and politically about as distant from Miller and Boas as it was possible to be. But considered from an *Indian* perspective, the published comments of the three could have sounded more alike than different and might have been equally frustrating and disturbing.

In these and other public statements about "the Indian question," the language of the discussions, no matter what the position of the writer, remains largely consistent and familiar, with certain terms—including *civilization* and *race*—appearing with predictable regularity. As these terms circulated in the period, however, they gained little in specificity, accrued little denotative weight, and accomplished their rhetorical work almost entirely through connotation. As Gail Bederman has observed in her discussion of "the discourse of civilization," the term *civilization* was used in so many ways and for such different purposes around the turn of the century that pursuing questions about its specific meaning leads to few revealing insights. For Bederman, then, "the interesting thing about 'civilization' is not what was meant by the term, but the multiple ways it was used to legitimize different sorts of claims to power." Matthew Frye Jacobson, writing about the same period, reaches a similar conclusion, observing that "the notion of 'civilization' in American thinking has historically represented a dense weave of ideas and assumptions." While Jacobson argues that *civilization* was primarily an economic concept, he also observes that the concept was "most often draped in the complementary logics of Christian moralism and white supremacy throughout the turn-of-the-century period."[8] Few of those who wrote for a mass audience felt compelled to define the term, no matter how often they used it. When Yale geographer Ellsworth Huntington did make an attempt at definition in a 1915 article for *Harper's,* his effort petered out in tautology and a shrugging reliance on his reader to just *know* what civilization is. Civilization, Huntington wrote, is dependent on

> those characteristics which are generally recognized as of the highest value. I mean by this the power of initiative, the capacity for formulating new ideas and for carrying them into effect, the power of self-control, high standards of honesty and morality, the power to lead and control other races, the capacity for disseminating ideas, and other similar qualities which will readily suggest themselves.[9]

The word *race* was also used so loosely in the writing directed toward a mass audience that it, too, carried more connotative than denotative weight and, as with *civilization,* those who used the word seemed generally unconcerned to give it a specific definition. Matthew Pratt Guterl has observed that while turn-of-the-century America was fascinated by questions of race and racial difference, references to those questions largely demonstrated a "remarkable looseness of fit in the language of race" that made the language adaptable to a variety of political purposes.[10] In discussions of the "Indian question," however, *race* was very frequently used in the context of comparisons between whites and Indians—both explicit and implied—that almost invariably addressed the distance and the distinctions between the two groups, as evidenced by their different rates of progress toward the goals of civilization (whatever that might be). These considerations of racial difference had been treated extensively by Lewis Henry Morgan in his influential 1877 book, *Ancient Society.* Morgan argued that all human groups move through two preliminary stages, savagery and barbarism, in their progress toward the ultimate stage of civilization, although they may move at very different rates. Having identified these universally shared phases of progress, Morgan was able to offer a confident conclusion: "It can now be asserted upon convincing evidence that savagery preceded barbarism in all the tribes of mankind, as barbarism is known to have preceded civilization. The history of the human race is one in source, one in experience, and one in progress." On the basis of this theory of universal human evolution, Morgan asserted that studying the American Indians was an appropriate way of understanding all of human history, no matter where it occurred, since the Indians' relatively slow rate of progress made them a kind of living museum of human development.[11]

Morgan's book had a major impact on the thinking of the emerging class of professional ethnologists and anthropologists, although, as Francis Paul Prucha has argued, his theoretical arguments were less important to Indian reformers and to those who were interested in shaping public opinion than were the more practical arguments of lay progressives.[12] Francis E. Leupp, who served as Commissioner of Indian Affairs from 1904 to 1909, even used a version of Morgan's theory to make a case for the *irrelevance* of all theories of race to the situation of the Indians: "The manifest inference," Leupp wrote in a 1910 book, "is that what we call the Indian problem is a human rather than a race question, and that its solution must be sought on common-sense rather than theoretical lines."[13] Even those who adopted Morgan's general theories did not necessarily adopt some of the significant parts of his discourse. While Morgan essentially devalued notions of separate races with different inherent capacities, for example, speaking of individual groups as "tribes" and reserving the term *race* for the "human race" (as he does in the sentences quoted above), adherents to his general theory were likely to continue to use *race* in vague and even contradictory ways. The Smithsonian ethnologist James Mooney, for example, prefaced his lengthy 1896 report on the Ghost Dance religion among the Sioux with an unequivocal confirmation of Morgan's position (and a clearly audible echo of his language): "The human race is one in thought and action. . . . There is nothing new under the sun." In leading up to this pronouncement about the unity of the "human race," however, Mooney conflates *tribe* and *race* in the very process of offering an argument against such a conflation:

> What *tribe or people* has not had its golden age, before Pandora's box was loosed, when women were nymphs and dryads and men were gods and heroes? And when the *race* lies crushed and groaning beneath an alien yoke, how natural is the dream of a redeemer, an Arthur, who shall return from exile or awake from some long sleep to drive out the usurper and win back for his people what they have lost? . . . The doctrines of the Hindu avatar, the Hebrew Messiah, the Christian millennium, and the Hesuananin of the Indian Ghost dance are essentially the same, and have their origin in a hope and longing common to all humanity.[14]

Mooney's prologue, like Momaday's prologue to *The Way to Rainy Mountain,* intends to locate specific moments in Indian history—in this case, the rise of the Ghost Dance movement—within the larger continuum of human history and thus to lessen the ideological and affective distance between the reader of his text and the Indian subjects of the text. Mooney wished to make the Ghost Dance seem less alien and exotic, that is, by suggesting that the basic structures of human experience are universal. Writing in 1896, however, Mooney seemed unable to broach the subject of human similarity and difference without using the word *race*—a term that he applied, significantly, to a "crushed and groaning" people.

The SAI itself, far from avoiding mention of race, fully embraced the term in its publications, issuing a statement in 1912 affirming that

> the Society seeks to bring about a condition whereby the white race and all races may have a better and a broader knowledge of the red race, its claims, its needs and its ability to contribute materially to modern civilization. The Society asserts the right of the Indian to an active voice in the rights and destiny of his race, and will ever seek to defend all just claims of the race.[15]

In 1916, the society began placing the phrase "A Journal of Race Ideas" beneath the title of its journal, changing that to "A Journal of Race Progress" the following year. The SAI did not seem very interested, on the other hand, in examining any of the contemporary theories *about* race or in staking out a consistent theoretical position of its own. Instead, as the language of its 1912 statement suggests, the primary objective of the society was more practical: to disinfect contemporary ideas of race by detaching the term from its associations with defeated ("crushed and groaning") or inferior peoples; to give rhetorical equivalence to the "white race" and the "red race"; and to construct new associations for the "red race"—in this particular statement, to associate it with knowledge, contributions, rights, civilization, and ideas.

In formulating their positions, the SAI spokespersons had essentially to demonstrate to their audience, especially their white audience, that Indians were not constrained or determined by their racial identification. (Franz Boas made a strong argument for detaching culture and behavior from race—an argument fortified with the data and discourse of the social sciences—but his argument was not published until 1911, and it obviously did not accomplish an overnight revolution in American attitudes toward the viability of theories of racial inferiority. Among those who were most resistant to Boas's work were his colleagues in the Bureau of American Ethnology.) Indian intellectuals had to demonstrate that they could *act* in ways that white America would approve and find unremarkable—in effect, to perform a new civic identity. This meant distancing themselves from the constructed Indian who had been the object of so much public curiosity, condescension, and even contempt and whose demise was so often predicted. There was, for members of the SAI and other Indian intellectuals, much public relations work to be done. The difficulty of getting the American public to take seriously the very concept of Indian intellectuals is illustrated by a notice that appeared in a local newspaper at the time of the SAI's 1914 meeting in Madison, Wisconsin. While the delegates, many of them lawyers, ministers, or other professionals, convened to articulate their positions on various political, legal, and social issues, the newspaper reported that "squaws and papooses in any number are here with their braves to take in the sights and learn what the white man can do for them."[16]

The need for educating the public was clearly articulated in a 1912 letter from Matthew Sniffen, secretary of the Indian Rights Association, to Arthur Parker of the SAI:

> One thing that is greatly needed at this juncture is to revive the interest that was formerly shown by the public in Indian affairs. . . . Unfortunately, the impression prevails in various quarters that the Indian question is practically settled; that the Washington Bureau is in good hands; that everything is lovely, and nothing now remains for the average American citizen to do in this connection, but to thank God it is so, and then proceed with a light heart to devote his attention to other matters. . . . You and I know, however, that this is merely crying Peace when there is no Peace, and that the work to be done by the friends of the Indian is not half accomplished. Consequently, your Society and ours must do all we can to bring the Indian situation before the public eye, AND KEEP IT THERE.[17]

The SAI had acknowledged this crucial aspect of its agenda from the beginning; in an early recruitment letter, sent on July 11, 1911, the executive committee of the young organization had noted that "a great many problems have arisen out of the question of race adaption [sic] to new conditions" and that as a result, the effort to "mould public opinion" had become "a vital necessity." The SAI's focus on public opinion was enthusiastically endorsed by the Commissioner of Indian Affairs, Robert G. Valentine, who told the delegates to the first convention in 1911 that "we have long needed an Indian public opinion about public affairs." A gathering of educated, public-minded Indians was, Valentine declared, "epochal" in its implications and its possibilities.[18]

SAI spokespersons undertook the monumental task of reconstructing the image of the Indians in the eyes of the public and responding to racist and paternalistic representations of them. An 1898 article in the *North American Review* by Lyman Abbott, an active Mohonker and virulent opponent of the reservation system, provides a good example of the kind of public statement that demanded a considered response. Abbott asked, rhetorically, whether the Indians were threatened with disappearance, and then proceeded with his answer:

> Certainly. The sooner the better. There is no more reason why we should endeavor to preserve intact the Indian race than the Hungarians, the Poles, or the Italians. Americans all, from ocean to ocean, should be the aim of all American statesmanship. Let us understand once for all [*sic*] that an inferior race must either adapt and conform itself to the higher civilization, wherever the two come in conflict, or else die. This is the law of God, from which there is no appeal.[19]

One way of responding to this sort of pronouncement about the necessary erasure of Indian identity was to draw a distinction between the "old" Indian, who was a source of consternation for the American public, and the "new" Indian, whom most American citizens had not yet met. Arthur Parker always insisted that the educated Indians of the SAI were *not* new Indians but old Indians who had successfully adapted (he preferred the term *adjusted*) to a new set of circumstances. Others, however, took a different rhetorical position. Parker's friend John M. Oskison, a Cherokee novelist and journalist who became an active SAI member, wrote in 1907 of the need for the public to recognize the emergence of a new Indian, capable of being self-supporting and living responsibly off the reservation. Oskison's article, published in *Everybody's Magazine,* emphasizes the difference between the "modern Indian" and the "dirty beggar" who was created by the old conditions, especially by the reservation system. Oskison bluntly describes his "new man" as being "Indian only in blood and traditions," thus attacking the premise that Indian behavior and promise are circumscribed by race and/or culture. Oskison even lets the reader see what the new Indian looks like. He begins the article by declaring that "a new series of Indian portraits is needed," and then provides a series of photographs: Indian men doing construction work, Indian students running printing presses and sewing machines, an Indian school official and an Indian Congregational minister, all of them in European attire.[20] In Oskison's terms, the old Indian was simply an Indian; the new Indian is, as the photographs attest, a dark-skinned, hard-working, progressive American whose racial identity is of less and less importance.

A similar kind of argument was made by Charles M. Harvey in an *Atlantic Monthly* article in 1913. This is the same Harvey who had pronounced in 1904, in the same journal, that "the Indian as an Indian is doomed by the law of the survival of the fittest." Using less apocalyptic language in the later article, Harvey predicted that the next United States census would find that a large number of Indians had become citizens and would therefore "no longer be regarded as Indians, except in a racial or historical sense."[21] Like Oskison, Harvey implied that in the common public perception, Indians cannot be citizens or self-supporting workers; to alter that perception required a demonstration that Indians were shaped in the past by historical circumstances rather than by race and were being radically reshaped, in the present, by new circumstances. Harvey dated the emergence of the new Indian from the passage of the Dawes Act in 1887, which, in Harvey's view, opened the doors of opportunity for Indian people. He is more blandly optimistic about the future than he was in 1904, seeing no reason to fear a re-closing of those doors; "the Indian," he wrote in 1913, "fits well into the new order."[22]

One of the reasons Harvey offered for seeing a relatively easy road to assimilation for the Indians was his conviction—not an uncommon one at the time—that they need not be held back by racial prejudice. The Indian, Harvey asserted, "has never been a slave. In his contact with whites in our time he arouses no prejudice. The superior race which refuses to associate on terms of equality with men of Black, brown, or yellow skins, raises no social barrier against the red man."[23] Harvey's statement, as smugly preposterous as it may seem now, still reaches out to a number of issues that were frequently addressed in turn-of-the-century discussions of the future of American Indians, in this case issues that were grounded in the inevitable comparisons between Indians and African Americans. These comparisons were certainly not new; Linda Kerber has, for example, examined the efforts of antebellum abolitionists to link the two groups. But for the abolitionists, according to Kerber, "the question posed by the Indian and the slave seemed to be the same—what would be the Americans' relationship to men of different color?"—and their assumption was that the answers to the question, whatever those answers were, would also be identical.[24] By the end of the nineteenth century, in the long aftermath of the Civil War and Reconstruction and with race riots and lynchings increasing rather than decreasing, things looked quite different. To a striking degree, the literature of the later period, especially the reformist literature, raises the comparison only to deny its usefulness, as Harvey does in declaring the two cases different because the Indian, unlike the African American, does not have to contend with racial prejudice.

Harvey's use of the singular pronoun and his reference to "the Indian" as a generic category was a stylistic commonplace of turn-of-the-century writing, so widely employed that it usually has no predictable political implications. The usage is worth pausing over briefly, however, if only to contrast it with the language of those who made a point of differentiating between white responses to the individual Indian person and to the generalized, generic Indian. In his 1911 book, George Bird Grinnell, an advocate of treaty rights who had traveled extensively among the Cheyenne, Blackfeet, and other western Indians, put it this way:

> Usually no prejudice exists against the individual Indian when he is brought into contact with white people, but against a body of them—as a tribe located on a reservation—there has usually been a very strong antagonism among the adjacent population. . . . I believe that this prejudice is less strong than it was a few years ago, and that ultimately it will cease to exist. Thus, in the future—provided intelligent effort shall be expended in teaching the Indians how to think like white men, how to work, and to work to the best advantage—they may become a self-supporting and self-respecting part of our population.[25]

Although Grinnell is here folding the question of prejudice into his own particular argument against tribalism and the reservation system, he still shared (at least rhetorically) the essential position taken by Harvey: the absence of prejudice against the individual Indian makes it much easier for him than for the African American to become successfully absorbed into the general population.[26] John Oskison took a similar position in a speech to the first annual conference of the Society of American Indians, announcing confidently that "prejudice against the Indian simply does not exist among people who can make or mar a career. . . . The Indian who fits himself for the company of those at the top will go up. He will go as swiftly and as surely as his white brother."[27]

These optimistic pronouncements about prejudice are part of a larger set of assumptions about Indians and race that often appeared in print. In general, comparisons between the (loosely defined) Indian question and the (equally loosely defined) Negro question led to the conclusion that the problems posed by the latter were much greater and more intransigent, for one primary reason: the Negro question was defined as a race problem while the Indian question, significantly, was not. Lyman Abbott argued in 1901 that the Indian problem could be solved by taking some fairly simple, clearly defined steps: abolishing reservations, ending the system of rations, and expecting each Indian to take care of himself. "In brief," Abbott concluded, "he should be treated, not as an Indian, but as a man." When he turned to the matter of African Americans, however, Abbott was less sanguine because he was unwilling to concede the irrelevance of race, specifically designating the Negro question as a "race problem" that was therefore "more complicated and more difficult" than the Indian question.[28] The distinguishing factor, for Abbott, was racial prejudice. The Negro question was a race problem because of deeply embedded prejudices—as the Indian question was *not* a race problem because of the absence of prejudice—and thus Abbott could see no immediate possibility of treating the Negro as a man rather than as a Negro.

An even more blunt statement of the difference between the two "questions" was offered by the (African American) commandant of cadets at Hampton Institute, Robert Russa Moton, whose observations were printed in the *Southern Workman* in 1903. Hampton, formerly an all-black school, had begun accepting Indian students in 1878. All Hampton students, black and Indian, were taken through the school's experimental combination of industrial-manual, military, and academic training. Moton's comments were cast as a defense of the Hampton program, which had come under attack from Richard Pratt and others who believed that the uplift of Indian students could not be accomplished by putting them together with black students, who would only hold them back. Moton, citing the authority of his experience of observing black and Indian students together, reached a set of conclusions meant to validate the Hampton educational agenda. Indians and Negroes were alike, he declared, in being intellectually and morally inferior to whites and in requiring both "mental and moral discipline"—a requirement that Hampton was well prepared to meet. But in other ways the two groups were strikingly different: the Indian had too much pride, while the Negro had too little; the Negro easily acknowledged authority, while the Indian did not; the Indian valued his traditions, while the Negro was "inclined to disdain and get rid of anything that is distinctly Negro." By educating the two groups together, each could, according to Moton, learn useful lessons from the other: "Each becomes in many ways a daily lesson to the other in the meaning and use of life." At the same time, Moton foresaw significantly different futures for them:

The question to be solved by the Indian is easy as compared with that of the Negro. With the Indian it is mainly a question of existence by civilization and amalgamation, or immediate extinction. Into the Negro's problem enter the factors of race hatred, social prejudice and political inequality, which make it not only complex and difficult but cast over its ultimate solution the shadow of uncertainty which only succeeding generations can remove.[29]

For Moton, the reputed absence of racial prejudice in the case of Indians meant that the Indian question could be resolved fairly quickly (even if one possible resolution was the quick extinction of the Indians). The Negro question, on the other hand, was a *race* question and therefore might not be resolved until the current generation of white and black Americans had been replaced—perhaps by more than one succeeding generation.

One of Moton's predecessors on the Hampton staff was Booker T. Washington,[30] a Hampton graduate who had returned to the school in 1879 at the request of its founder and head, Gen. Samuel Chapman Armstrong, to take charge of the male Indian students.[31] In his autobiography, *Up From Slavery*, Washington recounts the story of one of the duties he was asked to perform as part of his job, that of escorting an Indian boy from Hampton to Washington, D.C. The boy was ill and was to be delivered to the secretary of the interior, who was to give Washington a receipt for the delivery and then send the boy home to his reservation. Washington and the boy (who is not identified) began their journey on the Norfolk ferryboat. When dinner was announced on the boat, the two of them proceeded to the dining room; the Indian boy was immediately admitted and served, while Washington was told he would have to wait until the other diners had finished their meals and vacated the room. Washington tells the story in his book, without apparent rancor, as an illustration of "the curious workings of caste in America."[32] He had used the story earlier, in at least one instance, and on that occasion had attached a fuller explanation to the anecdote. At a speech before the Colored Young Men's Christian Association in Philadelphia in 1894, Washington told the story of the Norfolk ferryboat. This time, according to the newspaper account of the speech, Washington offered the story as evidence that "the prejudice against us negroes is not on account of our color, but because of the badge of slavery—the slavery we used to be in and the industrial slavery we are in now. . . . That Indian was a good deal darker than I am. But his people had never been in slavery, and my people had been and were, and that was the difference."[33] Washington's explanation is consistent with the one Charles M. Harvey later made in his 1913 *Atlantic Monthly* article: in race-conscious America, Indians have the advantage over African Americans because Indians were never slaves.

Washington's ferryboat story does indeed illustrate the "curious workings of caste" in the America of the late nineteenth century, though in more ways than Washington specifies. Washington was constrained by the Jim Crow codes of racial segregation; the boy was constrained by legal codes that made him a ward of the state whose movements were constantly regulated. The Indian boy was free to join the white passengers for dinner while Washington was not. But the reservation boy was not free to travel on his own, as Washington was; he was to be delivered by one supervisor to another, exchanged for a receipt, and then sent home to his reservation. At Hampton, this Indian boy and others could not choose to leave school—even for the summer or for family emergencies—as the black students could, and only the Indian students had to open their mail in the presence of a teacher.[34]

In assigning the cause of the prejudice against him to the historical fact of slavery and in suggesting that the Indian boy, in spite of his dark skin, had an advantage because Indians had not been enslaved, Washington was actually taking a position diametrically opposed to the position of some of the more vocal whites who were actively involved in Indian reform. From the perspective of these conservative reformers, the fact that African Americans were introduced to the culture of the United States through their experience of enslavement actually gave them an *advantage* over Indians, at least as far as their prospects for assimilation were concerned. At the basis of this argument were deeply racist (and widespread) assumptions about the propensity of African Americans to imitate or mimic those around them, especially whites, as well as equally racist (and widespread) assumptions about the innate self-assurance of the Indians that prevented them from acquiring anything useful from non-Indians.

Francis Leupp put these assumptions succinctly in his 1914 book, *In Red Man's Land*:

The Indian, instead of trying, like the negro, to copy his white neighbors, has usually stood aloof, maintaining a position in which a dignified recognition of the superior inventive genius of the white race is mixed with an assertion of his own equality in every other respect, and his entire content to remain as his Creator made him.[35]

Leupp had earlier (in 1910) raised the question of why American Indians had not produced a leader who could do for them what Leupp perceived Booker T. Washington to be doing for the uplift of black Americans. (Significantly, and not surprisingly, none of the whites with an interest in Indian affairs asked why there was no Indian version of the more radical Du Bois, whose reform agendas and attitudes toward cultural pluralism were actually much closer to those of Indian intellectuals than were Washington's.) Leupp's answer to his own question was based largely on his assumption that comparisons between blacks and Indians were fruitless, given their natural propensities and their recent histories. The common experiences of black people had drawn them together, Leupp argued, and their use of a common language helped to keep them together. It was therefore possible for a single leader to address the concerns and aspirations of all black people—whom Leupp considered to be, not coincidentally, eager to become as much like white people as possible. Indians, on the other hand, were congenitally independent, "full of race pride, disdainful of new and alien things"; in addition, they had retained their separate languages and separate traditions, which meant that no single leader could speak to them or for them. Leupp also argued that Washington's admonition to black Americans—most famously articulated in his "Atlanta Compromise" speech of 1895—to find the work that suited them and do it well enough to attract the attention and admiration of white Americans would be met with derision by an Indian audience, since "the only favor [Indians] have to ask of whites is to be let alone." Leupp's analyses led him to the general conclusion that the Indian problem, unlike the Negro problem, was "a human rather than a race question" and therefore not susceptible to race leadership.[36]

The monumental *Handbook of American Indians North of Mexico*, published by the Bureau of American Ethnology in 1907, included a lengthy entry on "Negro and Indian" written by Alexander F. Chamberlain of Clark University. Chamberlain focused much of his attention on the historical contacts and interchanges ("admixture" is his word) between African Americans and Indians, reaching a conclusion, strongly influenced by the ethnographic writing of James Mooney, that most cultural borrowings were unidirectional, with African Americans doing the borrowing. Chamberlain's conclusion relies on the notion, articulated by Leupp, that African Americans are imitative and Indians are not. The Indians therefore did not borrow much, while "the imitativeness of [the Negro] and his love for comic stories led him, Mooney thinks, to absorb a good deal from the Indian."[37]

Contrasting the status of American Indians with the status of African Americans was a favorite rhetorical technique of one of the most outspoken and intransigently patriarchal of the white reformers of the period, Richard Henry Pratt. Pratt had brought the original group of Indians to Hampton Institute, initiating that school's experiment in educating African Americans and Indians together—a plan that Pratt soon repudiated; subsequently he founded his own all-Indian school in Carlisle, Pennsylvania, where his largely inflexible theories of Indian education were translated into equally inflexible rules for students. Fundamental to Pratt's program was his idea that the farther Indians were removed from reservations and reservation culture the better their chances for assimilation and, indeed, for survival. Pratt therefore established an "outing" system, under which Indian students were sent to live and work in white communities as part of their Carlisle education; he adamantly opposed reservation schools (as opposed to the kind of off-reservation boarding schools for which he was providing the model at Carlisle) because they did too little to weaken the ties between the students and their home culture; he approved of military discipline and industrial education and disapproved of the use of tribal languages and too much study of academic subjects. In his particular take on the comparison between the Indian and Negro "problems," Pratt found evidence to support both his arguments for the Carlisle system and his fervently held belief that the reservation system was a moral and social evil.

Pratt argued that the United States had been able to absorb and civilize "ten millions of Black aborigines" in the course of its history, while the Indian population had been neither absorbed nor civilized after its subjugation, but had instead degenerated into a state of helpless dependency. These results, Pratt contended, were due entirely to the different systems of control imposed on the two populations, and especially to the policy of segregating Indians on reservations. While black slaves were forced to live among whites, adopting their habits and their language, Indians were forced to live apart from these "inestimable privileges." Slaves were forced to work and therefore learned the value of labor; reservation Indians were forced to depend on the government for the means of their survival. In the end, therefore, black people had it better than Indian people: "Slavery never more harshly grasped the negro as a race or compelled its intentions as relentlessly [as did federal Indian policy]. To enforce our decrees we used the whip on the negro but the gun on the Indian." Pratt's solution was to abolish the reservation system and force Indians to live among whites and to compete with them for the gains of civilization: "Can't you see that if the Indian could escape from the System and get out among civilized people, his eyes would open and he would then apprehend things as they are and be stirred to become a healthy factor in the country's affairs?"[38]

It can be difficult to determine exactly the racial attitudes held by men such as Pratt and Leupp, since their public statements were made in a politically charged environment and since both men were quick to offer broad generalizations about racial issues in the course of arguing for or against some particular policy. Both were, that is, political animals for whom a theory could be used to score a political point. Donal Lindsey argues, for example, that Pratt's enthusiasm for the outing system he developed at Carlisle, which he touted as the most effective means of smoothing the Indian student's rough edges, was due at least in part to his desire to locate his students as quickly as possible among white people and prevent the public from associating Indians with blacks. (The federal superintendent of Indian schools in 1901, Estelle Reels, recommended the Carlisle outing system for all Indian students in government schools. Her instructions to school superintendents strengthen Lindsey's argument about the racial underpinning of the outing system: Reels stipulated that the students be placed in "good white families"; the advantage for the Indian student was that he or she would have to "compete with wide-awake boys and girls of the white race."[39]) Pratt also came to disagree with his original collaborator in Indian education at Hampton Institute, Samuel Armstrong, that it would be appropriate for other all-black schools to follow the model of Hampton and begin admitting Indian students. Armstrong believed that it was best to place the Indians among the black students because "the aims and methods of most white schools render them unfit for Indians." Pratt couldn't have disagreed more, nor could he have been more confident that he was right. He explained his position in a letter to his friend and disciple, Carlos Montezuma: "All the great Negro Institutions do but consolidate and raceize the negro, and they see in my method of Americanizing and assimilating and abolishing race differences for the Indians, a threat to their work, and consequently they are not in sympathy with it, and never have been." Pratt also disapproved of Hampton Institute's stated aim of "developing race pride by producing race leaders" among its students—at least its black students; the school was not optimistic about the possibilities for Indian leadership. Hampton's magazine, the *Southern Workman,* carried an editorial comment in 1909 suggesting that, since the heterogeneity of the Indian population precluded the emergence of a leader like Booker T. Washington,

Indians would probably have to be satisfied with "shining examples" and "lesser lights" whose "modest achievements" could be an example to "the mind of the simple Indian." Pratt, on the other hand, avoided the whole question of race leadership, preferring that his Carlisle students shed as much of their racial identities as possible and "vanish" into the general population. Race leaders could only slow the process. Although Leupp and Pratt disagreed bitterly about many things, especially the value of off-reservation boarding schools as opposed to reservation day schools, they did share a commitment to what they and others termed the "vanishing policy," and it may well have been this commitment that led Leupp to dismiss the possibility that strong, racially identified leaders might emerge from the increasing ranks of educated Indians.[40]

Pratt's educational policies can seem unusually draconian in retrospect, especially his beliefs that Indian children had to be separated from their home environments and sent to off-reservation boarding schools if they were to make any progress toward assimilation and that academic study should be subordinated to manual training and work experience. Pratt was, without doubt, both rigidly paternalistic and pompously self-righteous in his attitudes toward Indians. (Even some of Pratt's contemporaries were appalled by his methods. F. F. Avery, superintendent of a reservation school in Miles, Washington, called Pratt's educational theories a "gospel of heartless selfishness" that saw Indian parents as "being beyond saving, or not worth saving—a part of conditions from which escape must be made at all hazards." Avery concluded, angrily, that "the resulting moral hurt may be incurable."[41]) As inflexible as Pratt's theories of education for Indians were, however, they were not, in their broadest outlines, inconsistent with the theories of other progressive reformers in education, many of whom were concerned with Americanizing immigrants and preparing them for industrial and agricultural vocations. John Dewey's Laboratory School in Chicago, which opened in 1896, was based on Dewey's idea that students learn through "active occupations" rather than through the "merely symbolic and formal"; hence his students, like Pratt's, were taught such practical skills as cooking, carpentry, and sewing. Pratt's statements about the civilizing goals of Indian education can sound like a rawer and much more rough-edged version of parts of Dewey's own credo, which emphasized "saturating [the student] with the spirit of service, and providing him with the instruments of effective self-direction." Pratt's vision of Indian education also resembles, at points, Jane Addams's vision of education for immigrant children—although hers does not have the militarist stamp of Pratt's. Addams wrote of the need, in working with immigrants, to "bring them in contact with a better type of American" and to introduce them to the practicalities of American life as well as to books: "We are impatient with schools which lay all stress on reading and writing, suspecting them to rest upon the assumption that the ordinary experience of life is worth little, and that all knowledge and interest must be brought to the children through the medium of books."[42] As a turn-of-the-century experimenter in education, then, Pratt was probably more typical than anomalous. Where his educational agenda differed most drastically and most controversially from those of other progressive educators was in his insistence that Indian children must be isolated from their families, homes, and native languages in order to limit their contacts, as far as possible, to whites who could serve as good role models.

That same conviction that Indians needed to be educated with whites lay behind Pratt's disagreements with Samuel Armstrong, and his reasons for disagreeing with Hampton's system of educating Indians and blacks in the same school eventually carried the day. Congress eliminated all funding for Indian students at Hampton in 1912 on the grounds that educating Indian and black students together was counterproductive. The eighty Indian students at Hampton signed a letter to Congress (although they apparently did not write it) protesting the cuts. The letter asserted, among other things, that "if the Indian is to keep his place in the world he must learn how to live with other men. . . . Surely the thrifty, hard-working Negro boys and girls at Hampton have much of good to give us."[43] In spite of their protest, John Hall Stephens of Texas, chairman of the House Committee on Indian Affairs, concluded that the government should not support integrated education but should provide schools that "separate these two races, and thus elevate the red race to the level of the white race and not degrade and humiliate him by sinking him to the low plane of the negro race."[44]

The comparisons between the Negro problem and the Indian problem came primarily from whites with an interest in Indian affairs and Indian reform; with a few exceptions, the SAI and individual Indian intellectuals, as well as black intellectuals, stayed away from such comparisons—and from each other. Du Bois and Charles Eastman both attended the Universal Races Congress in London in 1911, for example, but neither seems to have taken much notice of the other. Du Bois doesn't mention Eastman in his report on the variety of races represented at the Congress, published in the *Crisis,* and his biographer notes only that there was one unidentified Sioux from the United States present.[45] The distance that Indian intellectuals maintained from their African American contemporaries, which was clearly deliberate, was at least partially grounded in their recognition of the political liability of associating themselves in any way with the particularly virulent forms of racism directed at black Americans. Vine Deloria Jr. theorized in 1969, in comparing Indian activism with the black civil rights movement, that the U.S. government's attitudes toward blacks and Indians had been, historically, so different (if equally repressive) as to make collaboration between the two groups politically illogical: while the government had always tried to exclude blacks, Deloria argued, it had always tried to include Indians by erasing their Indianness and making them white.[46]

Indian spokespersons clearly found it more comfortable to compare their status with that of European immigrants, whom they saw as facing fewer racial barriers than did the black population but also as encountering fewer legal and cultural barriers than did the indigenous Native population. (The 1898 Supreme Court case of *United States v. Wong Kim Ark,* for example, had conferred citizenship on American-born children of immigrant parents, while specifically denying birthright citizenship to American Indians.) Carlos Montezuma liked to say, in his speeches and publications, that Indians would be much better off if they could be put on boats and then allowed to reenter the country as immigrants, with the same treatment and entitlements as new arrivals from abroad. Arthur Parker offered a more serious commentary in his 1916 article "Problems of Race Assimilation in America," in which he evaluated the relative difficulties of assimilation for European immigrants and Indians, while, in an unusual move for an SAI spokesperson, comparing both groups to African Americans. Of the three groups, Parker finds that the road to assimilation is easiest for the European immigrant: he is a white man (in Parker's formulation) who has relocated from one civilized country to another; he chooses to come to the United States, and he has time to prepare for his new life; he arrives expecting to work and already understands the value of money and property. The problems faced by African Americans, on the other hand, Parker sees as so enormous as to be almost insurmountable. These difficulties Parker attributes equally to three factors: the origins of American blacks in uncivilized Africa, the "race qualities of servility and imitativeness" that keep blacks from becoming self-reliant, and the prejudices of white Americans against the "darky habits of the Negro." In an admonition that seems laced with a cynical distrust of both white American tolerance and black American initiative and that reflects as well Parker's belief that all nonwhite populations, certainly including Indians, have to *perform* their abilities in a public way, Parker warns that "the Negro must demonstrate to the satisfaction of all men his equality and his capacity. Until then, civilization will hold the Negro in social and economic bondage and will count him an element to be exploited."[47]

When Parker turns to the assimilation prospects for American Indians, he locates the sources of difficulty almost entirely in the practices of white Americans and the policies of their government. Civilization was brought to the Indians, he explains, who saw no advantages in it and chose to remain aloof from it. But Parker's Indians were quickly overtaken by an invading culture they wished to have no part in: "The swift march of our modern economic life has been so great that the conservative Indian in his isolation has not quite understood his predicament." The reservation system, he adds, further isolated, confused, and disempowered the Indians. In spite of this history, Parker sees a much more promising future for Indians than for African Americans, largely because they don't face the massive obstacle of racial prejudice—and because, unlike European immigrants and African Americans, they have never been considered a labor force to be exploited. The Indian who escapes the reservation (and reservation habits of dependence), acquires an education, and becomes "engaged in the world's work" is, to all intents and purposes, already assimilated. The costs of assimilation for Indians, however, are high, since, like African Americans who have to renounce their "darky habits," and unlike European immigrants who are already culturally white, they must remake themselves—or at least their behaviors—in the image of white Americans: "To compete efficiently in civilization the Indian must conduct himself as a white man and under the white man's system of commerce. Then in order that the people about him may not regard him as a social or national menace he must actually have similar ideals and aspirations with other Americans."[48]

Although Parker thus separates Indians from both European immigrants and African Americans, arguing that the prospects for assimilation differ significantly for the three groups, he also suggests that Indians and African Americans share a history of victimization by white Americans that should make both groups expect little from white America in the future except exploitation of black labor and greed for Indian land. In the end, however, Parker returns to a focus on the differences in the way the two groups are perceived by white America, differences that outweigh any possible similarities. Full acceptance into American life he sees as a real possibility for Indians, because the assimilated Indians "constitute no grave social or race problems. Their aims and methods of thought are thoroughly American." African Americans, on the other hand, can expect to be at best tolerated and at worst exploited at every opportunity. To them, white America has this message: "In many respects you are unlike us and with some of us you are not over-welcome. However, we will tolerate you for after all you are a convenient laborer and may do even more for us, in time."[49]

Like his Indian colleagues, Parker was careful to make clear distinctions between the case of the Indians and the case of African Americans, acknowledging that the "Negro problem" was a thorny and worrying race problem that might not be solved for generations, rooted as it was in a persistent racial prejudice. If the Negro problem in America was generally perceived to be a problem with the Negro, Parker and other Indian spokespersons wished to make it clear that the Indian problem was not a problem with the Indian. Indians weren't a problem; Indians had a problem.

It may well have been because of this desire not to be classed with African Americans as part of the country's race problem that the Indian intellectuals and reformers did not address themselves in any significant way to the theories of race that were emerging in the early part of the century. The sources of these theories were various, ranging from the fieldwork of ethnologists like Boas to the racial classification schemes of eugenicists like Seth K. Humphrey and Madison Grant; what they had in common was the impulse to bring the methodological order of science to the vexing but fuzzy issues of race in America. While this racial science—or scientific racism, as the version represented by Humphrey and Grant has been rightly called—focused largely on the place of black people in a universal economy of races, the Smithsonian Institution, and especially its Bureau of American Ethnology, became a primary site for the study of the languages, traditions, and social practices of American Indians. The research centered in the Smithsonian, according to Frederick Hoxie, led to conflicting conclusions, especially concerning the significance of the racial identity of Indians. Some Smithsonian ethnologists concluded that racial characteristics were decisive in determining character, while others discounted race entirely and argued that environment was always determinative. Still others argued that race and environment worked together.[50]

The conflicting theories of racial development, even the discussions of the viability of race as a category for analysis, are centrally important to the history of American anthropology and ethnology as well as to the history of the construction of race in the United States. They are, however, less central to the history of Indian reform or Indian intellectualism around the turn of the century. Francis Paul Prucha has argued that scientific racism had little or no effect on the formulation of government policy toward the Indians in the nineteenth century; the significant influence, he contends, came not through science but through the Protestantism of the lay reformers. (It is probably more accurate to say that the effects on federal Indian policy of scientific racism and of the racial politics of the period in general were indirect and gradual rather than missing altogether.) In Prucha's formulation, the influence of the Protestant reformers was strongest in the period between 1865 and 1900, after which it began to decline, to be replaced eventually by the secular, social science approach that came with the New Deal and John Collier's directorship of the Bureau of Indian Affairs. The interim, which is essentially the period of this book, Prucha calls a transition period, with the Christian reformers gradually losing their influence while the social scientists had not yet fully established theirs.[51] (David Levering Lewis has described the period, less gently, as "a point in American history roughly equidistant between the espousal by the ruling classes of a fading creed of Christian uplift and their heartfelt embrace of a social gospel based on greed."[52]) Prucha is concerned entirely with white reformers and their influence on federal and state policies; I would extend his argument to include the Native reformers as well, whose positions and rhetoric were much more consonant with those of the white Protestant reformers than with those of the scientists or race theorists.

For the white reformers, the work of political and social reform continued to be central to the project of establishing a Christian civilization in America. Political issues were, for them, also fundamentally and unquestionably moral issues that required rational thinking and, above all, quick and effective action to produce visible changes. Some evidence of the extent of Protestant influence on the work of Indian reform is found in the (often overlapping) membership lists of the Lake Mohonk Conference and the Society of American Indians. The SAI list of associate (i.e., non-Indian) members for 1913 includes thirty who are identifiable as Protestant ministers. Perhaps more surprisingly, at least eight of the active (i.e., Indian) members in that year were also Protestant ministers.[53] More than one-fourth of the rosters of attending members at the Lake Mohonk Conference, from its first meeting in 1883 through its 1900 conference, consisted of Protestant ministers, their wives, and representatives of missionary organizations and other religious groups. Many other attendees were lay leaders in their churches.[54] The Lake Mohonk membership was also, significantly, primarily eastern and thus geographically removed from most of the sites of active contestation over the control and use of Indian lands. This distance allowed the Mohonkers to take a more theoretical stance toward land policies than did most of the westerners who spoke out on the issue, who were much more inclined to lobby for the immediate opening up of all Indian lands to white settlement. The general ethos that animated the Lake Mohonk Conference throughout its existence is suggested by the remarks of Lyman Abbott, a Congregationalist minister, in a speech made to the gathering in 1885: "The post-office is a Christianizing institution," Abbott announced; "the railroad, with all its corruptions, is a Christianizing power, and will do more to teach the people punctuality than schoolmaster or preacher can."[55] The political reform of Indian policy was, for Abbott and others at Lake Mohonk, undeniably a Christianizing project.

Because Abbott was so certain of the moral rightness of his ideas about Indians, and so vocal about them, a brief examination of his career is instructive for understanding the ideological bases on which much of the work of the white reformers was constructed. He was, early on, the protégé of Henry Ward Beecher, serving first as his successor as pastor of the Plymouth Church in Brooklyn and then, beginning in 1876, as his successor as editor of the *Outlook*—which at the time he began his editorship was called the *Christian Union*. Abbott remained as editor of the journal until his death in 1922. His concern for making the journal an organ for the expression of a Christian social conscience is suggested by the kind of works he published in serial form; they included Helen Hunt Jackson's *Ramona*, Booker T. Washington's *Up From Slavery*, Jacob Riis's *The Making of an American*, and Edward Everett Hale's *Memories of a Hundred Years*. Not only was Abbott's belief in the possibility of a Christian America not inconsistent with his belief in the possibility of a fully realized capitalist America; for him, it was *necessary* that a Christian America also be a capitalist America. He made this point explicitly in his 1896 book *Christianity and Social Problems:*

> The first duty a man owes is the duty of earning his own livelihood, and the livelihood of those who are intrusted [*sic*] to him. This is one of the foundation virtues. It underlies all civilization, all commercial well-being, all individual manhood. . . . The ambition to acquire, if acquisition is made subordinate to high and noble ends, is a noble ambition. . . . One object of Christianity . . . is to make all men capitalists. This object Christianity accomplishes wherever it succeeds in its mission, and the fact that churches

are capitalistic institutions is a witness that the hope of social reform lies in the church of Christ.[56]

Abbott's philosophy, as set out here, provides a capsule version of the theories that resulted in the passage of the General Allotment Act, or Dawes Act, of 1887—the legislation that mandated the division of tribally held lands into privately owned parcels, or allotments, to be granted to individual members of all allotted tribes. (Abbott was a vocal supporter of the legislation, and in fact claimed that the Dawes Act had its origins in discussions held in the editorial offices of his journal.) At the heart of Abbott's conception of a Christian civilization is the idea of individual self-sufficiency and ambition, an idea that he and other white Protestant reformers saw as completely antithetical to traditional tribal practices. For them, the reservation Indian was a generic figure, shaped—and limited—entirely by communal, tribal values and thus unfit for the kind of individualizing competition that characterized Christian citizenship. As Merrill Gates put it at the 1900 meeting of the Lake Mohonk Conference, "The deadening sway of tribal custom must be interfered with. The sad uniformity of savage tribal life must be broken up! Individuality must be cultivated."[57] For Abbott, Gates, and other Protestant reformers, the troubling fact about tribalism was not that traditional tribal spiritual beliefs and religious practices might be non-Christian or even anti-Christian; the problem was that the Indians' aversion to capitalist competition (at least as the reformers saw it) was clearly anti-Christian. Their plans for the conversion of Indians into Christian citizens began with the disintegration of the reservations and the transformation of their occupants into property owners.

Abbott's comments on the Indian question reinforce Robert Handy's observation that, after 1890, as American Protestants became more resolute and confident in their belief in the advance of Christian civilization, the emphasis on *civilization* gradually became more important to them than the emphasis on *Christianity.* "The concern for civilization," Handy notes, "which in the early nineteenth century had been secondary to the religious mission, was now often being put first, with religious mission as a means to the end of the Christianization of civilization. . . . Often unconsciously, an idealized Americanism had become the real center of interest for many Christians."[58] One result of that ideological (and rhetorical) shift can be seen in Abbott's repeated insistence that, in the case of Indian reform, some unpleasant sacrifices would have to be made to accommodate the inevitable progress of American civilization. Salvation, for Abbott, was primarily a matter of joining the winning side and making a go of it. Writing in the *Outlook* in 1901, he argued that the reservation system—the primary target of the Dawes Act—had perpetuated the habits of "barbarism" by separating Indians from the higher civilization around them. There was, he concluded, no moral or ethical reason to continue the reservations and a sound reason for getting rid of them. "Barbarism," he declared, "has no rights which civilization is bound to respect. In the history of the human race nothing is more certain than that civilization must conquer and barbarism must be subdued." Abbott acknowledged that many Indians would suffer under compulsory reforms and some might well die as a result, but such an outcome had its own moral justification, since "God's way of making men and women is through suffering and by struggle, and there is no other way."[59]

Abbott's morally certain position included a contempt for purely philanthropic or charitable approaches to the Indian question, approaches that he considered not just softhearted and ineffective but actually damaging to the moral and physical well-being of the Native population. A philanthropy designed only to protect the Indian from suffering or from falling victim to unscrupulous whites, he argued, "imperils, undermines, dwarfs, and destroys his manhood, under the impression that it is protecting his rights and providing for his well-being."[60] The muscularity of Abbott's Christianity fit well with the increasing signs, on the part of federal officials overseeing Indian affairs, of a desire to toughen and systematize the administration of Indian policy. *The Nation,* never one to wax sentimental, editorialized in 1904 that "the trouble with nearly every white philanthropist who addresses his attention to the Indian problem is that he lets sentiment dominate judgment."[61]

Francis Leupp put the matter frankly and succinctly in 1910, the year after he ceased being the chief administrator in the BIA:

> The Indian problem has now reached a stage where its solution is almost wholly a matter of administration. Mere sentiment has spent its day; the moral questions involved have pretty well settled themselves. What is most needed from this time forth is the guidance of affairs by an independent mind, active sympathies free from mawkishness, an elastic patience and a steady hand.[62]

Vine Deloria Jr. and Clifford M. Lytle have seen this complete dismissal of the "moral questions" by Leupp (and others) as an approving response to government efforts to make changes in the administration of federal Indian policies while not tinkering with the policies themselves. Leupp's statement, like Abbott's, seems intended to close off any further discussion of the moral, ethical, or political *rightness* of the allotment program and its attendant manipulations of Indian lands and lives and to refocus public attention on how best to get on with the business of making those manipulations more efficient. This bureaucratic perspective would be contested by, among others, Henry Roe Cloud, a (Winnebago) Presbyterian minister, educator, and active member of the SAI, who reminded the Lake Mohonk Conference in 1914 that, when the subject was Indian affairs, "every problem that confronts us is in the last analysis a moral problem."[63]

Neither Abbott nor Leupp identifies any specific sources of the "sentiment" and the "mawkish" philanthropy they castigate, although their language suggests two likely sources: women's Indian reform organizations, such as the National Indian Association (which was called the Women's National Indian Association from its founding in 1879 until 1901), and missionaries. The overlap between these two groups was extensive; many of the Protestant missionaries were women, and the NIA had early on chosen to direct its energies toward missions and leave the political reforms to male-dominated organizations such as the Indian Rights Association.[64] Another commentator on the "Indian problem," James McLaughlin, was more forthright in expressing his opinions about philanthropists and missionaries. McLaughlin, having spent thirty-eight years in the field as a reservation agent and inspector for the Indian Bureau, could speak with the gruff authority of the seasoned veteran. The Indian had been damaged, McLaughlin wrote, because "he has been coddled by a lot of fool friends whose hands he bit, or chased like a wild beast by fighting men who understood him no better than those who coddled him." McLaughlin was convinced that the problems posed by the uncertain status of the Indians would not be solved by missionaries or "bookmen" with their theories but by practical, tough-minded men with the right experience who could advise the government well. McLaughlin's own advice was that the government should give the Indians those things that were legally their due—land allotments, treaty and settlement monies—and then leave them alone to struggle with their futures: "It appears to me that it is the duty of the government to make some provision presently for the emancipation of these unhappy victims, to deliver them from the evils that guarantee a future of ungentle paupery, by giving to the Indian his portion and turning him adrift to work out his own salvation."[65]

Abbott, Leupp, and McLaughlin therefore agreed that what was needed to solve the Indian problem was more practical, hard-nosed administration that was resistant to sentiment of any kind; they did not agree, however, on general issues of policy. Abbott and McLaughlin both adopted the sink-or-swim position, arguing that anything less than a complete cessation of governmental and philanthropic grants would only encourage the Indian population, especially the reservation population, in idleness and dependence. Leupp argued, on the other hand, that the withdrawal of support needed to be gradual, on the grounds that Indians, by their very nature, were too diffident to succeed if they were simply thrown into competition with the white population. If the options were sinking or swimming, they would surely sink. What they needed, according to Leupp, was to be slowly coaxed into sufficient independence, through the *gradual* withdrawal of support, to allow them to manage on their own until they vanished as a separate and distinct population, through a combination of intermarriage, assimilation, and death by natural causes.

Leupp had articulated the rudiments of his "vanishing policy" in a 1900 article for the *Southern Workman* (five years before he became Commissioner of Indian Affairs), in which he began by proposing that the "line of nature" between the Indian and the white man was fixed and plain. Given their natural differences, it was futile, Leupp continued, to try to force the Indian to become something he was not and never could be:

> The duty of our higher civilization is not forcibly to uproot his strong traits as an Indian, but to induce him to modify them. . . . Our aboriginal brother brings, as his contribution to the common store of character, a great deal which is admirable, and which needs only to be developed along the right lines. Our proper work with him is improvement, not transformation.[66]

Taking a position that recalls Booker T. Washington's prescriptions for black education and uplift, Leupp further developed his argument in his 1910 book *The Indian and His Problem*. Leupp explained there his belief that education for Indians should be tailored to fit realistic Indian needs, prospects, and abilities; all the Indian student really needed from his academic education, he contended, was the ability to read the local newspaper, write an intelligible letter, and figure out whether the shopkeeper was cheating him. Otherwise, the student's training should be in practical manual skills. To expect to convert the Indian into a white man—to "transform" him—or even to expect too much of him as an Indian, was both futile and cruel:

> Nature has drawn her lines of race, which it is folly for us to try to obliterate along with the artificial barriers we throw down in the cause of civil

equality. The man whom she has made an Indian, let us try to make a better Indian, instead of struggling vainly to convert him into a Caucasian. Every attempt made by the Government, the politicians, or short-sighted educators, to blot out a distinction stamped upon him by a hand more powerful than ours, has accomplished nothing beyond making a strong man a hopeless and pathetic nondescript.[67]

Leupp's book was vigorously attacked in a review in the *Dial* by Fayette McKenzie, the (white) sociologist who was to be instrumental in the founding of the SAI only a few months later. McKenzie focused primarily on Leupp's insistence that Indians needed to be taught to be better at what they were already capable of doing rather than being given new skills to prepare them for a new life. McKenzie rejected as dangerously misguided Leupp's distinction between improvement and transformation, arguing that, as far as the Indians were concerned, the real choice was between transformation and *extinction*. Like Lyman Abbott, Richard Pratt, and James McLaughlin, McKenzie found the sink-or-swim approach to be the only viable one: "The Indian will never choose to jump the chasm which separates his stage of civilization from ours, yet his only hope of salvation lies in taking the leap. An Indian can survive in our civilization only by living in it and trusting to it, just as a man learns to swim only when he casts himself into the water."[68] (McKenzie's language in the review offers an interesting insight into his motivations for fostering the organization of the SAI, suggesting that he envisioned the society as consisting of Indians who had already taken "the leap" into a different "stage of civilization" and were prepared to encourage others to save themselves by taking the same dramatic action.)

Leupp's argument, with its premise that there are ineradicable, God-given differences between whites and Indians, was diametrically opposed to Pratt's argument that the things most closely associated with Indian identity—language, traditions, cultural practices—were the very things that most needed to be, and could be, eradicated. While Pratt wanted to erase all signs of what he called "Indianess," Leupp saw the racial and cultural distinctiveness of Indians as fixed. His largely political argument, that transformation was an impossibility and should not be a policy aim, was given a more specifically cultural interpretation by the University of Pennsylvania anthropologist Frank G. Speck, who essentially concurred with Leupp's contention that trying to transform the Indian into an imitation white person would only produce what Leupp had called a "nondescript" and Speck called an "anomaly." For Speck, the "Indianess" that Pratt abhorred was precisely what needed to be preserved and even encouraged, in the interest both of the Indians and of the country as a whole.

In a 1912 article entitled "Conservation for the Indians," published in the *Southern Workman*, Speck argued that Indian populations needed to be protected from the overzealousness of those reformers who would coerce the Indian "to deliberately lose his tribal and racial identity and cast in his lot in modern competitive industrial life with European immigrants." Taking a position that was not to find significant bureaucratic or public support for another twenty years, Speck called for the extension of a "cultural tolerance" to the Indians like that extended to immigrants. To deprive Indians of their languages, customs, and tribal identities, Speck argued, was to reduce them to anomalies—neither one thing nor another—and to deprive them of the racial pride that had, ironically, always won the admiration of white Americans. Indian people had much to contribute to the country, he noted, especially through their cultural productions—the "exuberant wealth of native Indian literature, music, and art." To allow the free expression of native arts would give a "most refreshing coloring" to American culture in general. Speck included in his argument a warning against the "too enthusiastic self-conceit of the dominant race," conjecturing that perhaps "one of our greatest but least realized faults is our enthusiasm for ourselves, possibly through failing to realize our own cultural setting."

Speck's was essentially a call for the extension of the philosophy of racial and cultural pluralism to include American Indians. His article, especially given its title, immediately invites comparison with the earlier and more well-known argument for pluralism made by W. E. B. Du Bois in his "Conservation of the Races" speech, given at the organizational meeting of the American Negro Academy in 1897. As Du Bois had done, Speck contended that the vitality of American culture depended on the distinctive contributions of its diverse racial and ethnic populations. There was, however, one crucially important difference in the positions of the two men. In what seems partly a specific rejoinder to Du Bois and other black cultural conservationists (he was writing fifteen years after Du Bois's speech and nine years after the publication of *The Souls of Black Folk*) and partly an effort to be sure the cases of blacks and Indians were not collapsed in the public consciousness, Speck singled out the Negro as an example of the complete *loss* of racial distinctiveness. The Indian, he argued, because of his refusal to yield up his independence, could still command the respect of white America, while the prejudice against the Negro was attributable to his readiness to conform:

The unenviable present social position of the Negro masses is undeniably partly due to the way in which they have faithfully allowed their native originality to become annihilated. In the first place the Negro, as a rule, submitted to slavery almost cheerfully after the first generation of subjugation, forgetting his native African language, institutions, virtues, such as they were, and all that made him stand for something independent. . . . The Indian on the other hand never submitted to even a momentary slavery, he has admirably clung to his language and many of his institutions, and thereby held himself apart from a debased cultural and moral subjugation to the dominant race.

The Negro's "experiment in mild submission," Speck announced, had obviously been a failure.[69]

Speck concluded his article by mentioning the newly formed Society of American Indians, which he urged to include a policy of cultural conservation in its program. His argument received a response a few months later in an article, also in the *Southern Workman*, written by one of the most active and vocal members of the SAI, Speck's old friend Arthur C. Parker.[70] Although Parker does not specifically mention Speck or his essay, he does specifically criticize the "conservative policy" that Speck had endorsed, naming it as one of the two radically different positions being taken by "earnest champions" of the Indian. The conservationist, according to Parker, works from a basic (if oversimplified) question: Why should any Indian "abandon his splendid traditions, his reverent religion, and his picturesque ceremonies for a mess of civilized pottage that is even now turning sour with age and infection? In a word, why should not broad America have room for her native people and leave them as they are?" The second position Parker identifies as that of the "extreme progressionist[s]," those like Richard Pratt and Lyman Abbott and the Lake Mohonk Friends of the Indian (although again Parker mentions no names) who contend that all races progress only through competition and struggle and that the only way Indians can survive is through learning from whites—as quickly as possible—how to live like whites in a white-dominated world. The central tenet in progressionist thinking is, in Parker's words, that "the persistent endeavor to advance, the struggle to attain, and the desire to obtain that which is better gives to a race its strength."

Having set out both positions, Parker then offers his own argument for a "sane middle ground" between the two. By introducing some practical and material considerations, Parker offers a corrective to the abstract (and largely ahistorical) theorizing of Speck and other social scientists—both professional and amateur. The problem with the conservationist position, he notes, is that it includes no advice about how the Indian who adheres to tribal traditions is to live successfully among whites—or, as Parker puts it, "how the Indian is to deal with the 'white problem.' " The extreme progressionist position, on the other hand, commits the basic error of "confusing civic and ethnic elements" by working off the assumption that cultural distinctiveness precludes patriotism and civic responsibility. The Indian who is being schooled for a life of competition among whites is often required to abandon his language, cut his tribal and family ties, and repudiate his traditions. He becomes "de-Indianized," and in the process he loses his racial pride and may even come to despise himself. Alternatively, he may eventually reject his education altogether, concluding that he has been manipulated and robbed, and then he may "go back to the blanket," more firmly committed than ever to a separate, traditionalist life.

Parker's argument for a "sane middle ground" rests on a series of pragmatic propositions that make up what he might have called his theory of adjustment. Beginning with the admonition that "absolute uniformity" is never necessary, Parker goes on to say that "as long as the Indian finds efficiency in his native ideas," there is no reason for him to abandon them. At the same time, it is essential for the Indian to leave behind any traditional habits that he might hold to for their own sake and to "adjust himself to modern conditions." In the increasingly competitive and even predatory society of the United States, such flexibility is especially necessary: "If there can be no adjustment there can be no hope for survival." Giving his own spin to the nearly ubiquitous sink-or-swim metaphor, Parker characteristically adjusts it rather than rejecting it: "The Indian of America may wear his own style of swimming suit and use his own special swimming stroke. He will progress faster and keep afloat better by doing so." Similarly, he adjusts Speck's observation that Indians have much to contribute to American aesthetic culture. His comments suggest that Speck's vision, which considered only Native contributions to the arts, is too narrow and reductive and excludes the Indian intellectual; the self-sufficient, self-aware Indian, Parker insists, "may add materially, not only to art and literature but to philosophy and politics."

In a final response to Speck's article, Parker concludes, as Speck had done, with a reference to the SAI, and again he aims for the middle ground. Parker explains that it is because the Indian needs to cultivate both his Indianness and his humanity, his local and his cosmopolitan identities, that the SAI had formulated its objectives as it had, recognizing both the need to promote "the advancement of the Indian in enlightenment that leaves him free as a man to develop according to the natural laws of social evolution" and the equally important need to "present in a just light the true history of the race, to preserve its records, and emulate its distinguishing virtues." In Parker's view, the Indian needed to be free to perform his part on the universal stage according to the same natural laws that applied to everyone else, but he needed to perform *as an Indian,* with his racial and cultural identity intact. His success on that stage could and should be a source of racial pride.[71]

Parker's article begins to suggest the reasons for the formation of the SAI and some of the reasons that its members launched their project with such enthusiasm. The organization offered an opportunity to escape or at least contest the usually unreflective paternalism that characterized the statements of white reformers and policy makers and gave Indian intellectuals a voice in the debates that directly and often disastrously affected their lives. Parker's article also suggests his awareness that the argument needed to be joined judiciously and on terms that had already been set (even if the terms needed to be adjusted). Indian intellectuals, that is, were conscious of their need to demonstrate not just their right but also their ability to enter the public arena *as* intellectuals—as informed thinkers able to situate their particular, local concerns within a cosmopolitan or universal context.

At the same time, Parker's article, with its confidence in the self-evident superiority of the "sane middle ground," a purely theoretical space that Parker envisioned as inhabited by the same generic Indian who inhabited the less placid spaces imagined by the white reformers, suggests the difficulties the SAI would face in entering the public sphere of debate and politics, some of which would prove very daunting indeed. Parker's experience is illustrative. No one embraced the work of the SAI with more initial enthusiasm and optimism. But by 1923, as a result of his experiences with the efforts of the organization to be genuinely pan-Indian, Parker had lost confidence in his own theories, concluding that "there is no such being or race today in America as 'The Indian.' To the contrary, there are between 300,000 and 340,000 persons of more or less Indian blood, each one of whom has his own vital individual interests."[72] As Parker and others were to learn, the Indian of intellectual debate and the thousands of Indians whose futures awaited the outcome of the debate, especially those struggling with the dispiriting realities of reservation life, often had very little in common.

CHAPTER 3 FOR THE GOOD OF THE INDIAN RACE
THE REFORM OF POLITICS

In 1887, William Barrows responded to the passage of the Dawes Act by publishing *The Indian's Side of the Indian Question,* a boosterish celebration of the possibilities opened up by the allotment program for extending Anglo-Saxon "sacrifice, and romance, and heroism, and humane and Christian devotion." Barrows was cheerfully confident that a population of allotted Indians would be a good proving ground for the robust principles of American civic religion: "For we will not admit that our common Christianity and our American civilization properly applied cannot make a fair Christian and a fair citizen out of an American Indian." Barrows did acknowledge, however, that "the Indian question" had become more and more complex over the years, acquiring in the process what he called its ten "faces": the Indian agent, the Indian contractor, the land speculator, the railroad builder, the philanthropist, the romantic admirer, the citizen friend, the man of visions, the Christian workingman, and the matter-of-fact man. The most obvious omissions from his list are, of course, the Indian people themselves, whom Barrows can envisage (in spite of the entirely misleading title of his book) only as the recipients of white bounty and the beneficiaries of a newly awakened moral sense among progressive white Americans. The Dawes Act had initiated a "new Indian era," Barrows asserted, and "it is with the superior race to make it a success or a failure. The whites are masters totally of the situation."[1]

Barrows is more egregiously blunt than most white commentators of the time in declaring the superiority and mastery of his own kind, but his general sense of white efficiency and Indian malleability was certainly widely shared, even among those who took the most active interest in Indian welfare. When the issue of how to resolve the "Indian question" arose, interested whites, no matter what their ideological or political perspective, were apt to adopt a discourse of instrumentality. Elizabeth Peabody, for example, writing in 1886 in sympathetic support of Sarah Winnemucca's efforts to establish independent Indian schools in Nevada, observed that one advantage of educating Indian children was that it could result in "making a healthy wild stock of natural religion on which to graft a Christian civilization worthy of the name." Francis

Leupp commented in 1907, while he was serving as Commissioner of Indian Affairs, that "in 'educating' the Indians our best plan is to take them as we find them and build on that foundation, instead of trying to sweep the foundation away and build anew from the bottom." James McLaughlin, writing in 1910 about his experiences among the Standing Rock Sioux, described the reservation agent's responsibility (in an unappetizing and somewhat confusing image) as "the task of taking the raw and bleeding material which made the hostile strength of the plains Indians, of bringing that material to the mills of the white man, and of transmuting it into a manufactured product that might be absorbed by the nation without interfering with the national digestion." Francis Leupp's successor as Commissioner of Indian Affairs, Robert Valentine, published an article, also in 1910, entitled "Making Good Indians," in which he declared his confidence that white Americans could, "with the right engineering for a few years, get [the Indian] well rooted as a productive citizen." The metaphors of grafting, building, manufacturing, and engineering used by these writers suggest the variety of ways that whites imagined themselves as creative agents responsible for shaping the pliant and inchoate material of an Indian selfhood they were inclined to represent as generic.[2]

This kind of public statement also helps to make clear the reason that the founders of the Society of American Indians saw their organization as crucially important—and the reason for their initial excitement about its prospects. The SAI promised to give Indian people an entry into an ongoing public conversation that was all about them but excluded them; to identify the most appropriate individuals to represent Indian perspectives to a larger audience; and to demonstrate the ability of those individuals who entered the public arena to perform the roles of informed, civic-minded citizens. The original circular letter sent to prospective members, over the signature of Fayette McKenzie, described in enthusiastic terms the ambitious goals of the organization:

> The chief reason we continue to have an Indian problem is because the public generally does not believe that the Indian is capable of education, culture, or high morality. I am therefore inviting the educated and progressive Indians of the country to meet in a National Conference in the fall of 1910. Even as the navigator Columbus discovered the old Indian in 1492, may we not hope that the city of Columbus shall discover the "new Indian" in 1910? . . . No such meeting of natives has ever been held in this country. No concerted effort for the welfare of the Indians has ever been

attempted by Indians. A glorious work is possible. The time has come when a "Mohonk by Indians" can do even more for the country than a "Mohonk for Indians."[3]

McKenzie continued to drum up support for what he saw as the momentous first meeting of the new Indian organization (the meeting was proposed for 1910 but did not take place until 1911). He wrote to one important prospective ally, Carlos Montezuma, conveying his belief that "this Conference will do in many unconscious ways a work which will dissolve the whole Indian situation, perhaps I should say resolve the whole situation into one so different that, almost without our knowing it, a revolution will have been accomplished. . . . I hope that you will spread the news of the large movement as widely and as often as you can."[4]

The launching of the society's journal, the first issue of which appeared in April 1913 under Arthur Parker's editorship, was a cause for further optimism and excitement. The National Indian Association, the largest of the women's Indian reform groups, called the issuing of the journal "something entirely and actually new under the sun. A real event in the history not merely of American journalism, but of the world's journalism."[5] Parker wrote to Alice Denomie—who was working as an unpaid assistant to the SAI and had become disheartened by the amount of work her volunteer position required—assuring her that the appearance of the journal was going to change everything. "Just wait for the famous Journal," he urged. "It will be a bombshell. We must send a copy to every member of the Lake Mohonk conference, the Indian Rights Association and the best people everywhere. It will go a long way to save us." Parker used the first issue to convey that same exuberant prediction to his readers: "This issue of the *Journal* and the next mark the beginning of a work, the vastness of which we can only dream."[6] Parker also used the occasion of the journal's launching to send a form letter to SAI members, reminding them of how much the society had accomplished in just two years. Primarily, according to Parker, it had demonstrated to a skeptical public how much Indians could accomplish in their own interests: "Never before has the public taken so much interest as now. Never before has the Indian race taken so much interest in itself as in these two years. Your Society is responsible for a large share in this awakening. We have shown that the Indian can organize powerfully and successfully."[7]

Although Parker continued to express confidence and determination through his editorials and articles for the *Journal,* even he was eventually overwhelmed by the immensity and complexity of the work the organization had set for itself. By 1917, Parker was acknowledging his frustration in his private correspondence, expressing his disappointment with "the results of all conferences" and his sense that the SAI, in trying to be truly pan-Indian and to incorporate a wide range of perspectives, had paralyzed itself "by our very 'democracy.' " In 1923, when the society had virtually dissolved, Parker was approached by someone who had hopes of keeping the organization alive. Parker responded by declaring it dead. By that point, the overworked Parker had become pessimistic about either interesting the general Indian population in new ideas or reinvigorating old interests and energies. "Few [Indians] have any very deep interest based on the idea of race," he wrote. "If there is such interest it is historical or sentimental and the blunting of the ideals of the old red man conspire to prevent the floating [of] any great Indian organization. . . . To go into the work too deeply only brings a heartache."[8] As Parker's comments here and elsewhere suggest, the SAI did eventually succumb to its own ambitions and to the inability of its members to agree on how to translate grand ideals and theories, vaguely stated, into a practical program that would be relevant to a thoroughly heterogeneous constituency. Many of those, like Parker, who tried to shape the SAI into a "great Indian organization" that would outlast them became frustrated and exhausted by the effort. Hazel Hertzberg, in her meticulous documentation of the rise and fall of the SAI, concludes that it was not "even remotely successful" in effecting significant change in the Indian policies of the government: "It was a reform organization which could not achieve reforms. And as in other reform movements unable to deliver concrete results, its members began to vent their frustrations upon each other, and conflicts hitherto minor began to assume major proportions."[9]

To survey the papers of the organization and those of some of its leading members is to become acutely aware, as Hertzberg was, of the personal conflicts and organizational in-fighting that dogged the SAI from the beginning. However, one also becomes aware that lying behind those conflicts was a mass of large, knotty issues and questions that were beyond the ability of even the most committed individuals to manage or control. The discussion of those issues in print and in open meetings often led to bitter conflicts and divisions of opinion about specific courses of action. To some of the participants, however, this public airing of hard questions came to seem a significant accomplishment in itself, the real raison d'être of the organization. The ultimate goals were, of course, a change in the wardship status of Indian people and in the conditions of life for them, but getting to those longest-range goals required a collective thinking through of complex issues in an effort to help create and shape something brand new—an Indian public opinion.

Because they needed both financial and political support from outside their own ranks, SAI leaders had to take into account the expectations of white sympathizers in shaping their statements and positions. They also had to negotiate their way around or through the paternalism of progressive reform groups like the Lake Mohonk Conference and the National Indian Association and, more important, of officials in the Indian Bureau. In addition, they had to confront their own, crucially important internal questions: about how to define their primary audience, about their relationship both to the Christianity that was so important to many white reformers and to those social science disciplines that were developing their own approaches to the study of Indians, and about what specific forms and directions their own progressivism would take. In short, they had to confront difficult questions about what it meant to be an Indian public intellectual at the beginning of the twentieth century. They disagreed more often than they agreed, but many of the participants in this process—as we shall see—were to find the rough intellectual give-and-take a measure of their success rather than a sign of their failure.

Some of the complexities of the SAI's position vis-à-vis other reform organizations can be illustrated by considering the conference sermon delivered by Washington Gladden at the second annual meeting of the society, held in October 1912. Gladden was among the best-known and most influential of the Social Gospel ministers, a visible presence in many areas of progressive reform (and an associate member of the SAI). He enthusiastically endorsed the young organization in his conference sermon, calling the attendees "a band of prophets and prophetesses to whom the scattered remnant of a mighty race is very dear" who had gathered to "reassert their claim to the birthright of humanity and to take the place that belongs to them among the people." Such a gathering Gladden found "touching and inspiring." When he turned to offering advice and exhortation to the group, though, his comments suggest how great a distance there was between the philosophy of the social gospeller and the practical needs and aims of the group whose existence he found touching. Race consciousness could be a good thing, he asserted, but only when it led to an awareness of what the race could contribute to the good of the whole. Any race "must be ready to take the task that no other race can perform and the service that no other race can render." The first object of the SAI should be, therefore, to inspire "all the rest of the race" to understand that the aim of life is service to others. "It is not your primary concern as Indians," Gladden admonished his listeners, "to get your rights recognized. It is your primary concern to get a clear conception of your duties, of your high calling as a people." To think this way would allow the SAI to become part of a great progressive movement, a new way of thinking about social change:

> The one thing which is getting pretty thoroughly demonstrated is, that the principle of every man for himself or every class for itself or every race for itself will not work; that it will bring chaos and destruction sooner or later to all who put their trust in it. I think that you are fortunate in setting forth on the enterprise at a time like this, when the old individualistic ethics is so palpably going to pieces; when it is becoming so evident that the only way of life for a man or a class or a race, is the way of unselfish service.[10]

There is much in Gladden's sermon that now sounds familiar. He echoed the sentimental, stereotypical notion held by much of the public that any surviving Indians were only a sad "remnant," and his admonitions were as peremptory and paternalistic, in their way, as the statements of the Lake Mohonkers and other reformers. His specific instructions to the Indians, however, ran exactly counter to much of what they were hearing from Indian reform groups. In declaring the philosophy of individualism chaotic, destructive, and finally moribund, for example, Gladden might have been pointing his finger directly at Lyman Abbott, Merrill Gates, and other Lake Mohonkers, who had insisted for years that the salvation of Indian people was to be found only through the cultivation of an aggressive, competitive individualism. That philosophy, Gladden wanted his listeners to believe, had been a demonstrable failure. Similarly, in telling his audience that they should not be primarily concerned with securing their rights, even though they represented a people "so long enthralled and repressed,"[11] Gladden implicitly disparaged the work of the white organization most closely associated with and akin to the SAI, the Indian Rights Association, whose primary purpose was to protect and enlarge Indian rights. His instructions to the Indian audience to devote themselves to a life of service, furthermore, did not accord well with the insistence of the Indian Bureau that Indians must learn to look out for themselves and sustain themselves through a life of remunerative work. (The postallotment policy of the Bureau was, as the superintendent of Indian schools put it, to "equip [the Indian] with the ability to become self-supporting as speedily as possible."[12])

Finally, Gladden's prescriptions for selfless service contradicted some of the society's own stated objectives, the first of which was "to promote and co-operate with all efforts looking to the advancement of the Indian in enlightenment which leaves him free as a man to develop according to the natural laws of social evolution." Another of the objectives of the SAI was "to promote citizenship and to obtain the rights thereof."[13] In eliding the whole issue of citizenship, Gladden overlooked what was perhaps the most crucial factor in the list of specific concerns for Indian intellectuals, the factor that most insistently distinguished them from other progressives. Not having the constitutional right to citizenship and therefore subject to the status of being wards of the state, Indian intellectuals invited, unwillingly but inevitably, exactly the kind of paternalistic condescension they received from Gladden. Whereas they set out to represent themselves as socially conscious reformers and thus the coevals of someone like Gladden, his approach had the effect of relegating them to the position of stateless dependents and supplicants, a remnant in need of instruction and care.

Gladden clearly had his own sure sense of what it meant to be progressive in 1912, a sense formed and refined through his many years of public engagement as a minister and social reformer. What it meant to be an *Indian* progressive, on the other hand, was a question that it was much less easy for anyone to be sure about—and a question to which Gladden apparently had not given much thought before offering his sermon to an Indian audience. The term *progressive* had a particular history for Indians; it had long been used in the discourse of Indian affairs and had acquired a specific set of implications within that context. The distinction between *progressives* and *traditionals* (or *nonprogressives*) became a form of shorthand, a reductive kind of code, widely used by Indian agents and white observers to describe reservation Indians (replacing the more common *friendlies/hostiles* distinction of prereservation years). One version of that code was set out by Herbert Welch, the founder of the Indian Rights Association, who described the Sioux in 1891 as split into two groups, each defined entirely by its attitude toward white culture and religion. The nonprogressive party was "pagan," according to Welch, hating everything belonging to the white world and maintaining a "hostility to the Government and to white civilization." The progressive party, on the other hand, "could properly be termed the Christian party, whose life was begotten, nourished, and trained by missionary enterprise and devotion."[14]

In his study of the Northern Utes, David Rich Lewis has outlined the way these terms formed, for reservation agents, a descriptive binary that had the effect of occluding the shifting, day-to-day realities of political and social life for many individual Utes. According to this binary, progressive Indians spoke English, lived in houses, worked primarily as farmers, and sent their children to school. Traditionals or nonprogressives preferred to live by herding and hunting, which made them nomadic rather than settled, and they were resistant to schooling their children. Not surprisingly, among the Utes as well as other groups, those who agreed to the allotment policy were assumed to be progressives, while those who resisted marked themselves as traditionals. The same pattern appears regularly in accounts of the postallotment period from various parts of the country. Thomas Wildcat Alford, for example, writing about the Absentee Shawnees of Oklahoma, notes that "there was a division among the tribe, when those under the leadership of chiefs John Sparney and Joe Ellis—called the progressives—accepted the allotments allowed by the government . . . Those under chiefs Big Jim and Sam Warrior, numbering nearly half the tribe—known to the government as the non-progressives—refused to accept such allotments." Significantly, Alford, himself an Absentee Shawnee, makes it clear that he is using the terms *progressive* and *non-progressive* as government-applied labels rather than as meaningful descriptors.[15]

When the SAI appealed to progressive Indians, therefore, as Fayette McKenzie did in his initial announcement and as Arthur Parker continued to do in his writing for the journal, they inevitably invoked both the accumulated meanings of the term as it applied specifically to Indian people as well as the more recent meanings it had acquired for reformist thinkers and activists such as Gladden. If the second set of meanings aligned Indians with a cosmopolitan ethos and a visible group of white elites, the alignment was qualified by the first set of meanings, which separated Indians out, distinguished them from any other population, and located them within a limiting and paternalistic paradigm. Progressive whites could and did see themselves as intellectual free agents, prepared to lead, counsel, and uplift others. Among those others were the "progressive" Indians, whom whites continued to see as a defined and special group, susceptible to uplift and advancement, but still Indians and therefore wards in need of direction and control.

Arthur Parker's six-year editorship of the SAI journal (1913–18) provides an opportunity to consider one Indian intellectual's attempt to negotiate the discursive terrain of the "Indian question" and to manipulate the discourse to make it serve what he believed to be the most pressing needs of Indian people. Because Parker was convinced of the need to negotiate and committed to the tactics of mediation, his writing is often so cautious, reserved, and occasionally imitative that it can convey little conviction or even, at times, little specific meaning. The language of his description of the purpose of the SAI, appearing in the inaugural issue of the journal, is not atypical. The plan of the society, he wrote, "is to develop race leaders, to give hope, to inspire, to lead outward and upward, the Indian American as a genuine factor in his own country and lead him to see that upon his individual effort depends his share in the salvation of his race and his value to his country."[16] There are many understandable reasons for Parker's vagueness and his use of catchphrases in statements like these—including his awareness of the extremely heterogeneous nature of the constituency, both Indian and non-Indian, that the journal and the society needed to attract and hold. Because he was so conscious of that need, Parker was insistent, especially as conflicts began to appear within the membership, that the society have ample room for a variety of opinions, and he took care to publish articles representing a range of ideological and political positions. He was also insistent that the society must not alienate white reform groups, since they had the resources to be of real political and material help to the SAI. As he wrote to the executive committee of the society in early 1912, "If our officers and our plans do not appeal to the Indians whom we seek to uplift and to benefit and if these do not appeal to influential non-Indians and Indian organizations, such as the various 'associations' and rights societies, we will fail to hold our own."[17] As a result, his writing can seem strained or flattened or ambivalent in its effort not to contradict or even strongly contest any of those positions. As a writer and editor, Parker seems to have considered it his role to please and to appease.

There are moments, however, when Parker abandoned his neutral, mediating role to offer a calculated argument, sometimes an emotional argument, and in those moments his writing becomes stronger, more compelling, and certainly more interesting. One of the most forthright of his arguments appeared in 1915 under the unpromising title, "Certain Important Elements of the Indian Problem."[18] Parker begins the essay by noting that the immense efforts of both church and state to remedy the Indian problem have produced few positive results. Both entities continue their efforts anyway, convinced that "Providence has entrusted a benighted people to their keeping" and blaming any of their failures on the intractability of the Indians. The real problem, Parker argues, is not with recalcitrant Indian resistance to white benevolence but with the myopia of a white America that has never understood, or even tried to understand, the nature and the seriousness of the injuries it has inflicted on the Indian population. Before whites can figure out how to *help* Indians, they must first understand what they have *taken away from* Indians. Parker then lists seven specific "charges" against "American civilization," accusing the American people of robbing Indians of their intellectual life, their social organization, their native freedom, their economic independence, their moral standards, their "good name among the peoples of the earth," and their civic status. For Parker, the most important results of these robberies are not poverty and disfranchisement, although these are real enough, but a psychological and emotional debilitation, a sense of debasement, bitterness, grief, and abjection. Every American Indian who has suffered from this oppression, Parker contends, feels that American civilization has "1. Made him a man without a country; 2. Usurped his responsibility and right of acting; 3. Demeaned his manhood; 4. Destroyed his ideals; 5. Broken faith with him; 6. Humiliated his spirit; 7. Refused to listen to his petitions." These are the results only of recent wrongs; there is a long history of more overt violence against Indian people—wars; the murder of women, children, and the old; the theft of land—to which Parker refers briefly, only to declare that history largely irrelevant to his real subject, which is the current state of things in Indian country, especially the psychological condition of its inhabitants.

This kind of bold and angry accusation is rare, not only for the usually diplomatic Parker but for his journal as well. In this case, he justifies making the angry charges against whites by subordinating them to the account of the psychological, emotional, and cultural damage that has resulted from white violence against Indians. Whites need to understand this "psychic equation," he argues, before they can make any progress in solving, or helping to solve, the problems they have created. The fundamental element in this equation, according to Parker's list, is the dislocation of Indian intellectual life. The deracination that has accompanied the imposition of Christianity, the English language, and the reservation system has deprived Indian people of the "thought world" that once was familiar and coherent, "yet nothing that could be easily or effectively understood was given to replace this mental life." The replacement for the old intellectual life must come, Parker argues here and elsewhere, through the kind of education that will equip Indians to live, without confusion, in the new world into which they have been thrust. Responsibility for initiating Indian education lies primarily, and necessarily, with the whites who control that new world: "Civilization through its schools must give back [to] the red man great ideals over which he may map his life and by which he may build his character."

The confidence Parker expresses here in the power of schooling as a means of aligning Indian consciousness with white realities, coupled with his anger and despair at the conditions prevailing in most of Indian country, helps to explain his general insistence that an organization like the SAI should be made up of educated and "progressive" Indians. His assessment, if pushed to its logical conclusion, would make Indians who have been educated by whites the *only* ones capable of a full intellectual life under the new dispensation, the only ones able to "map" their lives on an intellectual foundation that has not been discredited. Although Parker does not go so far as to equate formal education with the intellectual life, he does see education as prerequisite to escaping the entrapments of history and relocating the means of self-expression under the new dispensation: "The Indian has one door to true freedom—it is the door of education. Through it he may again find a greater life than that which his ancestors have lost."

Fayette McKenzie had written to Parker in 1911 with a plan for improving Indian education that particularly interested Parker. Noting that the best hopes for Indians "will proceed from and through the broader and higher leadership which will come from a broader and higher education," McKenzie recommended the establishment of an Indian university that would provide two years of college preparation and then two years of college-level work, after which students could finish their educations anywhere they chose. Parker responded to this suggestion with enthusiasm. "Your 'College' plan is of much interest to me," he wrote to McKenzie. "I can even imagine that progressive Indian communities like the Choctaws and Cherokees, and the like, would have their future politicians trained there. . . . I should like to see a school of this sort foster an Indian literature, not necessarily the old, but also the new. The poems of Pauline Johnson, Alex Posey, the writings of Eastman, Simon Pokagon, Zitkalsa [*sic*] and others might be rescued from oblivion or popularized still further."[19]

In this case, as almost always, Parker's visions of reform and uplift are sketched in general terms and focus primarily on those people who might best represent a newly imagined, bourgeois Indianness to the public; here, they are future politicians from "progressive" communities and published writers whose work would already be available to educated white readers.

Parker pursued the idea of an Indian university further in an article he wrote for the SAI journal in 1913. Having made the case that Indian students needed as much education as they could get if they were to compete successfully with whites, Parker then turned to the question of *where* Indian students should go to college. The answer, for him, was simple and unambiguous: the ordinary American university, he concluded, is "not good enough for the Indian. What the Indian has, ought to be the best. The American university is not the ideal school. . . . Therefore it is not good enough for the American Indian." The curriculum of the Indian university Parker envisaged would not be modeled on the courses of study in white schools, since "there is something better in life for the Indian than being like a white man," but would instead be open enough to allow each student to "develop his mind along the line for which he was best fitted by nature."[20]

McKenzie's and Parker's ideas for an Indian university met with considerable resistance—as did, for that matter, Parker's general belief in the urgency of organizing an educated, Indian elite. Richard Pratt, for example, argued strenuously, in as many venues as he could command, that separate education for Indians (in schools like his own Carlisle) was only a temporary expedient, a necessary evil, and that Indian students should be put into white schools as soon as possible. Once the students were merged into the public schools, Pratt argued, much of the reformers' work would be done: "Do not feed America to the Indian, which is a tribalizing and not an Americanizing process: but feed the Indian to America, and America will do the assimilating and annihilate the problem." The first three things that education should do for the Indian, according to Pratt, were to teach English, provide a usable, industrial skill, and cut all ties with tribal culture. "Book education" he saw as less important; in his list, it "logically comes last." Because Pratt saw the whole aim of Indian education to be that of training the Indian "to material usefulness and good citizenship," he took little interest in the possibilities of race leadership that animated McKenzie and Parker and apparently no interest in the group of Indian writers Parker names.[21] Pratt took specific exception to the Indian university proposal. He expressed his opinion in a letter to his protégé and admirer, Carlos Montezuma: "Of course I do not like Parker's idea of an Indian University, because all Universities are open to Indians and it is so much better [for them] to enter our own schools and universities for then they have to size up to the situation."[22]

While vocal, hard-line whites like Pratt could be an irritant to moderates like Parker, even more troubling were the Indian spokespersons who refused to consider the tactics of compromise that Parker found crucial, especially compromise with the Indian policies of the federal government. (Parker's own commitment to entertaining a variety of views is demonstrated by the number of times as editor of the SAI journal he published uncompromising opinions with which he strongly disagreed, including some of Pratt's.) Dennison Wheelock, an Oneida attorney and an early vice-president of the SAI (who had attended Carlisle), delivered a paper at the third meeting of the society in which he denounced any policies or practices, including educational practices, that segregated whites and Indians. Wheelock saw forms of segregation, beginning with the whole reservation system, as the government's way of demeaning Indians and duping them into thinking they were incapable of taking care of themselves. The message conveyed to the ordinary Indian by the Indian Bureau, Wheelock contended, was that "government schools are more suitable for the education of his children than white schools, because his children cannot learn as fast as white children, because the Indians are dirtier than white people's children, because if Indian children went to white schools they would get lonesome." Wheelock argued that the money currently used to provide a minimal, inadequate, and segregated education for Indian students could be much better used to support them in white institutions:

> Dotted everywhere in the land are the schools and colleges of the people of the United States, from whose portals come men and women not only able to live in civilization, but to make civilization. . . . If it is a good thing for the white man's children to attend Yale, Harvard, and other famous institutions of learning, why would it not be a good thing for the Indians to be permitted to attend those institutions also? . . . I am opposed to any scheme or policy which has for its object the separation of the Indian and white races; I am opposed to the establishment and maintenance of any Indian school while there are schools everywhere in the United States to which the Indians may be admitted upon equal terms with the whites, there to learn the truths of civilization at the feet of the same teachers who teach the white man's children.[23]

Wheelock's argument resembles Pratt's in its rejection of separate schools for Indians and its reference to a unified set of "truths of civilization," but differs significantly in its rationale. Pratt envisioned a system that coerced Indian students into learning *from* white students; Wheelock, on the other hand, advocated a system that allowed Indian students to exercise their right to learn *with* white students.

The vexed issue of Indian education, like most of the other matters debated by members of the SAI, was only one part of a complex of closely related issues, at the center of which was the vast and troubled reservation system. The system kept reservation Indians under the general control of the BIA and the specific control of local agents, always non-Indian and often poorly qualified political appointees, who oversaw virtually all aspects of life on the reservations, including the schools. Reform-minded Indians responded to the existence of the reservations in various ways. For some, like Gertrude Bonnin, who spent fourteen years living and working on reservations in Utah, the presence of thousands of Indians on reservations complicated decisions about the proper objectives and methods of any reform agenda and consequently about the primary constituency of the SAI. For others, like Parker, the major problem with the reservation system was that it made the citizenship status of all Indians murky and tenuous. For still others, like Carlos Montezuma, the reservations and the bureaucracy that ran them were so clearly the source of the entire "Indian problem" that both needed to be simply abolished before anything good could be done for—or by—Indians.

Bonnin's reservation work in the West led her to be increasingly concerned that the SAI was concentrating too much on the abstractions of theory and policy, addressing itself too exclusively to an educated, off-reservation, generally eastern audience (white and Indian), and not doing enough to address the day-to-day material needs of reservation populations. By 1916, Bonnin had become persuaded that the serious work of reform needed to be done on the ground, among the people with the most pressing needs. "I am more than ever convinced that this is a field too long overlooked," she wrote to one of the SAI vice-presidents that year, "and it is our first duty, to make an effort toward uplift work among our reservation Indians, ourselves; and in our own way."[24] While Bonnin criticized the SAI, gently, for taking too little account of specific local issues, she retained her confidence in the society as the best hope for meaningful reform. She kept Arthur Parker informed of her efforts to link reservation Indians to the work of the SAI—and of her frequent discouragement. One of her projects among the Indians of Utah was to organize groups of "returned students"—those who had been away to boarding schools and had come back to the reservation—and supply them with SAI information. "If we can get all Returned Students societies to become more inoculated with the motives and ideas of the S.A.I.," she wrote to Parker, "it will be untold benefit to the Reservations. . . . Then we will grow strong. We will see hundreds come into the main Society. This is what I desire most."[25]

Bonnin, herself a writer of fiction, poetry, and journalism who succeeded Parker as editor of the SAI journal for a brief stint in 1919, shared with Parker a belief that print publication had a power and efficacy that had not yet been exploited by Indians. One of her suggestions to him was that the journal of the society be made more accessible to reservation readers. "What do you think can be done in the way of publishing a leaflet, supplement to the Indian Magazine, especially for the Reservation Indians whose English vocabulary is very limited and powers of concentrated thinking still in the bud?"[26] She was frustrated as well by the inability of Indian reformers to succeed in getting their message out to a large general audience, exclaiming to Parker that "someone should write an 'Uncle Tom's Cabin' for the American Aborigine. Every Indian agent is a 'Legre' [sic] the slave killer. The task would be too difficult for an Indian. The perspective entirely too close. I can hardly write a few pages of a report on conditions in one agency, without being nearly consumed with indignation and a holy wrath."[27] Bonnin persevered in her efforts to link the reservations to the larger world through the SAI, despite her frequent exasperation with both her reservation constituents and her SAI colleagues. She wrote to Parker, at the end of her long stay in Utah, about her discouragement: "Every Indian who has attempted to do real uplift work for the tribes gets stung. No wonder that he quits trying; goes back to the blanket, and sits in the teepee like a boiled owl."[28] Bonnin herself, of course, did not go back to the blanket or choose to sit still; she went back to the East Coast instead, to work more directly with Parker and the struggling SAI and eventually to found the National Council of American Indians in 1926.

Bonnin was not the only one who nudged the SAI to give more of its attention to the needs of reservation Indians. For example, Parker received a letter from a white missionary on the Navajo reservation in Arizona, Sophia Hubert, thanking him for inviting her to attend the 1914 SAI conference in Madison and letting him know, with a strongly implied sniff, that the press of her duties would prevent her from making the trip. Missionaries and government agents, she reminded him, could not just pick up and head off to a conference, abandoning their manifold responsibilities, no matter how interested they might be in hearing intellectual debates on theoretical issues. Hubert went on to note that the Indians attending the conference would be "civilized and educated" people, whereas those she worked with "are in a very primitive and semi-savage state. I wish the Society could do something to help them *up*. They themselves, are quite content to remain as they are. They are not anxious for civilization."[29]

The rather prissily condescending and disapproving tone of missionary Hubert's letter sets it in contrast to the kinds of letters Parker often received from reservation Indians themselves. A 1913 letter from Lodge Grass, Montana, is fairly typical. The letter is typed on Crow Indian Mission letterhead, signed by Rides A White Hipped Horse, but written for him, according to a note at the top of the letter, by W. A. Petzoldt, the Baptist minister who headed the Crow mission for many years. Although the phrasing of the letter suggests that Petzoldt was actually composing rather than transcribing, we can assume that the letter represents at least the will of Rides A White Hipped Horse to make contact with the SAI, to bring himself to the society's attention, and to begin some kind of conversation:

> My dear Sir: I received your circular letter about the Denver Conference and the progress being made by the Society of American Indians. Also I have learned about your platform. I am an uneducated Indian and do not understand it all, but it has been interpreted to me by a good white friend and what I understand I am pleased with. . . . I am uneducated so that I do not even understand about the weight of the grain and other things I sell. But I want to work and make an honest living with my hands by work. In the plans and policies you are making do not forget the UNEDUCATED Indians in the backward tribes, and do not forget me. I am far away but I am trying to help the Society. This year, for the first time in the history of our tribe we celebrated Thanksgiving Day in the right way at the Mission. We had a great, good time. We are just beginning to understand some things that most of the progressive tribes already know but we are learning it for the first time.[30]

It is certainly to Parker's credit, and typical of his attention to all his correspondents, that he took the time to write a longish personal response to this letter. His response, however, is stilted and awkward; he talks down to the reservation man in simplistic language that verges on the insulting:

> I am very glad you are taking interest in this society of your own people. For the first time the educated Indians and other Indians who believe in good things for everybody have gotten together to work and make life better for all our Indian people. . . . I hope that you will learn many things as the years go on and that after [a]while you will understand how to make a living even if the white people about you try to take advantage of your lack of education. . . . I am glad that you had a good Thanksgiving day at the Mission. It is a great thing you are beginning to understand what true thanksgiving means. We will not forget the uneducated Indians or the

backward tribes. They are the very people we are trying to work for most. Some of them may not understand it because in our printing we try to appeal to the white man's intelligence so that he will be our friend.[31]

Parker's letter suggests that Rides A White Hipped Horse was not wrong in thinking that he and Parker (and the SAI) were "far away" from each other, intellectually as well as geographically. The letter also suggests the extent to which Parker saw the public work of the SAI, certainly including its journal ("our printing"), as meant to attract and impress a white audience, whose intelligence he clearly saw as different in kind from that of an illiterate reservation farmer in Montana. In a 1913 letter to J. N. B. Hewitt (Tuscarora), an ethnologist at the Smithsonian, written just a few months before his correspondence with the Crow farmer, Parker offered much the same commentary on his perception of the audience for the SAI's publications, although his language in the two letters reflects the deliberate adjustment of his tone and style to suit his audience. He explained to Hewitt that, while the society's publications had provided inspiration to reservation Indians, that effect was something of a fortunate byproduct; the real audience for the publications lived somewhere other than the reservation:

> With regard to the effect of the publications of this society, I think if you should look over the letters which I have received from day to day, you would find that they have proven an inspiration to the Indians, whom you term unlettered, for the subject matter has been read and interpreted to them and many of them have directed, in their simple, interesting way, letters of appreciation. The real value of the publications lie[s] in stimulating greater activity on the part of those who are educated up to a certain degree, in seeking to crystallize the sentiment of those with broader views and higher training.[32]

Parker mentions here the letters of appreciation he receives from the reservations; he does not mention the many complaints and requests for help he also received from the reservations. The SAI files contain dozens of examples of such letters, many about very specific, local conflicts, to which Parker evidently gave a great deal of his time and attention, taking the matters to the Bureau of Indian Affairs or to congressional representatives and pressing for solutions. A letter from a petitioner in Mayetta, Kansas, written in December 1913, is representative of the many requests Parker received:

Dear Sir

I will write a litter to get a advice on my busness in my dead mother land. I am a Pottawatomies Prairie band Indian my mother was an Indian but her husband is a white man my mother die 13 of November 1912 and she has been dead one year and one month and I have try every way to settle with him I have try to buy him out and tried to divied the land but he dont want to do right and so on his part there is to much improvement one his and he only want to gave me 60 acrs he want to gave me the poorest part and he has had the use of the land one year and has not pay me any leas money. . . . I want a patent for my part so I can do as I want to write a way and the agence sent a letter about 7 weeks ago and he has never heard from them yet or less he dont want to let me know I wanted to know for I wanted to build but they have never wrote so you write and let me know what to do right away so I will close[.]

Parker acted on this letter within a week, writing to the Commissioner of Indian Affairs, Cato Sells, with a succinct summary of the letter and a request that Sells let him know what the law provided in the case of deceased allottees and how the letter writer could obtain any of the land that was legally hers.[33] The extra work of this pro bono sort took its toll on Parker; he confessed to Gertrude Bonnin in 1917 that he felt "buried" by his obligations and guessed that he had more than one hundred letters on his desk, awaiting his reply.[34]

Parker says little about these kinds of interventions in his publications or his private correspondence. Perhaps he saw them as falling outside the scope of his work for the SAI, or perhaps he didn't want the "unlettered" reservation Indian to come under too much public scrutiny; it was always the educated, "progressive" Indian he wished to present to public view. (He wrote in the journal in 1918 that "the only just and logical way to understand the Indian and judge his capacity is to watch the Indian who is *away* from the reservation."[35]) Parker was also hesitant, from the beginning, about letting the SAI get too close, literally or figuratively, to people whose interests were primarily local. He wrote to Sherman Coolidge in 1911 to argue against having the 1912 conference in Colorado Springs, on the grounds that "it is too near the heart of an Indian country and we should be swamped by local parties who had not given our needs and problems especial attention." Chicago, he argued, would be "more likely to appeal to more progressive Indians." Parker concluded his argument to Coolidge by reminding him that "if we are to help our people we must perfect our organization before going to them and enlisting their local interest."[36] Whatever his reasons for doing so, Parker clearly made a distinction between his intellectual work, which he wished to make as public as possible, and his extensive and time-consuming work as a mediator between reservation Indians and government officials, which he considered "local" work and did quietly.

Parker did apparently make some concession to the requests of Bonnin and others that the SAI take more account of its reservation constituents, especially in its publications. After Parker's exchange of letters with Bonnin in 1916, the *American Indian Magazine* began to publish some kinds of materials that had not appeared before in the journal, at least not with any frequency: biographical sketches of individuals who were not officers or even prominent members of the SAI; fiction, including several stories with a reservation setting by Grace Coolidge, the (white) wife of Sherman Coolidge; poetry by Bonnin and others (including Parker himself, who signed his poems Gawasa Wanneh); short historical essays; a feature called "Men and Women Whose Lives Count," and brief notices about specific local issues on specific reservations. These changes seem to reflect an effort on Parker's part to make at least some accommodation for the kinds of readers who had never been part of the primary audience he sought.

The reservation-related issue that most captured Parker's attention, and that he was most eager to make public, was the civil status of Indians. Before the passage of the Indian Citizenship Act of 1924, Indian status was governed by a set of policies and regulations so byzantine and unstable that few claimed to have a good grasp of them. As Charles Eastman put it, "There has been so much confusing legislation on this matter, that I do not believe there is a learned judge in these United States who can tell an Indian's exact status without a great deal of study, and even then he may be in doubt."[37] No Indian persons had ever been constitutionally entitled to birthright citizenship, and the courts had refused to address the issue, declaring questions of Indian rights to be the province of Congress rather than the judiciary. The provisions of the General Allotment Act (the Dawes Act) began to address the citizenship issue, but in a complicated and piecemeal way, and amendments to the act produced even further complications. Under the original provisions of the act, Indians who accepted their land allotments automatically became citizens, even though the land was held in trust by the federal government. Any Indians who voluntarily left the reservation and "adopted the habits of civilized life" (according to the wording of the act) also became citizens. However, citizenship status did not automatically bring with it the right to vote—since determining eligibility to vote remained the responsibility of each state—and even citizen Indians were still under the guardianship of the Bureau of Indian Affairs. The Burke Act of 1906 adjusted the original terms of the allotment policy by delaying citizenship until the end of the mandatory twenty-five-year trust period, but also by allowing the secretary of the interior to declare any individual Indian competent to receive title to his or her allotment land, at the secretary's discretion, thereby shortening or even eliminating the trust period for these individuals.[38]

These complex and shifting regulations had the effect of thoroughly muddling the issue of the legal and civil status of individual Indian persons. Parker illustrated the maddening nature of this legal muddle by citing in the SAI journal the case of Sherman Coolidge, a full-blood Arapahoe minister and missionary and the first president of the SAI. Coolidge had been captured by the U.S. Army when he was seven years old; he was taken into the family of an army officer (named Coolidge) and subsequently educated, first in the public schools of New York City and then at military school. He next attended Seabury Divinity School in Minnesota; while he was there he was regarded as a citizen and, under the election laws of the state, allowed to vote. After leaving Seabury he moved to Wyoming, where, because of treaty regulations obtaining in that state, he was considered a noncitizen ward without voting rights. Then, in 1887, he was assigned an allotment of land in Wyoming and therefore, under the terms of the Dawes Act, he once again became a citizen of the United States—although, because he lived on a reservation, he was not considered a citizen of the state of Wyoming. His U.S. citizenship was again revoked, in 1906, when the Burke Act instated the mandatory twenty-five-year trust period for allotted Indians. Coolidge left Wyoming for Oklahoma; after two years, because he was not living on a reservation and had "adopted the habits of civilized life," he once more became a citizen and was able to vote. Coolidge was allowed to keep his citizenship status when he returned to Minnesota, but he could never, because he was an Indian, remove himself from the guardianship of the federal government, which retained ultimate control of his land and his children's trust funds.[39] (The Supreme Court had ruled in a series of cases between 1908 and 1916 that citizenship did not exempt Indians from the guardianship of the federal government.)

The legal complications, especially the Supreme Court's insistence that tribalism was incompatible with citizenship, created serious problems, with very real material implications, for tribes as well as for individual Indians. The

1903 Supreme Court case of *Lone Wolf v. Hitchcock* provides a landmark instance. The judgment handed down in this case was determined by the justices' conclusion that Indians who maintained their "tribal relations"—by which they apparently referred to both the social organization of tribes and the holding of tribal lands in common—could not claim the protection of the laws of the United States. The case resulted from the disposition of lands occupied by the Kiowa, Comanche, and Apache. Following the passage of the Dawes Act, their land was divided into individual allotments, with the remaining unallotted or "surplus" land—a total of three hundred fifty thousand acres—becoming public land available for settlement. Two million dollars was set aside in a trust account for the tribes to recompense them for the lost land. The three tribes brought suit, arguing that the financial compensation was too low and that the arrangement had not been approved by three-fourths of all male Indians in the tribes, a stipulation agreed on in a treaty that had been in force since 1867. In the end, the court declined to intervene. In rendering its decision, the court acknowledged that the existing treaty provisions had been violated but affirmed the right of Congress to commit such violations when it saw fit. As long as the Indians continued to maintain tribal relations with one another and to consider the land they occupied as tribal property, the court concluded, they were to be accounted wards of the state and to be fully subject to the authority of Congress. In the written majority opinion, Justice Edward D. White noted that this "power has always been deemed a political one, not subject to be controlled by the judicial department of the government."[40] In other words, the court affirmed that it had no responsibility at all for Indians who maintained tribal relations and therefore no reason to intercede when those Indians claimed their rights had been violated. Following that decision, the process of allotting Indian lands moved more quickly, since Congress was no longer bound to negotiate with the tribes, to secure their approval for any land settlements, or to honor any existing treaties.

The *Lone Wolf* case had attracted the attention of the Indian Rights Association, a large part of whose purpose was to protect Indians from exactly the kinds of abuses that stemmed from treaty violations. The IRA supported the Indians' appeal and had, in fact, hired and paid the lawyer who argued for the tribes before the Supreme Court. In acknowledging their defeat in the case, the spokesman for the IRA, Matthew Sniffen, interpreted the decision in language strikingly similar to that used earlier by Lyman Abbott in his declaration that "barbarism has no rights which civilization is bound to respect." The court, Sniffen wrote, "substantially declared it to be the law of the land that the Indians in their tribal relations have practically no rights whatever which Congress is bound to respect."[41] For the court, as for Lyman Abbott and other reformers, a tribal identity and a tribal ethos, especially the holding of land and property in common, precluded entitlement to the rights of citizens.

The codifying of the Indians' legal status became one of the major projects of the SAI, regularly providing an important plank in its platform (although the federal government was to take no significant action on the matter until the passage of the Indian Citizenship Act in 1924). Arthur Parker directed much of his attention to the issue of legal status, seeing it as prerequisite to any subsequent changes that might improve the situation of Indian populations and as a matter that could reasonably become the focus of a united lobbying effort by the SAI. He was an ardent supporter of the Carter Code Bill, introduced into the House of Representatives by Charles Carter, a Chickasaw congressman from Oklahoma and active member of the SAI. The object of the bill was to regularize and clarify—to codify—the provisions for Indian citizenship, in order to prevent the kind of confusion illustrated by the case of Sherman Coolidge. Parker urged the executive committee of the SAI, in 1912, to give the code bill priority in their planning. Getting the bill passed, he wrote, "may be the greatest thing we shall ever do. Certainly it will afford a basis upon which the Indian problem may be settled."[42] He also lobbied the Lake Mohonk Conference for its support, putting his appeal into the discourse of philosophical benevolence that was the lingua franca of the conference, a discourse that required casting the Indian in the role of the dependent other:

> The Indian as neither citizen, alien nor foreigner has occupied and now occupies a precarious position in our national life. . . . In his native state each Indian knew what his status was. It was a part of his intellectual life to know it. He felt himself a man and a master. In his present state, wherein he is ruled over and thought for, he feels himself the insignificant non-represented minor and ward that he is. Not knowing what his rights are or what will come next, he becomes chronically despondent, careless, and often degenerate. Out of an undefined status and the resultant uncertainty springs the host of evils deplored by the church, the school, and the Federal departments.[43]

In spite of his various efforts, Parker did not succeed in enlisting unanimous support from Indian rights organizations for the Carter bill.

Other SAI activists were equally frustrated and angered by the confused state of Indian rights, but some were not satisfied with a plan to simply define those rights more clearly, as the code bill would have done; they wanted more radical changes. Among the most outspoken and persistent of the radicals was Carlos Montezuma, who held out consistently, over the more than thirty years of his public life, for the complete abolition of the Bureau of Indian Affairs and the immediate granting of citizenship to all Indians. Montezuma had begun calling for the abolition of the Bureau before the SAI was organized, and he continued to insist on it in his speeches to the society, his writing for the society's journal, and the various venues in which he addressed the wider public. He even began issuing a broadside in 1916, to which he gave his Indian name, *Wassaja,* and which he filled with diatribes against the Bureau and complaints about the ineffectiveness of the SAI.

Montezuma was able to use his own extraordinary life story to his advantage as a way of getting the attention of the public, since it so exactly fit the "savagery-to-civilization" pattern that appealed to both the curiosity-seeker and the most optimistic of the reformers. He was Yavapai (although, because the Yavapai were also called Mohave Apache, he became known as Apache and usually referred to himself that way), born in southern Arizona around 1867. When he was about four years old, he was captured by Pimas and sold to a traveling reporter and photographer named Carlos Gentile, who gave him his new name, adopted him, and sent him to public schools, first in Chicago and later in Brooklyn. Montezuma subsequently attended the University of Illinois, making a name for himself as a debater and graduating when he was still in his teens; he then worked his way through Chicago Medical College and earned a degree in medicine. The first years of his career were spent as an Indian Service physician, at three reservation agencies and then at Pratt's Carlisle Indian School. He left Carlisle in 1896 to enter private practice in Chicago.[44]

Montezuma became acquainted with Richard Pratt while he was still in medical school, and Pratt immediately became a mentor and supporter, arranging for Montezuma to give public lectures, beginning as early as 1887, about his accomplishments and their implications for Indian policy. He was invited to speak at the Lake Mohonk Conference in 1893 and again in 1895. By 1909, Montezuma had clearly established a public reputation as an impassioned and politically engaged spokesperson for Indian reform. He was among the first people Fayette McKenzie contacted in that year to enlist support for his plan for the organization that became the SAI. In 1911,

Montezuma was approached by a representative of the Woman's Christian Temperance Union, Dorcas Spencer, who urged him to join Charles Eastman in attending the Universal Races Congress in London. Montezuma would be an ideal representative at the congress, Spencer wrote to him, because he was an "advanced, progressive man" who could "exert an influence to move others."[45]

Although Montezuma chose not to go to London, he continued to lecture throughout his life, using his autobiography as both a rhetorical hook and a dramatic example of his central message: the only Indians likely to succeed were those who, like himself, had been freed from both tribal life and the supervision of the Bureau of Indian Affairs and allowed to make their independent way in the world. Montezuma described the reservation as a "demoralized prison" that kept Indian people from competing on the same terms and with the same advantages as were available to immigrants arriving from other countries:

> I wish that I could collect all the Indian children, load them in ships at San Francisco, circle them around Cape Horn, pass them through Castle Garden, put them under the same individual care that the children of foreign emigrants have in your public schools, and when they are matured and moderately educated let them do what other men and women do—take care of themselves. This would solve the Indian question; would rescue a splendid race from vice, disease, pauperism and death.[46]

Montezuma did not hesitate to declare publicly that being taken away from his parents at the age of four and sold to a white man was the best thing that could have happened to him. "It looks cruel," he once told a congressional committee, "but see for yourself; do you need a better illustration? I claim that my people whom I left have been unfortunate and that I have been fortunate."[47]

In spite of his disagreements with the outspoken Montezuma, Arthur Parker invited him to become a contributing editor of the SAI journal. For one thing, Parker wanted the journal to represent differing perspectives, and for another, he could hardly overlook a full-blood Indian who had a medical degree, a successful public image, an already established public platform, and the strong support of the influential Richard Pratt. In his letter of invitation, Parker told Montezuma that he was inviting only college graduates to serve as contributing editors: "This will hold out the incentive to our brothers to break away from mere great white father schools and see something more beyond." Montezuma accepted the invitation, although he always maintained an on-again, off-again relationship with the journal and the society, using both as a platform to press for the abolition of the Bureau of Indian Affairs. Beginning in 1916, he was also using his privately printed broadside, *Wassaja* (which Montezuma advertised as "a little spicy newspaper"), to criticize both the Bureau and the SAI, which was never outspoken or aggressive enough to suit Montezuma. "As a society," he advised his colleagues, "we must not be timid and shrink and hold back on this stand against the Indian Bureau. . . . We must stir up righteous indignation and we must make the first move to abolish the Indian Bureau from the face of the earth; not until then shall we be perfectly free." Privately, he wrote to Pratt in 1916 complaining about the SAI journal's (and especially Parker's) refusal to take a strong stand. Changing its name from the *Journal of the Society of American Indians* to the *American Indian Magazine* had given the publication new reasons to sit on the fence, he wrote. "Since it is a magazine now, it can straddle most everything that comes along without a definite object like all magazines. Just to please its readers."[48]

America's entry into World War I in 1917 gave Montezuma added incentive to criticize the BIA and the SAI; it also allowed him to adopt the discourse of patriotism in his critiques. He used *Wassaja* to argue against drafting Indians into the armed forces, pointing out the injustice of forcing them to fight for the country that refused to make them citizens—and typically laying the blame at the feet of the Bureau of Indian Affairs: "The Indian Office keeps us Indians from our rights. It tells the country that we are competent to be soldiers, but are not competent to be citizens." In a 1919 issue of the SAI journal (this one edited by Gertrude Bonnin), Montezuma accused the society of always choosing neutral ground, of lacking the "divine impatience and godly aspiration" of a true American patriot such as Patrick Henry. The SAI's "cry for liberty should be loud and fearless. Whom should we fear? Are we not fighting for the right and for justice? Will Americans mock our cry while their sons die in France for these very purposes?" The Indian Bureau, Montezuma wrote, "defies justice, and most of all, it defies the righteous object of this world-war, namely, freedom, equal rights for all, Humanity, Democracy."[49]

Montezuma played the role of gadfly for years, prompting Parker, Bonnin, and others to send him regular appeals to tone down both his attacks on the BIA and his demands for immediate citizenship, in the interest of harmony among progressive Indian leaders. Montezuma remained outraged and outspoken, however, until eventually history, the American public, and the SAI caught up with him. It has been estimated that more than ten thousand Indian men served in World War I (roughly fifty-six hundred were drafted and thirty-five hundred enlisted), and Indian purchasers accounted for more than twenty-five million dollars worth of war bonds.[50] This widespread participation of Indians in the war effort gradually made the withholding of citizenship seem as unjust and absurd to the American public as Montezuma had always proclaimed it to be. The SAI journal began to publish articles like Charles Eastman's "The Indian's Plea for Freedom," in which Eastman posed a series of questions to the American public: "Is it not our due that we should call this fair land ours with you in full brotherhood? Have we not defended bravely its liberties and may we not share them?"[51] By 1918, the journal was able to reprint newspaper articles citing Indian contributions to the war effort as a reason for granting citizenship. Parker used the cover space to print photographs of Indians in uniform and his editorial space to extol Indian patriotism, pointing out in particular the large numbers of volunteers from various tribes who were on active service. He also argued strongly against the creation of all-Indian military units (an idea being pushed by the inveterate Joseph K. Dixon, among others) on the grounds that only by having served in an integrated unit would the Indian soldier "have proved himself a man as other men and able to cooperate in any activity America may demand."[52] As the language of his argument makes clear, Parker was still deeply interested in what Indians could do to demonstrate their capacities to white elites—whether by serving in a war or maintaining a measured and diplomatic tone in their publications. Montezuma, on the other hand, from the beginning had cared little about image and much about the need to demand immediate changes, and he was perfectly willing to create a fuss if it would help. Montezuma died of pneumonia in 1923, when he was in his mid-fifties. The following year, Congress granted birthright citizenship to all American Indians.

In spite of his disagreements with Parker and the SAI, Montezuma had encouraged readers of *Wassaja* to support the society and attend its conferences; but he had also encouraged them to resist being railroaded by those who had too many ideas and too little practical experience of real problems, especially problems on the reservations. In announcing the 1917 conference in *Wassaja,* he declared: "This is an Indian country: let the Indians attend and let the Indians rule. Heretofore the sentiment of the Indians has been lacking. Theorists have dominated."[53] Montezuma's phrasing here, ambiguous though it is, would seem to suggest that he is making a distinction between Indians, whose sentiments come from personal experience, and non-Indians, who have only theories about Indians. At the least, he is distinguishing between (legitimate) sentiment and (specious) theory and asking for help from the rank and file in overruling the theorists. (Given Montezuma's history of rabid opposition to the Bureau of Indian Affairs and his loyal support of Richard Pratt, who very definitely had his own set of theories about Indian affairs, the word *theorists* as he uses it is likely a code for bureaucrats.)

Montezuma's comments tap into a long-standing source of frustration for those activists, Indian and non-Indian alike, who were impatient with the proliferation of theoretical solutions to the "Indian problem" coming from many directions and the lack of significant progress in solving the real problems that Indian people, especially reservation people, were facing every day. Francis Leupp, who as Commissioner of Indian Affairs would have been on Montezuma's enemies list, agreed with him to the extent that he argued in his 1910 book for seeking answers to the problems "on common-sense rather than theoretical lines." The U.S. Board of Indian Commissioners expressed its impatience in a 1914 report on the administration of Indian affairs in Canada, chastising U.S. policy makers for letting their theories get in the way of the practical and humanitarian work that needed to be done. (The immediate reference was to the government's resistance to providing food rations to impoverished reservations on the theoretical grounds that rations encouraged dependence.) Reservation Indians in Canada were better off than those in the United States, the report claimed, because the Canadian government "has not starved her Indians into easy victims of tuberculosis and intemperance by subordinating a condition to a theory" in setting its policies.[54]

Even Arthur Parker, who had been eager to form alliances with the white reform organizations and to demonstrate that Indian thinkers could hold their own with their white counterparts and was therefore hospitable to theoretical debate, sometimes expressed (privately) his impatience with the complacency of white reformers, who could seem content to propound their theories and then consider the job done. After attending the 1912 meeting of the Lake Mohonk Conference, Parker wrote to Fayette McKenzie about the unhappy results:

> You probably noted that my rancor got the best of me there and that I was a little bit disgusted with some things and perhaps showed it. The infernal knitting, knitting, knitting, the click of the needles and the rattle of papers on the part of people in the hall who were reading novels and poetry seem

to afford an explanation of why the members of the Conference are sometimes quoted Mo-"Honkers." There is a big noise and a lot of dust flies—
whiz—and the whole thing is over. The sole memory is the lingering smell
of gasoline.[55]

Parker's remarks offer an ironic reflection on McKenzie's initial, enthusiastic
prediction that the SAI could become "a Mohonk by Indians" as well as on
the later complaints of Montezuma and others that the SAI generated a lot of
noise and dust of its own and little concrete action.

Laura Cornelius Kellogg, one of the founding members of the SAI, expressed her frustration with the divide between theory and action in her 1920
book, *Our Democracy and the American Indian*. "Any theory or policy which
intends to secure the ultimate welfare of the race," she wrote, "must first of all
consider how to secure real protection. . . . It is plain the Indian himself does
not know what theory to advance to save himself and his possessions, but he
realizes that the concrete thing he wants is to save them."[56] Cornelius, an educated Oneida who devoted much of her life to securing land rights for the
Iroquois and others (at times with apparently questionable judgment[57]), had
occasion to participate in—and contribute to—theoretical discussions of the
"Indian question" and also to observe at first hand the real circumstances of
reservation lives. Her sense of the irrelevance of theory to the immediate
needs of Indian individuals would have come from a familiarity both with
"concrete" needs and with the theoretical debates that, by 1920, had received
plenty of public airing.

Some of the theoretical positions being tried out came more or less directly from conversations taking place among professionals in the various social science fields. Arthur Parker and Fayette McKenzie came to their SAI
work with backgrounds and experiences that led them to try to bring the
work of Indian reform in line with Progressive Era directions in the social sciences. McKenzie was trained in sociology and economics, receiving his PhD
from the University of Pennsylvania in 1906, a year after taking a teaching position at Ohio State. Over the course of his career, McKenzie was involved in
working for settlement houses and black uplift as well as Indian reform; he
worked with the BIA to produce an Indian census, became president of Fisk
University in 1915, and was a contributor to the 1928 Meriam report, the document that lay behind the significant changes in Indian policy of the 1930s.
Parker, who was born on the Cattaraugus (Seneca) Reservation in New York,
went to work as a young man for the American Museum of Natural History

in New York, learning archaeology from F. W. Putnam. His friend Frank Speck, a student of anthropology at Columbia, introduced him to Franz Boas, who encouraged Parker to enroll in the anthropology program as well. Parker declined, remaining under the tutelage of Putnam and doing field work among the Seneca. In 1906 he was appointed archaeologist in the science division at the New York State Museum at Rochester, where he spent the rest of his working career, becoming director of the museum in 1925. At the time of his death, the *New York Times* obituary called him an "internationally known anthropologist, archaeologist, and museum authority."[58] Both men attempted, understandably but with problematic results, to bring the perspectives acquired in their professional training to bear on the work of Indian reform and uplift.

McKenzie contributed an article to the *Journal of Race Development* in 1912 and another to the *American Journal of Sociology* in 1914 in which he argued specifically for the importance of sociology—and trained sociologists—in setting the course of Indian policy. The earlier article, which Parker reprinted in the SAI journal, sorts the contemporary perspectives on the prospects for Indians into three large categories: those of the conqueror/biologist, the ethnologist/historian, and the statesman/sociologist. McKenzie's first category consists of those who are most pessimistic about the Indian future, holding to the Darwinian view that weaker races always succumb to stronger races and that there is little to be done about this natural process. In the second and "more humane" category are those who dispense with the evolutionists' conceptions of superiority and inferiority, simply declaring that Indians are different and should be left as they are to provide objects of study for the scientist and the historian. The third category, in which McKenzie clearly places himself, is the only one that offers significant promise: "Certain anthropologists and sociologists provide the ground upon which an optimistic statesmanship can build a positive and progressive program." The sociologist is likely to succeed where others have failed, McKenzie argues, because he understands that psychology and culture are not fixed but change as circumstances change—and because his knowledge gives him an optimistic faith in the possibilities for change. McKenzie casts the entire Indian reform effort as "a great sociological endeavor" with historic implications for the country: "Perhaps no other nation in the world has ever undertaken so thorough a plan for the salvation of a race through the transfer of culture. No greater glory could come to a nation than to succeed in bringing a primitive people into full participation in the best of its own civilization."[59]

McKenzie's 1914 article in the *American Journal of Sociology* is clearly addressed to an audience of professional, largely academic, sociologists. The discussion is framed by references to matters that would be familiar to readers of the journal (the relationship between theory and practice, the need for changes in academic practice); the real intent of the piece, however, is to broadcast McKenzie's message about the dire state of Indian affairs and the need for immediate, significant action. The Indian problem, he declares, "is fundamentally a sociological problem," one that needs trained professionals to "furnish the scientific basis for the Indian policies of the nation," although he notes that the sociologists have thus far taken little interest in it. McKenzie makes the case that becoming directly, actively involved in Indian reform would not be at all inconsistent with the intellectual and academic labors of his audience. Their contributions to sociological theory could only benefit from actual work in the field: "One of the great reasons for direct service on our part in the social movements of the world is that we may rectify, if not actually create, the splendid body of theory which we are to transmit to our students."

McKenzie's charge to the sociologists draws on the discourse of liberal progressive reform, especially as it was used by John Dewey in his writing about the reform of education. Dewey had stated in 1897 his belief "that education is a regulation of the process of coming to share in the social consciousness; and that the adjustment of individual activity on the basis of this social consciousness is the only sure method of social reconstruction." Dewey's phrasing as well as his sentiments are echoed in McKenzie's challenge to his readers: "The simple test of efficiency for us is, are we giving the Indian identical or equal opportunity with ourselves to share in and to control the social consciousness, as well as to share in the privileges, immunities, duties, and obligations of the members of our national social body? This is the only goal worth while in assimilation." McKenzie's most practical recommendation to the sociologists was that universities ought to support the work of Indian reform by endowing professorships in "race development." The study of the Indian past, he noted, was already supported by professorships in anthropology, ethnology, and history. "Should we not have men who can devote themselves to the problem of the Indian as he now is, and to the problem of the means by which he may realize his highest possibilities as a citizen and fellow-worker?"[60]

While McKenzie argued for the centrality of the discipline of sociology to the work of progressive reform, others reserved the central place for ethnol-

ogy. Robert H. Lowie, who trained with Boas and Clark Wissler at Columbia and did fieldwork among the Crow between 1910 and 1916, gave a series
of lectures titled "Culture and Ethnology" at the Smithsonian Institution in
1917. While Lowie's major purpose in his lectures was to argue (with Boas and
against Henry Lewis Morgan) that there is no direct "proportional" relationship between culture and race and that culture is the more important of the
two in determining the progress of a group, he also made clear the role of the
ethnologist in promoting as well as measuring progress. "The social builder
of the future who should seek to refashion the culture of his time and add to
its cultural values," he argued, "will seek guidance from ethnology, the science
of culture, which in [Edward B.] Tylor's judgment is 'essentially a reformer's
science.'"[61] Lowie's perspective on the close relationship between the study
of ethnology and the practice of reform is reflected in the 1907 *Handbook of
American Indians* (to which Lowie was a contributor) published by the Bureau of American Ethnology (BAE). The *Handbook* contains an entry for the
BAE, which explains that the difficulties the U.S. government has faced in
solving its Indian problem arise from the lack of reliable data about Indian
tribes as well as the lack of "a real appreciation of their character, culture status, needs and possibilities." One of the most important purposes of the BAE,
the entry notes, is to provide the kind of information that can guide the government toward the intelligent administration of Indian affairs.[62] Lowie's
linking of ethnology and reform also helps to explain why the *Handbook* contains entries for a number of the reform organizations that were functioning
by 1907 (included are the Boston Indian Citizenship Committee, the Indian
Industries League, the Indian Rights Association, the Lake Mohonk Conference, the National Indian Association, the Sequoyah League, and—oddly
enough—the Improved Order of Red Men). The inclusion of these organizations signals the BAE's sense of the commonality of the fundamental aims
of professional ethnologists and lay reformers; they were all, ultimately, in the
business of uplift and improvement.[63]

Others close to the SAI made similar connections between the social science disciplines and the work of Indian reform. The inaugural issue of the SAI
journal carried an article by J. N. B. Hewitt in which he argued for the teaching of ethnology in Indian schools, on the grounds that it could provide Indian students with the kind of knowledge of their tribal and racial pasts that
would become a source of pride. The field of ethnology, Hewitt asserted, provided the most comprehensive and relevant data for putting together a reliable portrait of Indian histories and cultures. He recommended that the SAI

take responsibility for assembling a textbook of American Indian ethnology for use in the schools, "not prolix or controversial, but summary and comparative in character, which should fearlessly embody the facts of American Indian culture and achievement in the past, without distortion or unfounded self-adulation."[64] Frank Speck used his professional perspective to argue for the preservation of as much of Indian culture as could be preserved, including "the exuberant wealth of native Indian literature, music, and art." His position was shared by the ethnomusicologist Natalie Curtis, who addressed an audience at the Hampton Institute anniversary exercises in 1905 on the subject of Indian music. Curtis, who was later to work at Hampton compiling a collection of black spirituals (and to become an associate member of the SAI), urged Hampton to do as much to preserve Indian music as it was doing with "Negro song," since Indian music was rightfully "the artistic heritage of America." She broadened her argument to bring it into line with the general Hampton ethos of uplift, connecting the preservation of tribal music to self-expression and self-respect—both essential preliminaries, she contended, to meaningful citizenship. "The real man must express *himself*," and the country at large must realize that "every man has his own note to sound in the rich harmony that is our national life."[65]

Parker agreed with McKenzie (as he usually did) about the role of sociologists. In the second issue of his journal, Parker seconded McKenzie's argument that the control of Indian affairs needed to be put into the hands of trained professionals, especially those trained in sociological theory and methods. The Indian problem, Parker argued, was a social problem and not a race problem, and it was to be solved by treating it in much the same way that other social problems—health, overcrowding, labor disputes, prostitution— were treated. The country needed a standard that could apply to everyone: "To bring [the Indian] to that standard is a task for the expert sociologist and not one for a bureau headed and filled with men without such training." Parker might have found the current administration of Indian affairs inefficient and even dangerous, but he was not ready to join Montezuma and Pratt in calling for the complete abolition of government oversight. Instead, adjusting McKenzie's call for academic chairs in race development, he recommended the creation of a Bureau of Race Development—headed by sociologists—that would set policies for all minority populations, thus eliminating the special status of Indians.[66]

The response from SAI members to this kind of call for a theoretical underpinning to plans for changes in Indian policy—especially with its implicit reliance on white academics—was predictably mixed. None of the essentially theoretical positions sat well with Montezuma, Pratt, and others who formed what Parker often referred to as "the Monte gang." From their perspective, there were two essential objections to the sociologists and ethnologists: first, the "Indianism" fostered by encouraging the preservation of cultural traditions was antithetical to any real progress toward assimilation; and second, the theorists, by using Indian schools as laboratories for their ideas, left Indian children confused and still badly educated. Chauncey Yellow Robe, a Sioux product of Pratt's Carlisle system who spent most of his working life as disciplinarian at the Rapid City Indian School in South Dakota, wrote to Montezuma in 1915 with a specific complaint about exactly the kind of practice Natalie Curtis had encouraged: "The idea of teaching the Indian Music in the Indian schools is an unprogressive—unAmerican one—it is purely an anthropological idea." Allowing Indian children to sing in their Indian language, Yellow Robe wrote, "should be discouraged rather than encouraged." Pratt was definitely of the same mind about the science of culture; as he wrote to Montezuma, "The tom-fooleries of ethnology are among the more ridiculous things in this world." Montezuma himself was consistently and loudly impatient with all those forms of "Indianism" that so attracted the ethnologists. The kinds of traditional art encouraged in some of the Indian schools he dismissed as "curiosities" that were "stamped all over with the marks of a savage existence." When Pratt left his beloved Carlisle and a new administration took over, Montezuma fumed that the school had become "only a curiosity shop where native industries are encouraged" and where "Indianism" threatened to ruin the school completely. He complained of other schools run by the BIA that the teachers "go into fads and stuff the fads into the Indian children. . . . It is experimenting and experimenting. Indian children are good material for them to experiment upon." These school practices Montezuma took as evidence that the Bureau really wished to "keep the Indians Indians forever."[67]

In spite of these significant areas of contention that divided Indian intellectuals and frustrated SAI activists, the public statements about the work of the society, coming from many quarters, remained remarkably positive throughout the life of the organization. Some recent accounts, such as Hazel Hertzberg's pioneering history of the society, call it a failure as a reform organization largely because it was never successful in pushing through the legislative changes it advocated. Arthur Parker's biographer similarly concludes that we must acknowledge that [the SAI] was a failure both as a reform organization and as a context for Parker's strenuous and enthusiastic efforts to secure Indian integration within the American cultural mainstream. Essentially, the SAI achieved nothing in terms of practical legislative change, and both its sphere of influence and its constituency were limited and ill-defined from the outset.[68]

The absence of demonstrable, direct effects on the course of legislation and policy as a result of SAI activity, on which these scholars base their conclusions, cannot be denied. On the other hand, the confidence and optimism of those who were actively involved in the organization, or who observed it at first hand, seems clearly more than an effort to defend a failure—even after the initial euphoric enthusiasm of the founders had long been tempered by conflict. Grace Coolidge, for example, in 1917 called the SAI "the truest expression and the brightest present hope of the Indian people," and even Montezuma, the society's arch-critic and perhaps the largest thorn in its collective flesh, advised readers of *Wassaja* in 1921, just two years before the final SAI conference, not to "let anybody try to make you believe that the Society of American Indians is dead. It is the greatest Indian organization in America."[69]

The differences between recent evaluations of the SAI, which conclude that it was largely a failure, and the much more optimistic pronouncements of those who were close to its work might be explained by considering the different expectations of the two groups. The recent critics have focused on legislative change—the ability of the society to lobby successfully for new laws and policies. The activists themselves, however, always defined their function in much broader terms. It is worth recalling in this context the language of the letter sent by the original organizing committee of the SAI, announcing the formation of the society: "An organization that shall voice the better judgment of the Indian people, and that shall command the attention of the United States, has become a vital necessity. In no other way can we so effectively mould public opinion and bring about conditions for the good of the Indian race."[70] Arthur Parker continued to hold to the premise that public "voicing" should be the primary role of the society, insisting in the journal that the society must be a forum for the serious discussion of a wide variety of views, whether any of those views resulted in concrete action or not. *"The political function of the Society is only one of its activities and not the greatest,"* he argued. *"New laws and a defunct Indian Bureau will not solve the Indian problem, though these ends may be helpful"* (italics in original). The great task of the

SAI, as Parker saw it, was to win a wide audience, and wide respect, for Indian ideas and voices, and the great challenge to the contemporary Indian was to "pluck the feathers from his war bonnet and make fountain pens of them." It was always Parker's belief that if Indian intellectuals could demonstrate their ability to articulate a clear set of aims based on universal principles, rather than generating a list of demands based on local injustices and problems, they would gain the respect of white intellectuals and elites in positions of power, and the changes in laws and policies would then follow in due course.[71]

Parker used the journal to remind readers of the ways in which the society had been successful in living up to its true aims and purposes. In the first place, it had brought together a group of Native men and women who were amply qualified to speak for American Indians as a whole and had given them a public forum. In a 1915 issue of the journal Parker offered the names of thirty-two individuals (nine of them women), all members of the SAI, who should, Parker argued, be recognized as "competent to be a board of review, an organ of counsel, the spokesmen for the red race."[72] In addition to empowering these Indian individuals and making them visible to the public, according to Parker, the society had also succeeded in bringing about changes in the general public's attitude toward Indian people. Changes could already be seen, he noted, in the treatment of Indians in newspapers and magazines. The SAI's own journal had accomplished much simply by its existence: "The very fact that we exist as a Society and that we publish a periodical is an answer to the question of what the modern Indian is." Members of the society were also increasingly in demand, he pointed out, to speak and write on Indian matters. All of these factors contributed to a significant and irreversible change in the "stream of public thought," which the SAI had helped to turn into "a straighter channel." Typically, Parker concluded this detailing of accomplishments by reminding readers of the importance of continuing to perform well before the public: "We must demonstrate that we have been worthy of confidence and that the higher regard we have found is deserved."[73]

Others in the SAI shared Parker's sense of what the crucial functions of the society were and how well they were being carried out. Thomas Moffett, the (white) superintendent of Indian missions for the Presbyterian Home Mission Board and an active associate member of the SAI, published a book in 1914 confirming the readiness of Indian people to accept the benefits of Christianity and urging the cooperation of sympathetic whites in assisting the Indian, as he put it, along the upward path to assimilation. Ironically, Moffett, whose paternalism is strongly imprinted on every page of his book, declares that the system of paternalism has now come to an end and that what is needed is exactly what the SAI provides—the opportunity for Indians to "think and plan" for themselves, to address the American public directly and not through guardians, and to develop a cohort of leaders. For these reasons, Moffett declares the formation of the SAI "an epochal event." Moffett continued to be optimistic, delivering an address to the 1916 conference of the SAI entitled "The Society of American Indians Is a Success" in which he confirmed his belief in the vitality of the organization, assuring his insider audience that if they had doubts, outsiders did not: "There is a zest and interest in this society wherever it has gone in a community that has been very striking. I believe the people outside of the Society think more of it than the people in it do." William J. Kershaw, who was at the time serving as vice president of the SAI, explained in a 1914 newspaper interview that the purpose of the organization was "discussion of the problems confronting the Indian and the nation." Before the formation of the SAI, Kershaw noted, "the Indian was the only person who was not engaged in a discussion of the Indian problem." Sherman Coolidge published an article in a 1914 issue of the society's journal—during his term as president—describing the function of the society as, first, providing a place where members can gather "for mutual encouragement, interchange of views and for consultation upon the live issues of the peculiar problem thrust upon them," and, second, as an encouragement to "go forth and create Indian public opinion among the white people and the Indians." Charles Eastman, who was to become president of the SAI in 1917, wrote about the society in his 1915 book *The Indian To-Day*, describing it, as Parker and Coolidge had, not as a political lobby but as an important site for intelligent, courageous, and open discussion. "These debates," Eastman wrote, "should at least open the public ear."[74]

The fact that individual SAI members continued to have an impact on Indian affairs beyond their work for the society is another sign of the organization's success in introducing an Indian perspective into the national conversations and giving its members the kind of exposure and status that allowed them to continue to voice an Indian public opinion and to influence white public opinion. Arthur Parker, for example, became president of the New York Indian Welfare Society in 1920. Gertrude Bonnin moved from the SAI to the Indian Welfare Committee of the General Federation of Women's Clubs and then, with her husband, founded the National Council of American Indians. In 1923, when Secretary of the Interior Herbert Work put together a committee of "prominent men and women of national vision" to advise him on Indian policy, most of the Indians invited to become members of that Committee of One Hundred had been active in the SAI—including Parker, Coolidge, Dennison Wheelock, John Oskison, Henry Roe Cloud, and two of the founding members of the SAI, Charles Eastman and Thomas Sloan.[75] As Frederick Hoxie has noted, the groundwork laid by the kind of work done by the SAI "encourag[ed] the emergence of new political leaders" and "made it possible for Indians to communicate with outsiders and with each other in new ways."[76]

Clearly, the activists of the SAI did not measure their significance or their success entirely by specific changes in legislation or policy, nor did they seem to expect to see such changes come quickly or easily. To declare their work a failure is, I believe, to apply a standard to which they themselves did not aspire and to bypass their own vision of what was new, exciting, and possible through their work. It is also to underestimate their success in bringing themselves and their concerns before the American public—in creating, that is, a space for an Indian public opinion. Understanding how important that entry into American public and intellectual life was to them, and how difficult it was, means that we can better understand the writing produced by people who were either personally immersed in these struggles or whose lives and thought were affected by them. Writers like Eastman and Bonnin, that is, did much more in their publications than simply offer their personal experiences to be consumed by a curious public; they wrote out of a deep understanding of the crucial issues in Indian affairs, the expectations of the public, and the need to use their own public discourse to reshape those expectations. They also wrote out of an awareness of themselves as both tribal people who necessarily carried a burden of representation and as American intellectuals and progressives whose experience made them particularly qualified to address broad civic issues—perhaps especially the issue of representation itself.

Three of the most productive and most well-known Native writers of the early part of the twentieth century were Sioux. Charles Eastman (Santee), born in 1858, and Gertrude Simmons Bonnin (Yankton), born in 1876, both had close associations with the SAI. Eastman was part of the original organizing committee of the society and later served a term as its president; Bonnin served as secretary-treasurer for a year and as editor of the journal (for three issues) after Arthur Parker left the post. Luther Standing Bear (Lakota), born in the 1860s,[1] was briefly a member of the SAI but was never active in the association, even though his younger brother Henry was a founding member. Luther Standing Bear began his work as a writer more than twenty years later than the other two: the first of his four books was published in 1928 and the last in 1934; Eastman's publications appeared between 1902 and 1920, while Bonnin's first book came out in 1901 and her second (and last) in 1921.

Standing Bear's publications, therefore, all came after the demise of the SAI, and their dates might seem to put his work beyond the chronological scope of this study. Reading the three writers together, however, and reading them in the context of the issues that engaged the SAI and its members, helps to place the intellectual work of all three and to clarify their aims as writers. Because all address their work to a primarily non-Native audience, considering the similar issues they choose to introduce to that audience is instructive. The differences in their approaches and their messages, however, are even more instructive. While Eastman and Bonnin, both writing before the SAI's final conference in 1923, work to define and to represent the modern Indian as a progressive in terms endorsed by the SAI, Standing Bear, whose work was produced in the late 1920s and early 1930s by someone who kept his distance from the SAI, moves independently toward a sharp critique of the very notion of Indian progressivism and of the institutions and practices on which the notion depended. His writing offers one engaged (and highly skeptical) Native person's reflections on the *results* of the Indian progressivism fostered by the SAI and on the ideas and tactics that had generated such hopeful energy among the SAI activists.

There is, to begin with, an important difference in the way Eastman, Bonnin, and Standing Bear position themselves as Native writers and as public intellectuals. Standing Bear consistently defines himself in his writing as Lakota, a chief and the son of a chief, the inheritor of a particular tribal legacy and the chronicler of a particular tribal history. Eastman and Bonnin, on the other hand, while clearly establishing their Sioux origins, present themselves primarily as representative American Indians, spokespersons for a pan-Indian consciousness for which their specific Sioux identity provides authentication. The titles of the publications of the three are indicative of these differences. Eastman's books include *Old Indian Days, The Soul of the Indian, The Indian To-Day,* and *Indian Heroes and Great Chieftains.* Bonnin's two published books are *Old Indian Legends* and *American Indian Stories.* Standing Bear's less generic titles include *My People the Sioux, Land of the Spotted Eagle,* and *Stories of the Sioux.* The perspectives of Eastman and Bonnin as writers, reflected in these titles, align them more closely with the pan-Indian reform philosophies of the SAI, as well as with its strategies and agendas, than do Standing Bear's more specifically Lakota books.

In spite of these differences, the publications of these three Sioux writers, not surprisingly, also have much in common. Each of the three eventually used his or her writing to address a white audience, and each was especially concerned to provide, through their published texts, calculated correctives to the erroneous assumptions about Indians that had been appearing for so long in white-authored texts. All three write nostalgically, even reverentially, about their childhoods and the contentment and coherence of the days before they started school that was disrupted by the rude shock of their transportation into boarding school life. In this autobiographical writing, all three contest two basic assumptions that their white audiences were likely to share: first, that Indian children who have not been schooled by whites are uneducated, and second, that the "wild," unschooled Indian has no conception of an intellectual life. All make it clear that they were thoroughly trained and educated as children in a coherent tribal system that was precisely fitted to the demands and exigencies of prereservation life for the Sioux. As Eastman puts it, "It is commonly supposed that there is no systematic education of their children among the aborigines of this country. Nothing could be farther from the truth." Standing Bear, in describing his childhood education, makes the similar observation that the "process of learning went on all the time. . . . Native education was not a class education but one that strengthened and encouraged the individual to grow." Bonnin details the "practical observation lessons" she absorbed from watching her mother work and listening to storytelling elders with whom she and her mother exchanged frequent visits.[2] The methods of teaching (as represented in these texts), accomplished without schoolrooms or books, integrated the child into the shared intellectual, ethical, and spiritual life of the group. When they come to narrate the circumstances of their entries into boarding school, therefore, all three writers make it clear that their families were not sending them away because they could not be educated at home; they were sending them off to acquire a specific set of *skills* that would equip them to contend with the pressures of white encroachment that threatened their homes, especially the skills of reading and writing in English.

Although they are all now primarily known as writers, all three were also accustomed to addressing white audiences through a variety of other kinds of performances as well: both Eastman and Bonnin lectured frequently, and Bonnin gave recitations and musical performances; Standing Bear toured and performed with Wild West shows, lectured, and later played Indian roles in Hollywood movies. All three frequently gave their performances in traditional Sioux regalia or in an appropriate costume, and all were often photographed in their regalia; for Eastman and Standing Bear, the clothing sometimes included a feathered warbonnet.

From the perspective of the contemporary reader, the public performances and the costuming on the part of these sophisticated, self-aware people may seem confusing or problematic, conscious as we now are of stereotyping, misrepresentations, and the manipulation of images of Indian people for ideological or commercial purposes. We are especially conscious of the way that images of the Sioux and other plains Indians, because of their association with the Indian wars of the late nineteenth century and because their clothing and regalia can be visually quite dramatic, have been used in the construction of the generic, picturesque, and warlike "Indian" of the imagined past. We may be made uncomfortable, therefore, by the seeming contradiction in the willingness of educated people—who knew and understood well the white public they were addressing, who specifically set out to *correct* stereotypes and misconceptions, and who acknowledged that changing public opinion was a necessary prerequisite to changing Indian lives for the better—to perform and pose in the very clothing that contributed to the stereotyping. In their writing, however, there is no sign of the discomfort the modern reader may feel. Eastman and Standing Bear specifically defended their wearing of regalia; Eastman defined his clothing as part of his educational mission, and Standing Bear asserted, even more emphatically than Eastman, that wearing the clothing was a means of protecting the self, even a means of survival. While all three were strong advocates for the extension of rights and protections to Indian populations, especially reservation populations, all three made it clear, through their public performances and their representations of themselves, that citizenship and assimilation were not at all the same thing. It was entirely possible, from their perspectives, to demonstrate one's "civilization" and one's Indianness in a single performance.

Of these three, Charles Eastman was the one most courted by the SAI, the one whose affiliation with the organization would have seemed most useful. Arthur Parker wrote to Eastman early in November 1911 to reflect on the events of the first SAI annual conference, held just the month before in Columbus. Eastman, apparently offended by some of the political wrangling that took place and by objections to his remarks at the conference, had withdrawn his name as a candidate for the chairmanship of the executive committee (a position equivalent to the presidency of the organization). Parker was diplomatic and conciliatory in his carefully phrased letter to Eastman, suggesting that the problems were due to a hotheaded few—he named Montezuma—and praising Eastman for his efforts to temper the debate. "You were the real statesman of the occasion," Parker wrote. He asked Eastman to reconsider his decision to distance himself from the organization (using an argument that would have been close to the heart of Parker, who was always concerned about representation and public image): "There are many ways in which you are our most representative man before the public and I want to feel that your heart is still with us in an active way."[3] Although Eastman had been one of the founding members of the SAI and had delivered the plenary address at the Columbus meeting, he evidently found the discord at the first conference disconcerting enough that, in addition to declining to run for office, and in spite of Parker's efforts to appease him, he seems not to have attended another SAI conference until 1918—at which late date he was finally persuaded to accept the presidency.

By the time of this 1911 letter, Eastman had done a great deal to warrant Parker's description of him as in many ways "our most representative man before the public." For the first fifteen years of his life, Eastman had lived what he called the "wild life" of a Sioux camp, speaking no English and expecting, by his own account, to continue a camp life forever. For several of those years, Eastman lived with his uncle's family. His father had fled to Canada in the troubled aftermath of the Sioux uprising of 1862; he had been captured there and returned to Fort Snelling in Minnesota where he was held as a prisoner of war. During his captivity he was converted to Christianity by missionaries and acquired a reading knowledge of English, eventually becoming, after his release, a settled farmer. He returned to his family convinced of the value of a school education and determined that his son should begin preparing himself to live among white Americans. On the instructions of his father, then, Eastman abruptly abandoned his old life to enter a series of schools, beginning with two boarding schools, gradually moving eastward in the process. After graduating from Dartmouth College and Boston University School of Medicine, he had served as government physician at Pine Ridge, arriving just in time to tend the wounded and dying after the 1890 Wounded Knee massacre. He had also served as Indian secretary of the national YMCA, as a lobbyist in Washington for the Santee Sioux, as outing agent at Carlisle, as physician at Crow Creek Agency in South Dakota, and as the principal fieldworker in the project of regularizing Sioux allotment records by giving every allotted Sioux a westernized name. In addition, and probably more importantly from Parker's perspective, he and his wife, Elaine Goodale Eastman, had collaborated on four books and a number of articles by 1911; he had begun a close relationship with the fledgling Boy Scouts of America; he had attended, by invitation, the First Universal Races Conference in London, delivering a talk in the same session in which W. E. B. Du Bois spoke; and he had lectured widely in the United States, often in full Sioux regalia. (Elaine Goodale Eastman noted that, beginning around 1906, Eastman made public appearances at least twenty-five times a year.[4])

Parker was aware that Eastman's visibility would be good for the SAI, an organization that needed to capture as much of the public's attention as possible. The problem was that Eastman seems to have had no stomach for political wrangling and, as his career constantly suggests, not much aptitude for it. He left both of his positions as a reservation physician, at Pine Ridge and at Crow Creek, as a result of disputes with the reservation agents, and his work as a lobbyist for the Santee Sioux led him into conflicts with another lobbyist for the Santee and eventually with the Santee themselves. In his writing, especially in *From the Deep Woods to Civilization*, Eastman represents the course of his career, and his maturing generally, as a process of increasing disenchantment with the grubby realities and blatant hypocrisies of American political life. (Elaine Eastman describes the early years of Eastman's career somewhat more prosaically, as "a series of dubious experiments," "repeated changes of occupation," and "abortive efforts."[5]) Eastman may therefore have embedded an irony in the title of *From the Deep Woods to Civilization,* given that the trajectory indicated by the title is a complex one, and any valorization of the "civilization" that is its end point is ambivalent at best.

Eastman acknowledges in this book that political realities were an unavoidable source of frustration and dismay to all Indians who lived under the oversight of a federal bureaucracy. His primary focus, however, is on his own particularly dispiriting experience. He recounts leaving the "deep woods" with the optimistic faith, encouraged by his father, that, as he came to know it better, the "civilization" of white America would reveal its superiority to the tribal culture with which he was familiar. Instead, in Eastman's telling, the culture of white America revealed to him its reliance on political systems that he increasingly found to be coercive and corrupt. His first real shock of realization came from his proximity to the troubles at Pine Ridge that eventuated in the Wounded Knee massacre, troubles that Eastman attributes directly to "dishonest politicians." He reports being stunned by his firsthand observation of the deliberate misrepresentation of the Sioux as dangerous troublemakers and their consequent violent subjugation. Until that moment, he says, he "had not dreamed what American politics really is." His further experiences on reservations and in American cities introduced him to more of what he calls the "savagery of civilization" and persuaded him that the country was suffering from "a civic disease."[6]

Eastman's flight from the political competitions that he found so disillusioning—and that dogged his personal life—is reflected in all of his writing and provides a way of contextualizing an important characteristic of his work: his persistent turning to the abstract, the ideal, the generic. Many of his recent critics have wanted to situate Eastman in a very narrowly defined political context and to measure him with an assimilationist yardstick. Since H. David Brumble III described Eastman in his 1988 book as being in thrall to a set of social Darwinist assumptions about the primitive immaturity of Native cultures, many subsequent readers, coming to Eastman's defense, have set out to unsettle Brumble's reading, arguing that Eastman's politics were probably in actuality more subversive, and certainly more complex, than they are in Brumble's account.[7] The most telling response to the kind of argument, like Brumble's, that would devalue the writing of Eastman (or any of his contemporaries) on the grounds that it is not sufficiently oppositional comes from Gerald Vizenor, who reminds readers of the particular—and particularly violent—circumstances of Eastman's extraordinary life, especially his participation in the shocking events at Pine Ridge in 1890. His experiences led

Eastman, Vizenor argues, to celebrate "peace and the romance of tribal stories" as a way of overcoming the disturbing memories of Wounded Knee. Those same events, preceded by the abrupt and dizzying changes in Eastman's life when he was fifteen, left him, Vizenor suggests, with the daunting challenge of redefining a sense of identity for himself as an individual and as a Santee Sioux: "What did it mean to be the first generation to hear the stories of the past, bear the horrors of the moment, and write to the future? What were tribal identities at the turn of the last century?"[8]

For Eastman as a writer and public figure, representing identity usually meant deliberately turning away from the disturbing details of specific recent histories, tribal or personal, and toward a more optimistic and idealized representation of "the Indian" as a figure grounded in history but not bound by it, a particular type of a universal ideal. The old Indian that Eastman had known as a child was no more to be found, he acknowledged, except in memory and imagination; but "as a type, an ideal, he lives and will live!"[9] The new Indian carried that internalized ideal with him into the civic and cultural life of America. For Eastman, the Indian ideal provided a model of democratic citizenship that set into relief the debasements of a society driven by materialism, greed, a love of ease, and the corruptions of political ambition. Eastman's writings, taken together, constitute a sustained argument for the conclusion he stated in a 1918 article for the SAI journal—that the American Indian is in fact the most appropriate representation of all that America has professed but failed to be: "I am proud to say," he wrote, "that the Indian has exemplified the American spirit; it is his contribution to mankind."[10] Eastman's presentation of his case fits comfortably with the general ethos of the SAI, at least as it was articulated by Arthur Parker, and perhaps even more comfortably with the ethos of those reform organizations that seemed to have more direct appeal to Eastman than did the SAI—the YMCA and the Boy Scouts of America. In his public presentation of himself, Eastman is both the SAI's representative man and the voice of one important strand of American progressivism.

Two of the objectives that the SAI leadership had articulated for the society from the beginning were to "present in a just light the true history of the race, to preserve its records, and emulate its distinguishing virtues" and to "direct its energies exclusively to general principles and universal interests." Both of these objectives emerge as guiding principles in Eastman's writing. He made very clear, for example, his intention of using his writing to set out a version of "the true history of the race" and provide a corrective to inadequate accounts. He prefaced *The Soul of the Indian* with an assertion that the nature of Indian religious life before white contact had never been adequately described and could only be described by an Indian, since "the religion of the Indian is the last thing about him that the man of another race will ever understand." Similarly, he prefaced *Indian Scout Talks* with an assurance that the information in the book was reliable and authentic: "These chapters represent the actual experiences and first-hand knowledge of the author. His training was along these lines, until he was nearly sixteen years of age." While he often cites specifically Sioux examples in these texts, or retells episodes from his own Sioux experiences, his emphasis—as indicated by his titles—is always on the idealized, generic, detribalized Indian, who embodies a collective truth and thus becomes more available to all, especially the white reader.[11]

In his long essay on Indian religion (*The Soul of the Indian*) Eastman announced that he had no interest in ethnology, which he likened to the piling up of dry bones; to treat religion from an ethnological perspective deadened it by reducing it to an object of scientific inquiry. What Eastman wished to convey, on the other hand, was the vital, personal significance of his faith, which could be shared by anyone who understood it right: "So much as has been written by strangers of our ancient faith and worship treats it chiefly as matter of curiosity. I should like to emphasize its universal quality, its personal appeal!"[12] For Eastman, the two objectives of getting Indian history right and locating the universal within the particulars of that history were essentially the same objective: the better a non-Indian audience came to understand Indian history and culture, the less alien it would become for them. An American audience might even come to understand that the Indian was, in fact, the true exemplar of the American spirit.

There are many other ways in which Eastman's writing reflects or echoes the published statements coming from the SAI, especially from its journal. Much of his 1915 book, *The Indian To-Day*, recapitulates positions taken in the journal, collecting them into a single volume issued under the name of the Indian who was, as Arthur Parker had suggested, one of the most widely known to the general public and therefore more likely than most to catch its attention. Both Eastman and Parker probably recognized that Eastman could claim authenticity more easily than could someone like Parker, not only because of his childhood experiences but because he *looked* like a "real Indian," especially in his regalia. (Gertrude Bonnin was to remark about someone else, a man named August Breuninger who was attempting to organize his own Indian society, that "he is unfortunate in not possessing a more Indian-face; therefore many will not have the confidence he asks them to repose in him."[13]) The title of *The Indian To-Day* suggests that it, too, was being offered as a corrective to ideas and perspectives being circulated by non-Indians, this time in the proliferating number of articles and books on the contemporary state of the "Indian problem" and the prospects for the Indian future.[14]

Eastman begins the book with an acknowledgment that, from one perspective, Indians are a vanishing race, but only in the sense that they can no longer exist in isolation from the larger population of the country and its ways of living. In a more important sense, he notes, the Indian "race" is "a thoroughly progressive one, increasing in numbers and vitality, and awakening to the demands of a new life." While Eastman frames the observations that follow with some ideas that are identifiably and peculiarly his own (and which I will discuss below), the book generally follows the pattern set by the SAI journal, focusing on the contemporary, progressive Indian and underscoring his capacity not only to participate fully in the civic life of the country but to make a significant contribution to it. Eastman has good words for white reform groups, especially the Indian Rights Association, and for the work of both the Hampton and Carlisle schools. He repeats some of the mantras of the SAI activists, mentioning the "pauperizing influences" of the reservations and insisting, as Arthur Parker, John Oskison, Sherman Coolidge, and others had done, that "the intelligent and educated Indian has no social prejudice to contend with. His color is not counted against him."[15] He reiterates another familiar point, about the ability of Indian people not only to move forward in their new civic identities but to do so quickly. Defenders of the federal government's Indian policies often argued that Indian people, because of their presumed backwardness, required the guardianship of the BIA for the foreseeable future. Theodore Roosevelt maintained, for example, that "it is impossible to expect to get the Indians up to the white level in one generation. It will take two or three to get them into a position where they will have a fair chance of surviving."[16] Eastman responded to this argument directly, drawing on his own experience:

> Who can say that civilization is beyond the reach of the untutored primitive man in a single generation? It did not take my father two thousand years, or ten years, to grasp its essential features; and although he never went to school a day in his life, he lived a broad-minded and self-respecting citizen. It took me about fifteen years to prepare to enter it on the plane of a professional man, and I have stayed with it ever since.[17]

Eastman also has much to say in his book about the necessity for an increased emphasis on education for all Indians. Unlike Richard Pratt (whom Eastman admired in general) and like the SAI spokespersons, he argued for more formal, "book" education that would produce more college graduates trained for leadership roles. He devoted a long section to an account of educated Indians who were already serving as leaders (the SAI journal also profiled educated Indians regularly). The first person on Eastman's list is Carlos Montezuma; the twenty others named include Arthur Parker, Gertrude Bonnin, John Oskison, Howard Gansworth, J. N. B. Hewitt, Sherman Coolidge, Frank Wright, Hiram Chase, Henry Roe Cloud, Stephen S. Jones, and Francis La Flesche, all of them active members of the SAI.

These success stories help to bolster what can be seen as Eastman's central argument in this loosely organized book, that "the Indian will soon adjust himself fully to the requirements of the age, be able to appreciate its magnificent achievements, and contribute his mite to the modern development of the land of his ancestors."[18] This seemingly offhand statement collapses into a brief sentence at least two fairly complex ideas, developed at much more length by Parker and others in their own writing about the meaning of the "new Indian." The first of these ideas is coded in Eastman's use of the word *adjust*, a word that emerges, probably most consistently and obviously in Parker's writing, to indicate a compromise (as discussed in chapter 2) between those who argued that the Indians had no choice but to embrace white culture fully and immediately and those who argued that for Indians to give up their cultural distinctiveness, including languages and tribal identities, was to commit racial suicide — or succumb to racial genocide. Parker, typically, had seen the possibilities of the middle ground, through the "adjustment" of tribal identities to contemporary realities rather than the abandonment of them. Parker, in fact, liked to say that he and his fellow intellectuals (including Eastman) were not new Indians but old Indians adjusted to new conditions.[19]

The second and closely related idea to which Eastman's statement reaches out is indicated by his reference to the ability of the adjusted Indian to contribute his "mite" to the "modern development" of the country. That idea, so modestly stated here, draws on the extensive debates about the place of pluralism in a democracy, and again Eastman echoes other progressive reformers, including both Parker and Du Bois, who contended that each race had a particular, unique contribution to make to the composite identity and well-being of the country.

Eastman, typically, offers more assertions and conclusions in this book than arguments, borrowing much of his language from others and eschewing the political complexities of any of his positions. There is another set of issues, however, that seems to engage him more deeply and about which he is readier to be discursive and analytical. These are the issues that align him with a different group of progressive reformers, those whose efforts were directed toward the civic and moral training of the young, especially as those efforts were channeled through the YMCA and the Boy Scouts. Eastman was drawn to the work of both of these groups, organizing Indian chapters of the YMCA between 1894 and 1898 (he helped to organize over forty, according to his biographer) and establishing his association with the Boy Scouts of America in 1910, the very first year of its existence.[20] His interest in writing for young people was evident in the books he published before 1910, including *Indian Boyhood, Red Hunters and the Animal People, Old Indian Days,* and *Wigwam Evenings.* In general, the style of his writing often reflects what one historian has called the "Progressive Era penchant for extreme idealism" that was encouraged by the philosophies of organizations like the Boy Scouts.[21] The writing after 1910, however, addresses more directly his reasons for choosing to focus his reformist sensibilities and efforts on a young audience. Eastman endorsed the character-building agendas of the YMCA and the Boy Scouts: he dedicated *Indian Scout Talks* to the Boy Scouts and the Camp Fire Girls; he called on parents to "give their fullest support" to the same two organizations in *The Indian To-Day* (177); and he noted in *From the Deep Woods to Civilization* that the program of the Boy Scouts "appeals to me strongly" (193).

The youth organizations to which Eastman was drawn, especially the Boy Scouts and the Camp Fire Girls, made Indian lore and the imitation of (presumed) Indian practices and traits a central part of their programming. (Eastman was not alone in supporting youth organizations that encouraged their members to "play Indian"; Arthur Parker's correspondence indicates that he enjoyed providing lists of names to youth groups that wanted to give their members "real" Indian names and that he sometimes helped such groups to locate Indian costumes.) In helping to spread the ethos of these organizations, however, Eastman gave his own particular spin to their progressive ideologies, anchoring them even more fully and explicitly in Indian history and culture than the organizers had already done and using his own experience as an exemplary case of the appropriateness of the Indian as a model for all young Americans.[22]

Throughout his post-1910 writing, Eastman reiterates two principal points that, in his treatment of them, are closely related: first, that a healthy, disciplined body is a necessary prerequisite to mental, emotional, and spiritual health, and second, that the training of Indian children in the old, "wild" days was actually a version of the kind of training given to the children of civilization—only more honest, more efficient, and more successful. The second of these points lies behind his contention that the Indian adult, the product of a genuinely Indian education, is the true exemplar of the spirit that all American education sets out to inculcate. That point also is reflected in the frequent analogies he uses, in the books addressed to young people, between the activities of the generic "uncivilized" Indian boy and the generic "civilized" boy. It is reflected as well in the language Eastman uses in describing his own early years, language that suggests the essential commonality of all boyhood concerns and experiences. While enjoying the free, "uncivilized" camp life that would be the envy of any boy, Eastman was also, he notes, being seriously educated and trained to look toward a future of responsibility. "From boyhood I was consciously trained to be a man," he writes in *From the Deep Woods to Civilization,* "to be in the broadest sense a public servant." With the aid of his "teachers" he constructed, like all well-trained boys, what he imagined to be "the foundations of my life career" and considered his "prospects" with confidence.[23] He presents himself in the days before he attended school, that is, as a Santee version of the ideally educated American boy who thinks of his life work in terms of his contribution to the public good.

Eastman makes a similar point about the religious beliefs he acquired from his early training, which he represents as a kind of pure distillation of the best elements of Christianity, without the corrupting overlay of a materialistic civilization. "I believe that Christianity and modern civilization are opposed and irreconcilable," he wrote in *The Soul of the Indian,* "and that the spirit of Christianity and of our ancient religion is essentially the same." The moral standards of the religion of the Sioux, he wrote in his 1918 article for the *American Indian Magazine,* are "nearer the Christ principle than the common standards of civilization."[24] The old version of tribal life, perhaps because it had essentially disappeared, provides Eastman with a set of ideals that can serve as generalized, depoliticized models for a new generation of young white Americans, who had no part in the causes of that disappearance, and as a measure of the failures of the previous generation, whose part was very large.

At the center of the set of ideals Eastman offers his readers, especially the young ones, is his strong emphasis on the health of the physical body. As a former agency physician, he was naturally interested in the inadequacy of health care on the reservations; he made that issue part of his analysis in *The Indian To-Day* of the general set of problems facing reservations Indians. He was more interested, however, in theorizing the place of the healthy body in a holistic philosophy of life, a place that he saw as foundational and essential. (He notes that he maintained his habit of exercising at least three hours a day throughout his college years.) In his advice to the Boy Scouts and Camp Fire Girls to whom he addressed *Indian Scout Talks,* he puts the idea in simple terms, informing them that the Indian boy always began his training for life by building a strong and efficient body. In the writing addressed to a more mature audience, he makes a more discursive case for the central importance of the healthy body. In *From the Deep Woods to Civilization,* he explains that his early training taught him to see the body as part of the physical universe in which he must learn to live harmoniously. He was taught to "adapt myself perfectly to natural things—in other words, to harmonize myself with nature. To this end I was made to build a body both symmetrical and enduring—a house for the soul to live in—a sturdy house, defying the elements." He explicitly equates that sturdy body with moral and spiritual health in *The Soul of the Indian:*

> The moment that man conceived of a perfect body, supple, symmetrical, graceful, and enduring—in that moment he had laid the foundation of a moral life! No man can hope to maintain such a temple of the spirit beyond the period of adolescence, unless he is able to curb his indulgence in the pleasures of the senses. Upon this truth the Indian built a rigid system of physical training, a social and moral code that was the law of his life.

Eastman offers yet another iteration of this point in *The Indian To-Day,* asserting there that the old Indian understood "that virtue is essential to the maintenance of physical excellence, and that strength, in the sense of endurance and vitality, underlies all genuine beauty."[25]

This conflation of the healthy body with a healthy morality and spirituality is certainly consistent with the ideologies of the YMCA and the Scouts, both of which set out to make better potential citizens of American youth by imposing early training on their minds and bodies. It is also consistent with other kinds of progressive reform efforts directed specifically to the strengthening of adult American bodies, especially the bodies of men. These were the kinds of reforms to which Eastman gave himself most enthusiastically, perhaps because they provided arenas in which he was more comfortable and effective than he had been as an agency physician or a lobbyist. To consider carefully Eastman's statements about this kind of reform, I believe, can also help to clarify some things about his own self-presentation that have seemed problematic to some of his readers. His emphasis on the body, for example, especially the fine-tuned Indian body, may help to explain why Eastman liked to lecture and be photographed in his Sioux regalia. That image of the Indian body, clothed in the material signs of its Indianness, was an essential part of the message he had to convey to white America about what Indianness means. *The Soul of the Indian* is introduced by a photograph of a bare-chested Eastman in a headdress, his eyes turned upward, his look meditative and serene. The image captures in visual language the portrait of the Indian that Eastman constructs in his text, in which the healthy physical body is an integral component of his spiritual philosophy.

Eastman approved of and encouraged other physical representations of Indianness of the kind that made some of his own contemporaries uncomfortable. He had no objection to costumed Indian performances in pageants (he wrote and produced his own pageant about the conspiracy of Pontiac) or even in Wild West shows, arguing that "the circus tent and the sawdust arena" were often the only venues available to Indians for representing themselves to a general audience. These performances he saw as giving Indian performers the best opportunity not just to entertain but to educate an uninformed audience that didn't understand Indian capacities or Indian histories. "The red man is a born actor," he explains, "a dancer and rider of surpassing agility, but he needs the great out of doors for his stage. In pageantry, and especially equestrian pageantry, he is most effective." The Indian performer could do what no one else could do as well, simply through "the realistic manner in which he illustrates and reproduces the life of the early frontier." He defends the use of Indian actors in Western films for the same reasons: the actors, he says, "are often engaged to represent tribal customs and historical events."[26] Eastman characterizes his own public performances as similarly educative, a means of correcting inaccurate representations by offering an authenticity— signaled by his appearance, including his clothing—that almost speaks for itself. Of his lecturing, he writes that his purpose was to "present the American Indian in his *true* character before Americans," to educate the public on "the Indian and his *true* place in American history" (my emphasis). The regalia he adopted—he calls it "our ancestral garb of honor"—became a component of his effort to educate his audiences, his particular contribution to the larger project of helping Indian people by reforming non-Indian people. Wearing the regalia, he says, made him something of "a pioneer in this new line of defense of the native American, not so much of his rights in the land as of his character and religion."[27]

In making this argument about his public appearances, Eastman may well have been responding to another Indian author who produced a book for boys, Francis La Flesche. His book, *The Middle Five: Indian Schoolboys of the Omaha Tribe,* first published in 1900, was dedicated "To the Universal Boy." Like Eastman, La Flesche asserted that his book was written to provide an accurate account of a (generic) Indian boyhood, to "reveal the true nature and character of the Indian boy." Unlike Eastman, however, La Flesche chose not to write about the boy's life before school, for reasons that he set out in his preface:

> I have made this choice not because the influences of the school alter the qualities of the boys, but that they might appear under conditions and in an attire familiar to the reader. The paint, feathers, robes, and other articles that make up the dress of the Indian, are marks of savagery to the European, and he who wears them, however appropriate or significant they might be to himself, finds it difficult to lay claim to a share in common human nature.[28]

Eastman took exactly the opposite position. His wearing of traditional dress was meant as a forceful, visual complement to the argument of his texts that the Indian, rather than being an exoticized variant, actually represented "common human nature" in its most undisguised and unvarnished form. Instead of putting the Indian boy in Western clothing, as La Flesche chose to do, Eastman preferred to put all American boys in Indian clothing.

We know that Eastman did not begin learning the English language until he was nearly sixteen years old; we also know that Elaine Goodale Eastman edited his writing, probably with a heavy hand, and that Eastman published nothing after his separation from Elaine in 1921. Much of Eastman's writing describes his experiences before he began to learn English, including the education that came to him through his tribal language. If his history suggests that he struggled to produce publishable English without his wife's editorial help, the history also supplies ample reasons for a struggle. In addition to using a second language he came to relatively late, he was also attempting to translate a philosophy and an intellectual system from its natural linguistic home into a foreign language. Eastman's reliance on physical images and performance—that is, on embodied, visual forms of his philosophy—should therefore not be surprising. The body and its performance did not require translation.

Eastman's biographer has acknowledged that he was never "a systematic thinker when it came to reform of federal Indian policy." One of his critics has made a more sweeping judgment, concluding that Eastman was not an intellectual and that he in fact became increasingly anti-intellectual over the course of his writing career.[29] Some of the details of Eastman's life and thought can make that conclusion seem plausible: his distrust of academic disciplines, especially the social sciences; his costumed performances; his persistent idealism; his valorization of the experience of the body; his address to young people, often in a simplified language; and his eventual abandonment of writing altogether. However, as a spokesperson for and teacher of a Sioux philosophy in which he was very well educated and to which he remained committed, Eastman assumed, deliberately and consciously, the role of the public intellectual. If, as Edward Said has written, the intellectual's purpose is "to represent all those people and issues that are routinely forgotten or swept under the rug" and the intellectual's task is "explicitly to universalize the crisis, to give greater human scope to what a particular race or nation suffered,"[30] then Eastman must surely be considered a significant figure in modern American Indian intellectual history.

Although Eastman was eighteen years older than Gertrude Simmons Bonnin, the early years of their careers have much in common. Both were products of Indian boarding schools: Eastman attended Flandreau Indian School and then the Santee Normal Training School in Nebraska; Bonnin attended White's Manual Labor Institute in Indiana and, briefly, Santee. Both left the Indian schools to attend primarily white colleges: Eastman graduated from Dartmouth, and Bonnin attended Earlham College in Indiana for two years. Both also worked briefly at Richard Pratt's Carlisle Indian School, Eastman as outing agent (1889–90) and Bonnin as a teacher (1897–99). Their early careers as writers are also somewhat similar, in that each published (as did Luther Standing Bear) the kind of material that was most in demand—and most expected—from Indian authors, particularly those with reservation experience: autobiography and retellings of traditional stories. Bonnin's first major publications were short stories based on her own experience, published in the *Atlantic Monthly* in 1900 and 1902. She also published less autobiographical short stories in *Harper's* in 1901 and in *Everybody's Magazine* in 1902. Her collection of retold Sioux stories, *Old Indian Legends,* was published by Ginn and Company in 1901. Although at the time of these early publications she seemed serious about continuing to work as a writer, her next significant publication did not come until 1921, when the magazine stories were combined with three new pieces and published as *American Indian Stories*.

Much of the critical commentary on Bonnin has focused, not surprisingly, on the second of these published volumes, even though most of the pieces in it (seven out of ten) were completed—and published separately—by the time she was twenty-six. The autobiographical stories have attracted particular attention, especially from literary scholars, lending themselves, as fiction, more readily to analysis than do the earlier translated stories of *Old Indian Legends* or the journalism and pamphlet writing that Bonnin was to do later in her career. The criticism has therefore concentrated on the work of a young woman, strong-minded and independent but also idealistic and frequently sentimental, who was to become in later life much more directly involved in the politics of the period than she was at twenty-six. Bonnin chose to republish these early stories in a volume she put together when she was in her mid-forties; by that point, she had moved to Washington, D.C., and had spent years working for the reform agendas of both the SAI and the Indian Welfare Committee of the General Federation of Women's Clubs. The three new pieces she added to complete *American Indian Stories* are specifically *about* reform work and specifically addressed to an audience of reform-minded (white) women: "Now the time is at hand," she writes in the final piece in the volume, "when the American Indian shall have his day in court through the help of the women of America."[31] The republication of the early stories alongside the reform stories suggests that Bonnin, as a veteran reformer, saw the early work as relevant to the efforts of organizations like the SAI and the Women's Clubs to secure rights for American Indians, especially the rights of citizenship. They preserve the emotional energy of the young writer who is fully capable of being outraged and appalled at many of the same injustices to which the older writer gave more methodical attention. *American Indian Stories* is most productively read, then, not only in the context of Bonnin's other writings but also as a 1921 publication, intended to address a particular set of issues that were crucial to Indian intellectuals and reformers of the post-World War I period, who were entering the 1920s still without the guarantees of citizenship.

Bonnin's autobiographical stories, like Eastman's, focus on the freedom of her early childhood and the demoralizing constrictions and dislocations that were imposed by her boarding school education. Both Bonnin and Eastman describe the moral code they absorbed as children, partly through the training that, as they represent it, came naturally with a free and self-sufficient, largely outdoor life. In reflecting on that early training, both emphasize the grounding of their spiritual and moral perspectives in a sense of relatedness to the natural world and all its living components. The universal sympathy and respect for life encouraged by this land-based philosophy they contrast with the rigidity and exclusiveness of institutionalized Christianity, which insists, in Bonnin's words, that "there is one God who gives reward or punishment to the race of dead men. In the upper region the Christian dead are gathered in unceasing song and prayer. In the deep pit below, the sinful ones dance in torturing flames."[32] This vision of a Christianity based on the prospect of an afterlife lived either above or below the earth omits entirely the present, living natural world that was central to the philosophies of both Eastman and Bonnin. In Bonnin's stories, the trauma of the Sioux child's experience of boarding school derives in large part from the confinement to an indoor life and the forced, abrupt confrontation with this version of Christianity, with its nightmarish representations of devils and hell.[33]

Eastman originally went to school, he writes in his autobiography, because his father had become convinced of the necessity for the Indian to learn to read and write English, so that, like the white man, he will "be able to preserve on paper the things he does not want to forget."[34] The father, as he is represented in this text, is fully persuaded that the new ways, including the new kind of education, are good and necessary, and he is enthusiastic about his son's new prospects. The departure for boarding school that Bonnin describes, on the other hand, is more emotionally tense and more ominous. The child in her stories—presumably a reimagined version of the eight-year-old Gertrude Simmons—is eager to try the adventure of travel and school, while her mother has only reluctantly resigned herself to sending her small daughter off in the care of white, English-speaking Christians who will introduce her to an alien life. The mother suffers at the parting and knows that her daughter will soon suffer as well: "She will need an education when she is grown, for then there will be fewer real Dakotas, and many more palefaces. This tearing her away, so young, from her mother is necessary, if I would have her an educated woman. . . . But I know my daughter must suffer keenly in this experience."[35]

The mother in these stories is one avatar of an important figure in Bonnin's thinking and writing: the traditional Indian woman who has taught her children well but must remain behind and suffer as her children leave or are taken from her. Bonnin's anxiety about the mother who is left behind suffuses the letters she wrote to Carlos Montezuma—to whom she was briefly engaged to be married—in the spring and summer of 1901. At that point, Bonnin had resigned her teaching job at Carlisle and was finishing a course of study at the New England Conservatory of Music in Boston. By June 1901 she had returned to South Dakota to work at the Standing Rock Reservation, in part to be near her mother. Bonnin's letters to Montezuma during this period convey ambivalence and indecision about her future, both personal and professional. She is indecisive about marrying Montezuma, especially since it would require that she join him in Chicago (he apparently refused to consider taking a job as a reservation physician, as Bonnin had suggested he might do); she is also indecisive about how best to direct her intellectual energies and ambitions, and much of her frustration seems to come from a conflict between her personal ambitions and her sense of responsibility to her mother and the other "old ones" who have remained at home.

Bonnin worked to resolve the conflict. Before she left Boston in the spring of 1901, she wrote to tell Montezuma that she was planning to return to South Dakota to learn what she could from the reservation people: "I do not mean to give up my literary work—but while the old people last I want to get from them their treasured ideas of life. . . . The old folks have a claim upon us. It is selfish and cruel to abandon them entirely."[36] By early April she had determined to stay at home for at least a year, and by mid-April she was able to articulate a fuller rationale for her decision. If one is always torn, she explained to Montezuma, between wanting to be kind to those who are nearest and wanting to have an influence in the wider world—in this case, to help one's own mother and thousands of other mothers at the same time—then her plan for returning to the reservation offered a good solution to this dilemma: "I can write stories and have them published in the East for the so-called civilized peoples. This is combining the two."[37] Six weeks later Bonnin had refined her plans further to accommodate marriage to Montezuma: "I shall gather all I can [on the reservation] and do the writing when I am in our own home. . . . Would it not be a great work to write *many* volumes of Indian legends?"[38] She set about her story-collecting in earnest, writing to Montezuma in June that she had made an appointment with a local informant to come and tell her stories and adding, "I have a good time talking Sioux with the old folks." By the middle of June, she was able to report that things were going well: "Yes—I have got many fine old legends! And my publishers are very anxious to keep a hold on my work."[39] The relationship with Montezuma soured after the intensity of that spring and summer, and the correspondence faltered. Before the middle of August, she had married Raymond

Bonnin, a Sioux. The letters she wrote to Montezuma during the course of their courtship and engagement were signed "Zitkala-Sa," the name under which her publications appeared; when she wrote to him on August 26, 1902, she signed the letter "Mrs. Gertrude Bonnin." The stories she collected and translated during that period—that is, after the 1901 publication of *Old Indian Legends* and before her marriage to Raymond Bonnin in August 1902—were never published during her lifetime.[40]

The correspondence with Montezuma, as brief as it is, throws an interesting light on Bonnin's sense of herself as an educated Indian woman with a full awareness of both her ability to make her way successfully in the non-Indian world of the East and her responsibility to the old ones left at home, those who were victims rather than beneficiaries of the intrusions of the white world. It also makes clear the absence of any conflict in Bonnin's mind between her aspirations as an intellectual and her desire to collect, translate, and modify traditional stories and offer them in readable form to a non-Indian audience. The correspondence suggests, in fact, that she saw this kind of project as entirely appropriate work for her as an educated, conscientious woman and a daughter of the Sioux.

The letters to Montezuma also indicate that Bonnin was intensely aware of, and somewhat defensive about, the fact that her choices put her in direct conflict with Montezuma's friend and mentor—and her former employer—Richard Pratt, whom Bonnin thoroughly disliked. She even suggests that her dislike of Pratt, whom she calls "woefully small and bigoted for all his imposing avoirdupois," is a significant motivation for her writing: "just the hate of him fires me to work again even when I would most like to fold my hands."[41] The work Bonnin was doing at that point—collecting and translating stories on the reservation and defending traditional Sioux life—would clearly not have pleased Pratt, whose considerable energies were given to urging the breaking up of reservations, the swift death of Indian languages and traditional practices, and the end of most federal protections for Indians, including Bonnin's old ones. "You know how Carlisle scoffs at all Indian-ism," she wrote to Montezuma. "If you have faith in the Indian becoming 'civilized'—it is not because you agree with Carlisle!" Bonnin bristled at Pratt's overbearing paternalism and his insistence that Indians could survive only by imitating whites and learning from them:

I will never speak of the whites as elevating the Indian! I am willing to say higher conceptions of life elevate the whole human family—but not the

Indian more than any other. Until Col. Pratt actively interests himself in giving college education to Indians I cannot say his making them slaves to the plow is anything other than drudgery![42]

In 1902, Bonnin produced the brief essay "Protest Against the Abolition of the Indian Dance," an argument for preserving one form of the "Indianism" that Pratt (and Montezuma) deprecated and, once again, citing the welfare of the old ones as a primary consideration. "The old illiterate Indians, with a past irrevocably dead and no future," she wrote, deserve to retain the rituals and pleasures that sustain them: "What American would shuffle off an old parent as he would an old garment from his body?"[43]

There are many ways of understanding Bonnin's personal and ideological differences with Pratt. She spent a year and a half as a teacher at his Carlisle school, leaving in January of 1899 with a distaste for teaching—especially, it seems, for Pratt's kind of teaching. Her first three published stories, appearing in the *Atlantic Monthly* in early 1900, contained stinging critiques of the treatment of Indian children at a boarding school that remains unnamed in the stories but is administered by a distinctly Pratt-like figure. The stories also openly criticize the incompetence and cruelty of the boarding school teachers, who use psychological and physical coercion to distance the students from their origins—including their own former selves—as fully as possible. The narrator sees her experience as both student and teacher in boarding schools as a painful process of deracination and diminishment: "Like a slender tree, I had been uprooted from my mother, nature, and God. I was shorn of my branches, which had waved in sympathy and love for home and friends. The natural coat of bark which had protected my oversensitive nature was scraped off to the very quick."[44]

Not surprisingly, the publication of these stories elicited a quick and strong response from Carlisle and other boarding schools. Hampton's newspaper, the *Southern Workman,* immediately denounced the stories as the "bitter reminiscences" of someone whose experience was atypical, concluding its review with the hope that the author, through the help of kind friends, might settle down and lose her sense of "unrest" so that any sequels to the stories might be "brighter and more sunny." The Santee Normal Training School's *Word Carrier* was less gentle in its rebukes to the former Santee student, calling the stories exaggerated inventions designed for maximum dramatic effect. The author has only "contempt and disgust" for her characters, the reviewer contends, and the stories reveal that Zitkala-Sa "is a person of infinite conceit," ungrateful for "all that has been done for her by the pale faces, which in her case is considerable." Fortunately, in the eyes of this reviewer, the upstart Zitkala-Sa is not representative of all Indian girls: "They average far better." The *Word Carrier's* review was reprinted in the Carlisle paper, the *Red Man,* in June 1900. The *Red Man* carried another brief comment on Bonnin's stories in a subsequent issue, this time using them to convey to the Carlisle students a small lesson about attitudes and deportment. People like Zitkala-Sa, the article begins, "always insist on sitting on the cold side of a hill," storing up "dark pictures" and forgetting their happier experiences. "Those who make light of small trials," on the other hand, "and push them aside that sunshine and cheer may enter are the people who make the world worth living in."[45]

These responses, especially those from Carlisle, only intensified Bonnin's desire to write freely, as we have seen from her letters to Montezuma, and may have helped inspire a subsequent story, "The Soft-Hearted Sioux," published in *Harper's* in 1902. That story explores the problem of the returned student, in this case a young Sioux man who comes back to the reservation from an eastern boarding school prepared to use his new learning, including his new faith in Christianity, to help those at home. The young man finds that his search for the "soft heart of Christ" has left him unequipped for the very hard realities of life at home on the reservation, including illness and starvation. The local medicine man condemns him in public: "He is a fool! Why do you sit here giving ear to a foolish man who could not defend his people because he fears to kill, who could not bring venison to renew the life of his sick father? With his prayers, let him drive away the enemy! With his soft heart, let him keep off starvation!"[46] The story thus contains an implicit critique of the Carlisle philosophy that separating Indian children from the old ways of their families is necessary for the survival of the children and, ultimately, their families. Bonnin's returned student no longer knows how to survive in the reservation world, nor does he know how to help those who need him. As a result of his bewilderment, his elderly father dies of starvation.

Others of Bonnin's published works also focus on the distress and suffering of elderly Indians who have no access to outside help or who may have fallen victim to policies, such as the allotment program, that were often encouraged by well-intentioned whites with no real understanding of reservation realities. Her narrative poem, "A Sioux Woman's Love for Her Grandchild," published in the *American Indian Magazine* in 1918,[47] when Bonnin was beginning a brief term as editor, tells the story of an elderly Sioux woman whose grandchild wanders away from her, just as two dangers approach: a prairie storm and the troops of Custer's cavalry. The other Sioux who are fleeing the soldiers urge her to come with them to save her own life, but the old woman chooses to remain behind, unwilling to abandon the lost grandchild and thus—so the poem suggests—guaranteeing her own death. "The Widespread Enigma of Blue-Star Woman," a story first published in Bonnin's 1921 collection, details the struggle of another elderly Sioux woman against a different kind of antagonist, the bureaucracy of the BIA. Blue-Star Woman, who doesn't understand either English or the workings of bureaucracies, has been denied an allotment because she can't document her family history. Her efforts to obtain a piece of land on which to live bring her into conflict with another old one, a man named High Flier, who is trying to prevent the loss of Sioux land through fraudulent allotments. Both eventually fall into the hands of opportunistic, grasping Indian strangers who, in collusion with a corrupt and bribable reservation agent, cheat both of the old ones out of half the land and money that are due them.

This story, which is undated, was probably written around the time Bonnin began her official connection with the Indian Welfare Committee of the General Federation of Women's Clubs in 1920, given its very explicit appeal to women to take an active interest in the fate of the western Indians. The old Sioux chief in the story, High Flier, writes a letter of appeal (dictated to his English-speaking granddaughter) to "a prominent American woman," asking her to investigate the process by which the Sioux land is being allotted, a process that the old man suspects is corrupt. He decides to burn the letter rather than mailing it, hoping that action will make its airborne message find the eastern benefactress more quickly. Because he builds his fire close to the reservation agency buildings, he is arrested as a troublemaker and imprisoned. In a politically interesting if aesthetically awkward moment in the story, High Flier has a vision, in his jail cell, in which a "great galaxy of American women" gather around the Statue of Liberty, willing the giant female figure into life. The massed energies of the women cause Liberty's torch to shine, casting its light "into the obscure and remote places of the land." For the first time, and because of the united will and strength of these American women, "her light of liberty penetrated Indian reservations. A loud shout of joy rose up from the Indians of the earth, everywhere!"[48] High Flier's burned letter of appeal is therefore salvaged, through the agency of Bonnin's story, and sent on its way to its intended audience of privileged eastern women.

Bonnin's concern for those left at home on the reservation, and her determination to bring them to the attention of the public, continued to shape her work as a reformer and social activist. With her husband, she spent roughly thirteen years with the Ute Indians on the Uintah Reservation in Utah before moving to Washington, D.C., in 1917 to work full time as secretary of the SAI and, in 1918, to take over from Arthur Parker as editor of its journal (both were unpaid positions). In 1920 she began her Indian welfare work for the General Federation of Women's Clubs, and in 1926 she and Raymond Bonnin founded the National Council of American Indians, using their Washington location to lobby directly for fair treatment of reservation Indians. In Utah, Bonnin had run sewing classes for the Ute women, persuading them to give one day a week to sewing clothes for the elderly; she had also opened a lunchroom to serve food to the Ute who came in to the reservation agency to transact business with the agent. She was outraged by how much of the reservation business was kept secret from the people whose lives were most affected. "We must have data from the Indian Office," she wrote to Arthur Parker, "relative to amounts of Indian funds, proposed expenditures and payments to Indians, that as a people we may know the business transactions on each and every Indian reservation. At present we are kept in the dark."[49] Once she became an active member of the SAI—while she was still in Utah—Bonnin pelted Parker with letters about the organization's responsibility to the reservation Indians whose poverty and minimal knowledge of English kept them largely beyond the reach of the SAI's efforts at uplift. "I almost feel that I should beg your pardon for writing you so frequently," she wrote to him. "I am so determined that our work for the Indian race shall not drag because of any negligence on my part."[50] In Utah she also became, notoriously, a vigorous and outspoken opponent of peyote, urging a legal ban on its use and tirelessly citing its damaging physical effects and its cost to people who had little money to begin with.

When Bonnin attended the 1916 meeting of the SAI in Cedar Rapids, she was interviewed for the local newspaper, the *Evening Gazette*. Her comments (which were primarily about the sewing classes and the agency lunch program at Uintah) were prefaced by an error-riddled introduction:

Zitkala-Sa (Red Bird) is an Indian woman of culture and refinement. She is a graduate of Earlham college, Richmond, Ind., a graduate of the New England conservatory of music, Boston, and formerly a teacher in the Indian school at Carlisle. She is a member of the Sioux tribe, and is married to a white man. Mrs. Gertrude Bonnin left the civilization of the east to go into the desert of Utah that she might bring unto the untamed Utes the message of the white man.[51]

Bonnin attended Earlham but left before graduating; her husband, Raymond Bonnin, was Sioux; and whatever complex of motives took her to Utah with her husband, those motives were certainly not collapsible into a simple wish to bring the white man's message to some "untamed" Indians. Bonnin worked to protect the well-being and the interests of the Ute *against* white incursions, and if she was conveying messages, it would be much more appropriate to say that it was Indian voices, especially Ute and Sioux voices (like that of the fictional High Flier), she wished to translate to a white audience. Bonnin sent her messages back east from the reservations, in the form of stories, letters, and pamphlets, as often as she could.

Unlike many of her SAI colleagues—certainly including Montezuma—Bonnin continued to put the reservations and a traditional Sioux ethos at the center of her philosophy as a reformer and a thinker. Like Eastman, she held that the Sioux religious sensibility she had internalized as a child not only did not distance her from the non-Indian world but was, in fact, the source of her strongest sense of connection to it. The study of Indian "folklore," she wrote in the introduction to *Old Indian Legends,* "strongly suggests our near kinship with the rest of humanity and points a steady finger toward the great brotherhood of mankind."[52] The effects of an educational system like Pratt's, Bonnin repeatedly suggested, smothered that deep sense of kinship by deliberately suppressing a Native sensibility and so, in effect, worked against education's intended goal of smooth assimilation.

In two of her published pieces, "The Indian's Awakening," a poem published in the SAI journal in 1916,[53] and "A Dream of Her Grandfather," a story included in *American Indian Stories,* Bonnin affirms the importance of the symbiotic relationship between her strong sense of tribal connectedness and her work as an educated, politically aware activist. The speaker of the poem laments the loss of a sense of tribal identity, represented by her "eagle plumes and long hair," taken away by an educational system that might have been founded on good intentions but that in practice left her isolated and confused: "From you my own people, I've gone astray. / A wanderer now, with no where to stay." The laments of the speaker are answered by a disembodied voice that leads her, in a vision, into the Indian spirit world and eventually to a village where the inhabitants of this world are telling stories by the fire.

When the speaker expresses her shock at encountering so many people she thought were not only dead but lost to memory, one of the Indian spirits assures her that she's wrong. " 'My child, We are souls, forever and aye,' " their spirits dispersed throughout the visible, natural world and therefore always available to the memory of the living: " 'Now various stars where loved ones remain / Are linked to our hearts with Memory-chain.' " The spirits of the Indian dead retain their own memories, and what they remember are "Old Earth trails"—the landscapes of the physical world in which they once lived. Nature thus links the living and the dead, the modern educated woman and her tribal forebears, through a deep, instinctive, shared memory. The speaker returns from her visionary journey restored to a sense of her ineradicable Indian identity and determined not to waste the "Gift of Life" in grief and regret for what might have been lost.

The brief story "A Dream of Her Grandfather"[54] follows a similar pattern but was probably written later than "The Indian's Awakening," after Bonnin had moved to Washington, and seems specifically directed to other women, both Indian and non-Indian, who were involved in Indian reform. The story describes another vision, this one received by a woman whose grandfather had led one of the first delegations of Sioux to travel to Washington to negotiate with federal officials. The grandfather had fallen ill and died in Washington. His educated granddaughter has now come to Washington to carry on the "humanitarian work" of her grandfather, taking on the problems of "welfare work among her people." She dreams one night that her grandfather has sent her a cedar chest; opening it, she releases a vision of "a circular camp of white cone-shaped tepees, astir with Indian people." The village crier calls the people out of their homes to hear his message, spoken in the Dakota language (which the dreaming granddaughter understands): " 'Be glad! Rejoice! Look up, and see the new day dawning! Help is near! Hear me, every one.' " This vision, like the one in "The Indian's Awakening," is restorative; the end of the vision leaves the granddaughter "thrilled with new hope for her people." In this case, however, the message from the world of the dead is specifically about the future, about the brighter prospects (especially for reservation Indians) made possible by the "help" that is on the way. That help, as the story implies, will come from educated Indian people like the granddaughter who have access to those with the power to make changes.

Although all of Bonnin's published writing helps to provide a context for her public self-presentation, that is especially true for these pieces that confirm the need for a deep, *conscious* connection between the contemporary, educated Indian and a traditional tribal past—including a tribal language. Like Eastman, Bonnin saw forms of public performance as an important part of the work she could do for Indian people, and, again like Eastman, she frequently performed in full regalia and was often photographed wearing it. Her performance career began early, starting with her success as a prize-winning orator at Earlham. She also frequently performed as a musician (she played violin and piano) and sometimes combined her music with her oratory. In the spring of 1900, while she was studying music at the New England Conservatory, she accompanied the Carlisle band on a tour; the group's Washington, D.C., appearances included a performance for President and Mrs. McKinley at the White House. Bonnin (who had adopted the name Zitkala-Sa by this point) contributed to the tour program by reciting a portion of Longfellow's *Hiawatha* and playing her violin. One of Carlisle's newspapers, the *Indian Helper,* reported enthusiastically on her success: "A Dakota girl, in Dakota costume of beaded and fringed buckskin, with her long black locks combed very smoothly over the ears and braided in two braids, she was decidedly picturesque and typical in style, and the recital from start to finish would have satisfied Longfellow's highest ideal of native grace and eloquence." A week after this notice appeared, the *Indian Helper* ran an even more effusive comment, calling Bonnin "our Minnehaha who takes each audience by storm and holds it breathless till she chooses to release it. Her rendering of the pathos and beauty and truth of Longfellow's lives is a revelation to her hearers, while her violin wins all hearts." (These notices appeared in March 1900; by June, the other Carlisle paper, the *Red Man,* was publishing its attacks on Bonnin's stories.[55]) While her long stay on the Uintah Reservation gave her few opportunities for public performance, she did collaborate in 1913 with a young white musician, William Hanson, on the production of an opera. Their *Sun Dance Opera,* which drew on Bonnin's musical knowledge as well as her knowledge of the traditions and rituals surrounding Sioux versions of the Sun Dance, incorporated interludes of traditional song and dance. The performers included both white and Indian students from the local Uintah Academy.[56]

In 1916, when Arthur Parker gave Bonnin's name (along with Eastman's) to a Chautauqua booking agent who was looking for Indian speakers, Bonnin was receptive to the recommendation, noting in a letter to Parker that they seemed to agree in thinking of "lecture work as a desirable field for our cause."[57] Her later work for the General Federation of Women's Clubs included regular lectures, and she used her position in the SAI not only to give speeches at its meetings but also to give costumed performances. She offered a reading of the "Eulogy of Sitting Bull" at the 1918 meeting, wearing full regalia, and she took a role in Eastman's costume pageant, *The Conspiracy of Pontiac,* when it was performed at the 1919 meeting. Her pamphlet *Americanize the First American* and her book *American Indian Stories,* both published in 1921, included the same photographic portrait of Bonnin in braids and beadwork, and there are a number of extant photographs of her in a full-length, elaborately beaded dress.

Although we can ultimately only speculate about Bonnin's specific reasons for choosing so often to appear before the public in tribal regalia, in her case, as in Eastman's, the choice of clothing is completely consistent with the perspectives on her Indianness that she articulates in her writing. The clothing provides a physical representation of those visions of the past—including her own childhood past—that she includes in her poems and stories, using visual imagery to invoke the role she chose for herself and advocated for others: the old Indian successfully adjusting to new ways, the grandchild grown up but still a grandchild. There are some suggestions that Bonnin was aware that the work she might accomplish through her clothing and her performances could not be done so well in any other way. As she wrote to Arthur Parker, "I have often wished for a wireless, wordless means of communication . . . [since] words are such clumsy weights upon one's thought."[58] When she decided to succeed Parker as editor of the SAI's journal, she explained the decision to Carlos Montezuma in self-effacing terms that suggest her frustration with the effectiveness of her own writing:

[I] want to assure you that when the time comes, I shall not be afraid to handle the magazine. It has long been my private opinion that able writers should seek the large magazines with a million readers, so that every stroke of their able pen might reach the greater number; and do more for the cause of the race. . . . Therefore, if Mr. Parker is a more able writer, he should be released to contribute to the hundred millions of Americans, and then it will seem more right that I do the best I can, according to my lights.[59]

The regalia and the music were wordless forms of communication to which she turned often. And while she continued to produce her own stories, poems, and speeches, Bonnin seemed most comfortable translating and performing the words and even the visions of others.

4. *Gertrude Bonnin (Zitkala-Sa) in regalia, ca. 1913. (Courtesy of L. Tom Perry Special Collections, Harold B. Lee Library, Brigham Young University, Provo, Utah.)*

The publications of Luther Standing Bear differ from those of Bonnin and Eastman in several ways: they are less theoretical and philosophical and more revealing of the particular details of the writer's own life and career. His work is also less consistent in the positions it takes from one book to the next. Standing Bear's books in fact reflect a fairly radical change in his thinking, between the publication of *My People the Sioux* in 1928 and *Land of the Spotted Eagle* in 1933, about a number of the issues that concerned all three writers, especially Indian education and the effectiveness of progressive reform agendas in improving the lives of Indian people. By the time of the latter book, Standing Bear had become disillusioned with the kind of reforms encouraged by the SAI and cynical about many of the results. Even the 1924 Indian Citizenship Act that conferred birthright citizenship on Indians—a significant goal of all the Indian reform groups—Standing Bear angrily declared in his 1933 book to be "the greatest hoax" ever perpetrated on the Indians.[60] The differences between *My People the Sioux* and *Land of the Spotted Eagle* seem attributable to at least two major factors. The first is that, between the publication of the two books, Standing Bear returned to the Pine Ridge Reservation for a visit after an absence of sixteen years. The conditions he found there shocked and appalled him. Describing his visit in an article for the *American Mercury* in 1931, Standing Bear declared that "I found the destruction of my people continuing; I found conditions worse than when I left them years ago." No one at Pine Ridge had enough to eat. The young people seemed weakened by hunger, and the old were "pictures of lost hope. . . . The system has crushed them; they are nonentities."[61] Having witnessed this startling evidence of the failure of years of Indian reform to give the reservation Sioux any more control over their own lives, leaving them even more destitute and hungry and hopeless, Standing Bear revisited and revised his attitudes and perspectives, especially his confidence in the good will of white America.

A second reason for the striking differences between the two books is that the later one reflects Standing Bear's familiarity with the contemporary literature about Indians. *Land of the Spotted Eagle* is organized as a series of direct and sometimes angry responses to a particular set of generalizations that had appeared regularly in the writing produced by white authors. He asserts at the beginning of that book that even though whites understand little about the ideas, motivations, or desires of Indian people, they still continue to "write much of the visible and exterior life with explanations that are more often than not erroneous."[62] Perhaps because he was not concerned to appease whites and solicit their support for any particular project or piece of legislation, Standing Bear is more forthright than any of his predecessors in simply declaring white writers dead wrong about a number of issues. His writing in *Land of the Spotted Eagle* doesn't negotiate; it flatly refutes.

My People the Sioux is largely autobiographical, a fairly straightforward account of Standing Bear's childhood, his schooling at Carlisle, his impressions of the troubles at Pine Ridge in 1890, his travels with Buffalo Bill Cody's Wild West Show, and his eventual move to California to work as an actor in Western movies. While the book offers some criticisms that grow out of Standing Bear's experience of the white world, these are rather muted and directed primarily at Hollywood representations of Indians. The tensions and anxieties expressed in the book are largely personal, and they center on Standing Bear's recollections of his experiences as a Carlisle student. Much of what he recalls as particularly shocking and disorienting—train travel, haircuts, uniforms, rigid scheduling, the enforcement of English-only rules—is also treated in accounts by other former boarding school students. What distinguishes his Carlisle narrative from other boarding school reminiscences is Standing Bear's focus on the problem that seemed to worry him most—figuring out how to please, simultaneously, two men (who could hardly have been more different from each other) whom he admired and whose approval he very much desired: his father and Richard Pratt.

Standing Bear (like Eastman) went to school at the urging of his much revered father—to whom he dedicates this book—in the first group of students Richard Pratt brought to Carlisle.[63] He recalls assuming at the time that his trip to the East was a kind of rite of passage, a way of proving his bravery to his father, another step in a boy's training to be a respected tribal citizen: "My idea was that I was leaving the reservation and going to stay away long enough to do some brave deed, and then come home again alive. If I could just do that, then I knew my father would be so proud of me." After only a short time at Carlisle, Standing Bear realized that the school had an entirely different agenda in mind for him, one that he saw as not just separating him from his traditional Sioux father but as an actual form of betrayal of his father. He records his struggle to find a way to reconcile school and home, to be both a good student and a good son:

> I now began to realize that I would have to learn the ways of the white man. With that idea in mind, the thought also came to me that I must please my father as well. So my little brain began to work hard. I thought that some day I might be able to become an interpreter for my father, as

he could not speak English. Or I thought I might be able to keep books for him if he again started a store. So I worked very hard [at Carlisle].

Standing Bear's work paid off. He succeeded well enough to become a favorite of Pratt, who sent him to Rosebud and Pine Ridge to recruit more students, chose him to lead the Carlisle band when it played for the opening of the Brooklyn Bridge, and named him as the model Carlisle student who would accept John Wanamaker's invitation to come to Philadelphia to work in his store. In preparing for that move, Standing Bear recalls, he prayed "that I would be able to fulfill all the hopes of my school and race, and that it would please my father." When the elder Standing Bear came to Carlisle for a visit, the son was relieved by the absence of the conflict he had feared between his father and his new mentors and gratified by the respect that the representatives of home and school displayed for each other in their first direct meeting: "Doubtless they wished to convince him that I was a boy they were pleased to have in the school. The school people were glad to have had him with us, as he was so neat and clean, and conducted himself in such a gentlemanly manner, even if he was an Indian right off the reservation."[64]

Standing Bear did manage to find a way to use the skills he acquired at Carlisle to help his father, by accompanying him to Washington as interpreter (Pratt went, too) when the elder Standing Bear visited the Bureau of Indian Affairs with a petition from the reservation. The anxieties of the young Standing Bear were thus moderated by his successes, and in recounting them, he seems unambiguously proud of his independence, his initiative, and his accomplishments. He is able to make two significant statements: first, that "my father was very proud to think that he could depend on me for the sake of the whole tribe," and second, that "Captain Pratt was very proud of me."[65] The school narrative thus leads to an implicit affirmation of the possibilities for pleasing both mentors, for using the skills learned in the white world to make things better for those at home, for being successful as a Sioux son and a model Carlisle student.

The school narrative of *My People the Sioux* connects the earlier sections of the book—which provide stories from the life of Standing Bear's father and from the history of the Sioux as well as reflections on his own childhood education—with the later sections that recount his work as a performer in Wild West shows and Hollywood films. (Although Standing Bear doesn't mention this, his father had also spent one season as a show Indian, with an organization called Doc Carver's Wild America Show.) Standing Bear's emphasis on the performative nature of many of his school experiences makes his later performance work seem a logical, even natural extension of the life he was accustomed to, in which white people *watched* Indians. On the original train journey to Carlisle, Standing Bear and the other children were acutely aware of being objects of curiosity; crowds gathered when the train stopped, and when the children were taken off to have a meal, "the white people were all crowded up close to the windows on the outside, watching us and laughing their heads off at the way we acted."[66] Richard Pratt says of this train trip that "crowds met us at every point, and when we reached Chicago, the papers having published our coming, many thousands of people were in and about the station to see us, and such was the pressure that the railroad authorities were compelled to run our cars out in to a private yard with a high fence around it to keep us from the crowd." (Gertrude Bonnin also recalls the extreme discomfort of being watched by staring adults and pointing children on her train journey to boarding school, and again of being constantly "watched by those around me" as a young teacher.[67]) At Carlisle, Standing Bear and his fellow students were frequently put on display for whites, sometimes in organized performances by the bands, choirs, and drill teams, and at other times in simulations of unrehearsed, ordinary behavior: "Captain Pratt was always very proud to 'show us off' and let the white people see how we were progressing. Sometimes we were drilled for days before starting out to an invitation for dinner, so that our deportment should all be correct and proper."[68]

In his accounts of his work with Buffalo Bill, Standing Bear not only speaks without regret or chagrin at having been a "show Indian," he speaks with obvious pride in recalling a job he considered well done. He seems especially pleased to know that he gained the approval of Cody—as he had earlier been gratified by the approval of his father and Richard Pratt. Standing Bear considered himself successful both as a performer and as an interpreter and general assistant to Cody: "Buffalo Bill was well pleased to note how well the Indians minded me in all our work." Cody's confidence in him led to his choosing Standing Bear to put on a special performance when the show came to London—to dance, alone, in front of the box of King Edward. The dance was evidently a success: "The King had been very dignified thus far and had not even smiled. But when I got down to doing my fancy steps and gave a few Sioux yells, he had to smile in spite of himself. I saw that I had made a hit with him, and was very happy." In addition to performing, Standing Bear took upon himself the responsibility for keeping the Indians in the troupe as far away from alcohol as he could and eventually for managing their money so that they wouldn't spend it too quickly. Once again, he concluded that he had done a good job: "To this day I am proud of the success I had while abroad with the Buffalo Bill show, in keeping the Indians under good subjection."[69]

After leaving Cody's show, Standing Bear performed for a while in New York with a show organized by his brother Henry and then with the very successful 101 Ranch Show in Oklahoma before moving on to California and the movies. He is strongly critical of the representation of Indians in Hollywood films, largely because the Indian roles were frequently taken by whites—and always taken by whites if the role was a major one. Standing Bear is disturbed by the resulting distortions:

> I have seen probably all of the pictures which are supposed to depict Indian life, and not one of them is correctly made. There is not an Indian play on the stage that is put on as it should be. I have gone personally to directors and stage managers and playwrights and explained this to them, telling them that their actors do not play the part as it should be played, and do not even know how to put on an Indian costume and get it right; but the answer is always the same, "The public don't know the difference, and we should worry!"[70]

Interestingly, what bothers Standing Bear about the Western movies is not that Indians were performing their Indianness—playing Indian—for a white audience, but that they were *not* doing it; the whites were doing the performing, and getting it wrong. Buffalo Bill, on the other hand, did things right, from Standing Bear's perspective; his performances made it possible for Indians to demonstrate, with pride, some of the things they were very good at doing: riding, shooting, dancing, and wearing their costumes correctly. Like Charles Eastman, Standing Bear wanted to see more Indians performing for the public, rather than fewer.

The critique of white representations of Indians that Standing Bear offers at the end of *My People the Sioux* becomes one of the organizing principles of *Land of the Spotted Eagle*. In the earlier book it was primarily the movies that were the object of his criticism; in the later book, Standing Bear rejects other forms of representation as well, especially the written texts produced by white authors. His preface makes clear his conviction that whites have never gotten their representations of Indians right and probably never will. In a direct response to those white writers who proclaimed of the Indian, as had the ethnologist Frank J. Monsen, that "his life is an open book," Standing Bear

5. *Undated photograph of Luther Standing Bear, in headdress, with the cowboy actor William S. Hart. (Courtesy of the Denver Public Library, Western History Collection, B-708.)*

asserts unequivocally that "the inner life of the Indian is, of course, a closed book to the white man."[71] That fact, however, had not prevented whites from arrogantly continuing to disseminate their misinformation, according to Standing Bear, causing serious harm to the people they misrepresent:

> Irreparable damage has been done by white writers who discredit the Indian. Books have been written of the native American, so distorting his true nature that he scarcely resembles the real man. . . . So, through the very agencies that reach the mass of people, that purport to instruct, educate, and perpetuate true history—books, schools, and libraries all over the land—there have been graven false ideas in the hearts and minds of the people.[72]

Standing Bear was clearly familiar with these white-authored texts, and his own book is offered as a strong corrective to the existing histories, an account from an Indian's point of view of the virtues of the old life that whites were so eager to obliterate and of the debasements of the new life that replaced it. Many of the issues he addresses are therefore familiar ones: boarding school education and the influence of the returned student, the retention of tribal traditions, the preservation of languages, the status of women in tribal cultures, the equating of assimilation with survival.

In his *American Mercury* article, Standing Bear had observed that, when he lived on the reservation, he was known as a "bad Indian," a "chronic disturber."[73] He takes up that role again in this book, moving as far away as possible from the "good Indian" roles he had described with apparent pride in *My People the Sioux:* good student, good employee, good manager, a keeper of the peace. The voice of this book is defiant, oppositional, often angry, and distrustful of institutions and practices that he had accepted with equanimity in the former book. Repeatedly he contrasts Indian ways of doing things with the ways that whites have forced on Indians, or with practices that whites have held up as models for the Indians, and repeatedly he declares the Indian ways superior. One of the more common tropes in white accounts of Indian life, for example, is that the forced labor of women in tribal life is a good indicator of the superiority of American "civilized" life, in which women are venerated and protected from the brutalizing effects of labor. Standing Bear is having nothing of it:

> Women and children were the objects of care among the Lakotas and as far as their environment permitted they lived sheltered lives. . . . Whether,

from the Caucasian point of view, the position of the Indian woman in the tribe was a hard one is not the question. People are fitted for life as are trees, plants, birds and animals. If a Lakota woman were given the chance to continue living the free hardy life of her ancestors or to become transported into the toil of mill, factory, or laundry, it would be only good sense on her part to prefer the still pure air of the plains and the cheery fire of a comfortable brown tipi beside a rippling stream.[74]

Standing Bear is especially contemptuous of the boarding school education that so many had claimed to be the necessary beginning of a process of incorporation and assimilation for American Indians—and that Standing Bear himself had earlier written about with pride in his own accomplishments as a student. This time, he denounces white-controlled education for, among other things, encouraging competition among the students and thus ensuring that some of them will be embarrassed and humiliated. This time, his references to his experiences at Carlisle are to the "confusion and pain" he felt at being forced to compete with other students, rather than to the pleasures of being commended by Captain Pratt.[75]

Standing Bear also expresses his anger at the boarding-school practice of forcing the children to speak English and thus distancing them from their native languages. Many lost their original languages that way, he observes, and many others simply refused to speak them once they left school because they had been taught that those languages were primitive and limiting and would stigmatize them: "I soon began to see the sad sight, so common today, of returned students who could not speak their native tongue, or, worse yet, some who pretended they could no longer converse in the mother tongue. They had become ashamed and this led them into deception and trickery." Standing Bear notes that he never lost his knowledge of his original language, a fact that he sees as fundamental to his continuing sense of himself as fully and unambiguously Sioux. Languages remain alive through the speaking of them, he argues, as a people remain alive through their language: "A language, unused, embalmed, and reposing only in a book, is a dead language. Only the people themselves, and never the scholars, can nourish it into life."[76] Although Standing Bear never names the writers who have misrepresented the Indians or the scholars who have attempted to keep a language alive by recording it in books, one of the people he may well have had in mind in this case is Natalie Curtis. Curtis's 1907 publication, *The Indians' Book,* was a compilation of stories and songs that Curtis collected from a number of Native informants, recorded, and transcribed. The "Dakota" section of the book includes an entry on music that is attributed to three informants, White Bone, Iron Bird, and Standing Bear—Luther's father. The songs in the section, which appear in both original and translated texts, were collected at Rosebud and Pine Ridge. Luther Standing Bear would have had reason to distrust this effort to preserve Sioux songs in a written text, as he would have had ample reason to reject Curtis's characterization of all American Indians as belonging to one of the "child races."[77]

The loss of language is only one of the problems Standing Bear identifies with boarding school education; in general, he suspects that what education at the hands of whites primarily does for Indian students is to turn them into imitators of the most superficial and inessential parts of white culture. His own Carlisle experience he now sees as a coercive effort to force him "to remake myself, if I could, into the likeness of the invader."[78] In *My People the Sioux*, he had spoken admiringly of his father's adoption of Western clothing for his visits to Carlisle and to Washington: "He wore a gray suit, nice shoes, and a derby hat . . . He looked very nice in white men's clothes. He even sported a gold watch and chain." He is less admiring in that book of the dandyism of his own postschool appearance but also clearly forgiving of his youthful attempts to look the way he thought he should—and to look as good as his father had:

> The clothes I wore were the very latest style at that time, and I felt quite "swell" in them. But I have to laugh now at my appearance. I looked like one of these Jew comedians on the stage. I wore a black suit with a cutaway coat which had quite a tail, a small derby hat, a standing collar, and my cuffs stuck out about half an inch below my coat sleeves. . . . All I lacked to resemble Charlie Chaplin was a cane.[79]

This friendly attitude toward the Indian in white man's clothing—admiring in one case, gently self-mocking in the other—gives way to cynical contempt in *Land of the Spotted Eagle*. In this book, Standing Bear sees the stylish clothes as one sign of all that has been lost in the name of a "progressivism" that is really only empty imitation: "Today the young Indian who dons a white collar and assumes the mannerisms of the white man and adopts his ways to the destruction of his morals and physique is called progressive. Thus, still, is the Indian deluded."[80]

Standing Bear's contempt for the concept of the progressive Indian, as he expresses it in *Land of the Spotted Eagle*, reflects his anger and dismay at seeing material evidence of how little good had been accomplished by the rhetoric or the policies of the progressives. In fact, from his perspective, the effort to cultivate progressive Indians had actually worsened things generally, especially for those on the reservations. White progressives had owned and defined the term: "White men seem to have difficulty in realizing that people who live differently from themselves still might be traveling the upward and progressive road of life." By trying to remake some of the Lakotas (such as himself) into imitation white men and abandoning those who didn't seem susceptible of conversion, white progressives had created a painful example of the failure of their grand project of Indian uplift: "The Lakotas are now a sad, silent, and unprogressive people suffering the fate of all oppressed. Today you see but a shattered specimen, a caricature, if you please, of the man that once was."[81] Addressing the familiar distinction between progressive Indians and "blanket Indians," Standing Bear is unapologetic about taking the side of the conservatives. "Going back to the blanket," he asserts, is what has "saved [the Indian] from, or at least stayed, his final destruction." While white reformers—especially those who had put their confidence in the allotment policy—had industriously pushed the argument that, in order to survive, Indians must be gotten out of the blanket and into trousers with pockets that could hold cash, Standing Bear insists that survival actually depends on resisting the argument and those who make it: "Many an Indian has accomplished his own personal salvation by 'going back to the blanket.' " In his usage, the meaning of the phrase is literal as well as metaphorical: "To clothe a man falsely is only to distress his spirit and to make him incongruous and ridiculous, and my entreaty to the American Indian is to retain his tribal dress."[82]

The conclusion of this book contains an impassioned, even apocalyptic vision of the fatal results of abandoning traditional tribal culture, in even the smallest of its manifestations. In a rejoinder to Richard Pratt and others who declared that Indianness must be destroyed if Indians are to be saved, Standing Bear states unequivocally that if the Indian gives up his traditional music, exchanges buckskin for "factory shoddy," and stops telling the stories of tribal heroes, "he will be a dead Indian. . . . His spirit will be gone, and though he walk crowded streets, he will, in truth, be—*dead!*"[83]

As Gerald Vizenor has suggested, Standing Bear was writing the close to one chapter in the history of Indian resistance and reform and sketching the outlines of the next one.[84] His angry denunciations of progressivism came after the SAI, the Lake Mohonk Friends of the Indian, and Richard Pratt had all vacated the public stage, and after the passage of the Indian Citizenship

Act. He was therefore not so much engaging in the debates about the "Indian problem" as he was pronouncing, in the strongest terms, his sense of the failure of most of the reform agendas, as well as the actual reforms, including the Indian Citizenship Act, for the simple reason that they did not much improve the lives of most Indian people: "Not one agent was removed from office, Indian boys and girls are still segregated in school life, and the reservation and reservation rule still exist."[85] Standing Bear did not exhort his Indian contemporaries to improve and "raise" themselves; on the contrary, he encouraged cultural entrenchment, a reappropriation of the highly symbolic and much-reviled blanket. The new chapter in the history of Indian reform that Standing Bear anticipated would not be about acceptance or assimilation but about cultural and political sovereignty.

CONCLUSION

A PRESENT AND A FUTURE

The intellectuals of the SAI generation, in their efforts to craft a progressive, pan-Indian perspective and represent it to the public, encountered the kinds of difficulties and frustrations that, in hindsight, can seem unavoidable and even predictable. The major problems they faced arose from their effort to realize what now seems the impossible ambition with which they began: to articulate positions that were, inevitably, highly charged politically and yet to do so without taking the kinds of clearly defined political stances that might alienate any of their major constituencies, white as well as Indian. If this attempt meant that their specific political actions were circumscribed and their victories on specific political issues were limited, it also meant that their significant contributions lay elsewhere and were less immediately visible. In their efforts to formulate tenable positions, as well as in their negotiations with one another, they forwarded the process of shaping an Indian public opinion by helping to define the issues that were most urgent, clarifying the problems that Native intellectuals were facing, and energizing individuals who might not otherwise have found a forum for their ideas or a channel for their actions.[1] In all of these ways, the SAI provided an important intellectual grounding for succeeding generations of Native spokespersons and writers, who are still addressing problems that by now seem all too familiar.

The SAI had tried to shape a unitary model of the progressive Indian, one that was constructed not only with an eye to meeting the expectations of white progressive reformers but that would also be recognizable in any context, on or off the reservation. The subsequent history of the concept of the progressive Indian, a concept that was fundamental to the public discourse of the SAI, offers one useful example of the ways in which such constructions evolved and changed as they were later reshaped through their testing in different contexts. Luther Standing Bear, in 1933, was already contesting the SAI's model and the conservative-progressive binary out of which it grew, arguing that a progressivism constructed to accord with white expectations was so antithetical to Indian histories, cultures, and traditions that it could be considered an agent of genocide. Survival for the Indians, in Standing Bear's terms, was a matter of remaining as resolutely conservative and resistant to imposed models of progressivism as possible. The Cherokee writer and activist Jimmie Durham revisited the conservative-progressive binary in 1974, this time to deny the relevance of the old formulation to the new Indian politics of resistance. Speaking as a representative of the American Indian Movement (AIM), Durham explained that the people whom the Bureau of Indian Affairs considered most conservative, politically and culturally, were the same people that AIM defined as progressive: "So our progressives," Durham declared, "are what look like to you our 'conservatives.' "[2]

Durham's new formulation, which essentially reaffirms Standing Bear's argument, explodes the old binary by denying the validity of the familiar distinction between "traditional" and "progressive." His formulation, however, still relies on those old terms and their histories for its meaning; one needs to know the histories in order to recognize the revolutionary intent of his declaration. The use of the terms, therefore, positions Durham's statement within the long (and changing) story of Native contestations of white efforts to impose material and discursive control over Native subjects. Such a statement, that is, implies that while Native spokespersons may have been working aggressively since the early years of this century to detach Native self-representation from representations of Natives by others, the issues that have always shaped both forms of representation have not disappeared, although they may have been reconfigured. As Stephen Cornell has put it, "The new Indian politics is part of an old Indian struggle," the "resurgent phase" of a contestatory movement with a very long history—a history in which, I would argue, the SAI generation played a significant role.[3]

Understanding the issues that engaged the SAI generation and shaped their public discourse can provide a critically important context for situating Native political issues in the present. More important for my purposes here, understanding those engagements can allow for a more informed and responsible reading of the productions of contemporary Native writers, whose work often combines old issues and old language with new contexts to produce, as Standing Bear's and Durham's statements do, a fresh synthesis, a revised rendering of a familiar history. These writers are returning to many of the same essential issues that concerned the SAI generation—returning because those issues are still vital—but with a new perspective and a full consciousness of how their work is and is not continuous with that of their predecessors. They are also, importantly, addressing those issues with a significantly different sense of audience.

In the following pages I wish to revisit very briefly some of the concerns that were shared (to a greater or lesser extent) by Charles Eastman, Gertrude Bonnin, Luther Standing Bear, Arthur Parker, and others of their generation in order to consider the ways in which these concerns are being reexamined and reconfigured by the writers who are their intellectual heirs. These concerns include: the need to revise the historical record from a Native perspective and to verify an indigenous intellectual tradition; the divide between reservation life and urban (or simply off-reservation) life, especially as exemplified, for the SAI generation, by the problems of the returned student; the precarious position of Native elders as the carriers of traditional knowledge; and the necessarily performative nature of Indian address to a white audience. While these concerns are still very much present, they can look different now — not only because the historical determinants have changed but also because Native readers have increasingly become a significant part of the implied audience for contemporary writing. For an audience more concerned with political and intellectual self-determination than with accommodation to white expectations or adjustment to white demands, the essential question is not so much how to live *in* white America as it is how to live *with* white America.

The work of revising the historical record through the incorporation of Native perspectives and interpretations — a fundamental motivation for writers such as Eastman and Standing Bear — is everywhere evident in the recent writing. The fictions of James Welch and Louise Erdrich provide especially clear examples; Welch's *Fools Crow* and Erdrich's *Tracks,* for instance, both ground themselves fully in the historical archive in order to reconsider its data from a Native position.[4] Both authors return to critical moments in the history of Indian-white conflicts, writing from the (reimagined) perspective of Native participants in the events: Welch examines the final years of Blackfeet resistance to white encroachments before the 1870 massacre on the Marias River and the confinement of the Blackfeet to reservations; Erdrich revisits the Ojibwa struggle to survive epidemic disease, hunger, forced land allotments, corrupt reservation agents, and greedy lumber companies in the first quarter of the twentieth century. Like their predecessors, these writers are concerned to correct misconceptions or errors and to fill in gaps in the written record. In addition to questioning the reliability of the historical *archive,* however, Welch and Erdrich are equally concerned with the reliability of a historical *narrative* that takes seriously only one kind of archive and one way of reading histories, discounting the evidentiary value of oral stories and the hermeneutic value of tribal epistemologies. Their revisionist narratives therefore challenge the sufficiency of the received (and largely univocal) historical narrative through multivoicing and, especially, by incorporating the kinds of elements (dreams, visions, prophecies, totemic animals) that were traditional ways of making meaning in tribal narratives. For these writers, the need to represent the strong differences between two kinds of American narratives—Native and non-Native—is as important as was the need for Parker, Eastman, and others to make a space for Native persons, histories, and perspectives within an existing, unitary American narrative.

Among the earlier writers, both Bonnin and Standing Bear were deeply skeptical about the shared sense of political and cultural legitimacy implied by the unitary narrative. These two writers channeled much of their skepticism into their portraits of students who return to the reservation from boarding schools where they have been immersed in a Christian version of Americanism as well as being taught a set of unfamiliar skills and behaviors. Bonnin's portrait of the "soft-hearted Sioux," whose boarding school experience incapacitates him for the hard life of his reservation home, and Standing Bear's portrait of his own dandified student self, grotesquely out of place back on the reservation, are precursors of a series of representations of young Indians who leave reservations or other Indian communities and, when they attempt to return, are disturbed to find that they have exchanged a fairly comfortable relationship with their communities for a reciprocally anxious relationship with those at home.

D'Arcy McNickle's novel *The Surrounded,* published in 1936, just three years after Standing Bear's *Land of the Spotted Eagle,* offers a protagonist who is a somewhat more self-conscious version of the bewildered returning students represented by Bonnin and Standing Bear. McNickle's Archilde Leon has learned from his experience of boarding school and of working in the city that "when you came home to your Indian mother you had to remember that it was a different world."[5] Remembering that, of course, does not diminish the difference between home and elsewhere or prevent it from ultimately becoming, in McNickle's novel, disastrously undermining. Louise Erdrich's Albertine Johnson, in *Love Medicine,* returns from nursing school to a family so concentrated on the particular entanglements, frustrations, and resentments engendered by reservation life that her return is sufficient to trigger violent eruptions. Although Albertine goes home in 1981, nearly fifty years after Standing Bear described his return from school and sixty years after Bonnin published the story of her "soft-hearted Sioux," the essential narrative of the returned student remains largely intact: the student's immersion in the material and ideological world of non-Indian America brings into focus the immense differences—the bad fit—between that world and the world of Indian America, represented microcosmically by the reservation. For the one returning, and as a result of the return, both worlds can become, to a disconcerting extent, other worlds.

The implications of the return narrative are widened in N. Scott Momaday's *House Made of Dawn* (1968) and Leslie Marmon Silko's *Ceremony* (1977); in these novels, the immediate source of alienation is not a school but a war—specifically, World War II. Momaday's Abel and Silko's Tayo learn from their military experience that they are valued as soldiers but not as citizens; without their uniforms, both become nearly invisible in the American political and cultural landscape. Their near-invisibility is one sign of how little their Indianness figures in the ideological and rhetorical constructions of the America that welcomed their bodies into its military service. At the same time, their absence from home and their transportation to alien geographical and psychological spaces has estranged them from home. As Abel's Navajo friend Benally notes, "Once you find your way around and get used to everything, you wonder how you ever got along out there where you came from."[6]

In describing the experiences of these fictional characters, Momaday and Silko cast a much colder eye on the possibilities of military service as a means of legitimation than had SAI spokespersons, for whom Indian participation in World War I had provided an argument for the extension of birthright citizenship to all Indian people. Military service could be read as patriotism, and patriotism could be read as an essential qualification for citizenship. The evidence of Indian military service was a major factor in the passage of the Indian Citizenship Act in 1924, but, as the contemporary writers are well aware, citizenship did not mean either equality or autonomy for Indian people. The failure of citizenship to translate into sovereignty or self-determination or assured access to civil rights lies behind the deep distrust of American state authority (represented by the police as well as the military) in Momaday's and Silko's novels. Military service becomes, in their novels, another form of deception, another source of failed or empty promises, another reason to resist the blandishments of the rhetoric of assimilation.

Indian education was an important issue for Eastman, Bonnin, and Standing Bear, and all approached the issue by first explaining that their own attendance at white-run schools was a deliberate choice on the part of their parents, a decision based on the parents' awareness of the need for their children's generation to acquire certain practical skills—skills they would require in their negotiations with white America. The parents, in these accounts, were sending the children to school primarily to receive a *training* the parents could not provide. All three writers made it clear that they had already received a comprehensive *education* before they went to school, one that prepared them for the tribal life they had, as children, both anticipated and desired. Their early educations were based on indigenous intellectual traditions that predated, by many hundreds of years, the English-language instruction of Indian students in white-run schools or the production of Indian-authored texts.

These indigenous traditions are centrally important to the work of Silko, especially to her novels *Ceremony* and *Almanac of the Dead*. For Silko, much more is at stake than the valorizing of an educational process that white America has tended to belittle or ignore. Her fiction defines indigenous intellectual traditions as the *only* ones with any ultimate legitimacy or potency in the Americas, contrasting their longevity and their power to clarify experience, both individual and collective, with the obscurities, distortions, and dangers that Silko sees as resulting when European systems of thought are transported to the Americas and become hegemonic. In Silko's view of postcontact history, indigenous traditions have allowed Native people to survive that history by exposing the racist violence inherent in the colonizing imperatives of the imported traditions and providing an alternative to them. A less apocalyptic (or perhaps just more comically apocalyptic) treatment of the encounter between indigenous and imported traditions appears in Thomas King's trickster novel, *Green Grass, Running Water*, in which female figures drawn from native North American traditions (First Woman, Changing Woman, Thought Woman, Old Woman) must work hard to prevent various male representatives of imported traditions (including Adam, Noah, Jesus, and Captain Ahab) from wreaking havoc on the continent. In both Silko's and King's treatments, the possibilities for a synthetic, inclusive American tradition—of the kind reflected in Eastman's prescriptions for the training of non-Native children in Native philosophies—collapse in the face of white arrogance and obduracy.

The characters in King's novel also assume a deliberately performative role in their relationships with white characters and white culture—donning masks, changing their names, sometimes playing white and sometimes playing Indian. One (Blackfeet) family in the novel, for example, runs a café that pretends to serve a Sioux specialty, dog stew, because they know the white tourists visiting their Canadian reserve are looking for something authentically and exotically Indian. These characters understand that whites *expect* them to perform (customers arrive at the Dead Dog Café by the busloads to sample the daily special, willingly suppressing the correct suspicion that they are actually eating ground beef) and that erecting a performative barrier between themselves and curious whites is their best means of both protection and profit. Other characters who adopt a similar kind of cagey, performative relationship to the dominant culture can be found in the fictions of Gerald Vizenor, whose tribal tricksters play survival games with comic exuberance, as well as in the stories of Sherman Alexie. One of Alexie's characters, a Spokane elder named Etta Joseph, takes advantage of the arrogance and credulity of the white anthropologist who has come to interview her, keeping him off balance by feeding him stories alternately designed to meet his textbook expectations and to explode them, before she finally offers him a plain statement. In her long life, Etta explains to her interviewer, she has had to perform by acting white for fifty-seven minutes of every hour; in the remaining three minutes she gets to be Indian, "and you have no idea, no concept, no possible way of knowing what happens in those three minutes."[7] The performing characters of King, Vizenor, and Alexie are clearly following their own hidden transcripts; they are also accepting (and making good use of) a performative role that has become theirs almost by default. If the SAI generation chose performance as a political strategy that might give them a space on the stage of American public life, these more recent writers often use their own performativity and that of their characters for the different strategic purpose of protecting what remains to them from too much public scrutiny.

Gertrude Bonnin's work demonstrates her fear that the tribal elders who had taught her generation would disappear and take their wisdom and knowledge with them; in her stories, the culture-bearing elders are endangered. The work of one group of Bonnin's successors—those who by now can be considered the older generation of contemporary writers—often expresses this same sense of precariousness in the representation of elders. The grandmothers who appear in Silko's *Ceremony*, Welch's *Winter in the Blood*, and Momaday's *The Way to Rainy Mountain* provide interesting examples of the presence of a continuing anxiety about the transmission of cultural values and tribal knowledge. The grandchild senses in the grandmother—who is in each case either blind or nearly sightless—a serenity, knowledge, and completeness that the grandchild lacks. Yet in Welch's novel the grandmother says nothing, in Silko's novel she says little, and in the strongest memory of his grandmother that Momaday records in his memoir, she is praying in Kiowa, a language her grandson doesn't understand. These elders are isolated from their grandchildren through their blindness or their silence or their incomprehensibility, which signal troubling psychological and cultural differences between the generations that it will be up to the grandchildren to resolve. In the work of the next generation of contemporary writers, on the other hand, the elders, like Etta Joseph, tend to be far less isolated and far more secure. Alexie's stories, Susan Power's stories in *Roofwalker*, and Craig Womack's novel *Drowning in Fire* include grandparents who are not only articulate but can even be loquacious, providing guidance to the grandchildren they may fear losing to urban America. In William Yellow Robe Jr.'s play *The Star Quilter*, the wise, articulate character whose final monologue carries the thematic weight of the play is a blind grandmother—the same figure who is completely silent in *Winter in the Blood*, nearly silent in *Ceremony*, and untranslatable in *The Way to Rainy Mountain*.

The contemporary writing also frequently reaches back, beyond living elders, to reanimate voices and lives from the past, sometimes the deep past. Womack's *Drowning in Fire* and LeAnne Howe's *Shell Shaker* alternate scenes from present and past, conflating ancestral lives and contemporary ones to produce stories about the ways in which identity is both constructed and understood in a tribal context that makes memory more relevant than chronology. Sherman Alexie's stories of modern Indian life are haunted by the figure of Crazy Horse, a hero of nineteenth-century Native resistance, and the young female protagonist of Betty Louise Bell's *Faces in the Moon* is visited in a vision by another resistance hero, Quanah Parker, whom she declares to be her real father. Figures from traditional tribal stories are present in the literature as well. The Ojibwa creator/trickster Nanabush presides over Tomson Highway's *The Rez Sisters*, sometimes hovering around the edges of the central action of the play and at other times orchestrating moments of life-and-death significance. In Hanay Geiogamah's play *49*, the mythic Night Walker moves across temporal boundaries, protecting a group of contemporary young Indians from the police and, in alternating scenes, instructing their equally young ancestors about faith in the tribal future. What the contemporary writing suggests over and over is that addressing questions of Indian identity in the present requires the invocation of elders, ancestors, tribal heroes, and tribal stories. The embrace of tribal traditions, the confidence in their ultimate accessibility, and the faith that traditional values can be transported into the spaces of urban life—and translated to fit those spaces—mark a distinction between these contemporary writers and their turn-of-the-century predecessors, whose consciousness of the need to be taken seriously by a skeptical white America often led to the suppression or censoring of their relationship to tribe and tradition.

Louis Owens, writing in 2001, posed a question about the challenge to contemporary Native writers that, even while it uses a very different discourse, strongly echoes a fundamental question that the intellectuals of the SAI generation had confronted: "After five hundred years of war, of colonial infantilization and linguistic erasure, cultural denigration, and more," Owens asks, "how and where does the Native writer discover a voice that can be heard at the metropolitan center?"[8] In Owens's formulation, the history of white repression of American Indian bodies, voices, and political values ultimately devolves, for the contemporary writer, into what is essentially a question of audience. We have seen how the earlier intellectuals responded to the challenge defined by Owens not so much by *discovering* an appropriate voice as by consciously *shaping* an address to a metropolitan audience of white elites—through their writing and other kinds of public performance—out of a sense of political necessity and an awareness of new political opportunities. But we have also seen how that almost single-minded focus on the metropolitan center troubled some of them, such as Gertrude Bonnin, who was concerned about the marginalization of the urgent needs of reservation populations and worked to bring them more fully into the range of the SAI's agendas and its publications.

In the introduction to a 1998 collection of essays, *Speaking for the Generations,* Simon Ortiz commented on the need for Native writers to reach the widest possible audience. The voice of the Native writer, Ortiz declared, "still needs to be heard in every corner of the Americas and beyond. About this there is no doubt."[9] Ortiz's declaration democratizes the audience for Native writing, substituting "every corner" for the metropolitan center that interested Owens and the SAI intellectuals, and occluding any useful distinction between Native and non-Native, local and cosmopolitan. Writing in that same collection, however, other writers expressed their sense of audience more narrowly and specifically. Gloria Bird declared that "my primary audience is Native people. We have so much work to do," and Luci Tapahanso named "our children and grandchildren" as the principal audience for her work.[10] Even given these differences, the statements from all three writers about their sense of audience could hardly be at a farther remove from Arthur Parker's comment to a reservation correspondent that "in our printing we try to appeal to the white man's intelligence so that he will be our friend" or his description of SAI publications as "seeking to crystallize the sentiment of those with broader views and higher training."[11] The sense of urgency expressed by the SAI generation is still present when Native writers speak of their roles—the consciousness of so much work to be done, as Gloria Bird puts it—but the perception of *where* and *how* the work needs to be done has undergone changes that can be considered revolutionary. The contemporary writers have shifted white elites out of the center of their vision of audience, in some cases replacing them with a specifically Native readership. This move, made possible by the emergence of a Native audience that was not yet available to the SAI, is as strategically political as was the SAI's courtship of white elites. As Thomas King has explained, speaking for contemporary Native writers in general, literary production is being seen not only as an important form of self-representation but also as an agent of political autonomy that "allows us the opportunity to *create for ourselves* and our respective cultures both a present and a future" (emphasis added).[12]

This sense of collaboration between Native writers and Native audiences in the project of sustaining and strengthening Native communities that King articulates marks one important difference between the current generation's perceptions of the nature and purpose of intellectual work and the stated aims of their predecessors. Yet both generations, and their work, clearly belong to what Leslie Marmon Silko has called "the long story of the people," a complex narrative that includes the history of Native relationships with a white America whose expectations for Indian people, and demands on them, have never remained constant.[13] The earlier intellectuals often felt compelled to appease white elites, who constituted for them the metropolitan center and who had the power to make policy decisions with significant, long-lasting effects on all Indian people, no matter how distant from the center they might be. For many of these intellectuals, appeasement required the public occlusion of tribal traditions, narratives, and lifeways—that is, it meant deliberately keeping Luther Standing Bear's closed book not only closed but out of sight of the public, as a matter of survival. With increasing opportunities for Native people to go public, especially through the publication or performance of their own scripts, and with an increasing focus on political and cultural self-determination, there has also come an increasing sense on the part of Native intellectuals that the Native audience, from whom nothing needs to be hidden or perhaps can be hidden, is the one that really matters.

NOTES

INTRODUCTION

1 Pokagon's speech is reprinted in Frederick E. Hoxie, ed., *Talking Back to Civilization: Indian Voices from the Progressive Era* (Boston: Bedford/St. Martin's, 2001). My references are to pages 31 and 35.

2 B. O. Flower, "An Interesting Representative of a Vanishing Race," *The Arena* 16 (July 1896): 240.

3 Frederick E. Hoxie, "Red Man's Burden," *Antioch Review* 37 (Summer 1979): 326–42; Rosemarie K. Bank, "Representing History: Performing the Columbian Exposition," *Theatre Journal* 54 (Dec. 2002): 589–607; Robert A. Trennert Jr., "Selling Indian Education at World's Fairs," *American Indian Quarterly* 11 (Summer 1987): 203–20. Trennert's research led him to conclude that the ethnographic exhibits and, of course, the Wild West shows were much more interesting to fairgoers than the Indian school exhibits, which drew relatively few visitors.

4 Henry Adams, *The Education of Henry Adams* (New York: Modern Library, 1931), 343.

5 Sarah Winnemucca (Paiute) toured the East in 1883–84, lobbying for more schools for western Indians; Susette La Flesche (Omaha) and her husband, Henry Tibbles, began touring on behalf of the displaced Ponca Indians in 1879; Pauline Johnson (Mohawk) launched her career as a performer of her own literary compositions in 1892.

6 Rosemarie K. Bank, *Theatre Culture in America, 1825–1860* (Cambridge: Cambridge University Press, 1997), 61.

7 Philip Deloria, *Playing Indian* (New Haven: Yale University Press, 1998), 126.

8 Kathryn Shanley, "Writing Indian," in *Studying Native America: Problems and Prospects,* ed. Russell Thornton (Madison: University of Wisconsin Press, 1998), 146.

9 Robert Allen Warrior, "Reading American Indian Intellectual Traditions," *World Literature Today* 66 (Spring 1992): 239; Robert Allen Warrior, *Tribal Secrets: Recovering American Indian Intellectual Traditions* (Minneapolis: University of Minnesota Press, 1995), xvi, 10.

10 Elizabeth Cook-Lynn, "American Indian Intellectualism and the New Indian Story," in Devon A. Mihesuah, ed., *Natives and Academics: Researching and Writing about American Indians* (Lincoln: University of Nebraska Press, 1998), 137.

11 Craig S. Womack, *Red on Red: Native American Literary Separatism* (Minneapolis: University of Minnesota Press, 1999), 1, 11.

12 Luther Standing Bear, *My People the Sioux,* ed. E. A. Brininstool (Boston: Houghton Mifflin, 1928), no page number; *Land of the Spotted Eagle* (1933; reprint, Lincoln: University of Nebraska Press, 1978), xv, 248.

13 Gerald Vizenor, *Fugitive Poses: Native American Indian Scenes of Absence and Presence* (Lincoln: University of Nebraska Press, 1998), 15. Vizenor distinguishes between

"Indian," which he calls the "commemoration of an absence," and *"indian,"* a simulation, and contrasts both with "native," which signals an actual presence. In my own discussion, I have used a number of terms (Indian, American Indian, Native) almost interchangeably, trusting that the context will make the references clear.

14 Gerald Vizenor, *Manifest Manners: Postindian Warriors of Survivance* (Hanover, N.H.: University Press of New England, 1994), 5.

15 James C. Scott, *Domination and the Arts of Resistance* (New Haven: Yale University Press, 1990), xii, 4.

16 The Supreme Court specifically denied birthright citizenship to American Indians in *Elk v. Wilkins* in 1884, ruling that assimilated Indians could become naturalized citizens, but only when the government judged them fit for citizenship. In the 1898 case of *United States v. Wong Kim Ark,* the court ruled that all children born on United States soil were automatically citizens, with the exception of the children of American Indians, for whom citizenship was still available only through naturalization. Birthright citizenship was finally granted by Congress in 1924. See Rogers M. Smith, *Civic Ideals: Conflicting Visions of Citizenship in U.S. History* (New Haven: Yale University Press, 1997), esp. 393–94, 439.

17 Francis Paul Prucha, ed., *Americanizing the American Indians: Writings by the "Friends of the Indian", 1880–1900* (Cambridge: Harvard University Press, 1973), 175–76. Thayer's comments originally appeared in the *Atlantic Monthly* in October 1891.

18 Letter to Arthur C. Parker, July 11, 1911, Papers of the Society of American Indians (hereafter SAI papers).

19 Others included the American Indian League, the Indian Industries League, the Massachusetts Indian Association, the Northern California Indian Association, the California Indian Association, the Bureau of Catholic Indian Missions, the Boston Indian Citizenship Association, the American Indian Association, and the Zayante Indian Conference of Friends of Indians.

20 *World's Work* 8 (July 1904): 4943.

21 James Harvey Robinson, *The New History: Essays Illustrating the Modern Historical Outlook* (New York: Macmillan, 1912), 23.

22 Daniel T. Rodgers, "In Search of Progressivism," *Reviews in American History* 10 (Dec. 1982): 114, 127.

23 Herbert Croly, *The Promise of American Life* (1909; reprint, Cambridge: Harvard University Press, 1965), 400.

24 *Quarterly Journal of the Society of American Indians* 1 (Apr.–June 1911), back cover.

25 Prucha, *Americanizing the American Indians,* 29, 43, 340.

26 Here my argument diverges somewhat from that of Warrior, who, while recognizing the sincerity and commitment of the SAI reformers, still sees them as assimilationists who generally supported, with "blinding progressivistic optimism," the Indian policies of the federal government. In my own analysis I hope not so much to refute this conclusion as to elaborate on it.

27 *The American Negro Academy Occasional Papers,* no. 2, 1897.

28 In discussing the influence of the eugenics movement on the writing of W. E. B. Du Bois, Daylanne English observes that modern intellectuals, even those we associate pri-

marily with oppositional stances, "were not necessarily entirely alienated, as a result of their racial identity, from now-discredited but then-normative ideologies." See "W. E. B. Du Bois's Family *Crisis,*" *American Literature* 72 (2000): 292.

29 Ross Posnock, *Color and Culture: Black Writers and the Making of the Modern Intellectual* (Cambridge: Harvard University Press, 1998), 13, 54. Posnock has also observed that the cosmopolitan perspective is "an instrument of cultural democracy that, historically, has been particularly congenial to those on the periphery." See "The Dream of Deracination: The Uses of Cosmopolitanism," *American Literary History* 12 (2000): 807.

30 Edward W. Said, *Representations of the Intellectual* (New York: Pantheon, 1994), xiii, 44.

31 Arthur C. Parker, "Progress for the Indian," *Southern Workman* 41, no. 11 (Nov. 1912): 630, 633.

32 Cook-Lynn, "American Indian Intellectualism," 111; Melissa L. Meyer and Kerwin Lee Klein, "Native American Studies and the End of Ethnohistory," in Thornton, *Studying Native America,* 197–98.

CHAPTER 1. A MIGHTY DRAMA

1 Some tribes were exempted from the provisions of the Dawes Act, including the Five Civilized Tribes living in Indian Territory, the Osage, Miami and Peoria, Sac and Fox, and Seneca. A few tribes had already been given allotments before 1887: the Crow and Omaha in 1882 and the Umatilla in 1885. The provisions of the Dawes Act were later amended by the Burke Bill of 1906, which postponed citizenship for most allottees until the end of the twenty-five-year trust period.

2 Vine Deloria Jr. notes that the IRA "advocated allotment as a means of vesting Indians with political rights and of providing them an economic livelihood, rather than as a policy to eliminate all traces of Indian culture. Thus the view of the IRA differed considerably from that of such people as Theodore Roosevelt, who saw allotment as a process of grinding up the tribal mass and producing standardized Indian citizens." See "The Indian Rights Association: An Appraisal," in Sandra L. Cadwalader and Vine Deloria Jr., eds., *The Aggressions of Civilization: Federal Indian Policy since the 1880s* (Philadelphia: Temple University Press, 1984), 7.

3 Frederick E. Hoxie, *A Final Promise: The Campaign to Assimilate the Indians, 1880–1920* (Lincoln: University of Nebraska Press, 1984), 64.

4 Francis Paul Prucha, ed., *Americanizing the American Indians: Writings by the "Friends of the Indian", 1880–1900* (Cambridge: Harvard University Press, 1973), 258–59.

5 *Southern Workman* 29 (Sept. 1900): 531; *Southern Workman* 33 (Mar. 1904): 182–83.

6 These figures are taken from Charles M. Harvey, "The Last Race Rally of Indians," *World's Work* 8 (May 1904): 4807.

7 John Higham, *Strangers in the Land: Patterns of American Nativism, 1860–1925* (New York: Atheneum, 1973), 75; David Glassberg, *American Historical Pageantry: The Uses of Tradition in the Early Twentieth Century* (Chapel Hill: University of North Carolina Press, 1990), 67.

8 W. E. B. Du Bois, "The Star of Ethiopia," *Crisis* 11 (Dec. 1915): 91.

9 Interestingly, although Indian figures were ubiquitous in civic pageantry produced by white Americans, black figures seldom appeared. Black Americans were evidently too present and visible, while the Indians could be more easily relegated to past history or even to prehistory.

10 Glassberg, *American Historical Pageantry*, 114, 178, 182.

11 Ibid., 50.

12 Janet E. Chute, *The Legacy of Shingwaukonse: A Century of Native Leadership* (Toronto: University of Toronto Press, 1998), 220, 308 n. 88.

13 W. D. Lighthall and L. O. Armstrong, *The Book of the Play of Hiawatha the Mohawk during the Siege of Hochelaga and the Battle of Lake Champlain* (1909), unpaginated.

14 William N. Fenton, " 'Aboriginally Yours': Jesse J. Cornplanter, Hah-Yonh-Wonh-Ish, the Snipe," in Margot Liberty, ed., *American Indian Intellectuals of the Nineteenth and Early Twentieth Centuries* (Norman: University of Oklahoma Press, 2002), 206–7; Richard W. Hill Sr., "Developed Identities: Seeing the Stereotypes and Beyond," in Tim Johnson, ed., *Spirit Capture: Photographs from the National Museum of the American Indian* (Washington, D.C.: Smithsonian Institution Press, 1998), 139.

15 Charles Eastman, *The Indian To-Day: The Past and Future of the First American* (Garden City, New York: Doubleday, Page, 1915), 106.

16 L. G. Moses, *Wild West Shows and the Images of American Indians, 1883–1933* (Albuquerque: University of New Mexico Press, 1996), 317 n. 4.

17 On the question of Sitting Bull's actual role in the Little Bighorn fight, James Welch notes that "depending upon which scholar you read, he was making medicine in his tipi, he was riding herd on the women and children in the center of camp, or he was cowering behind them. These various accounts of his whereabouts were furnished by Indian people who were in the village." See *Killing Custer: The Battle of the Little Bighorn and the Fate of the Plains Indians* (New York: W. W. Norton, 1994), 157. General O. O. Howard, in his *Famous Indians I Have Known* (New York: Century Co., 1908), declared unequivocally that at the time of the Custer fight, Sitting Bull was "miles away" (306).

18 Moses, *Wild West Shows*, 25–50.

19 Program for "Buffalo Bill's Wild West," 1895, copy in the author's possession; "Buffalo Bill," *Outlook* 115 (Jan. 24, 1917): 136.

20 Luther Standing Bear, *My People the Sioux*, ed. E. A. Brininstool (Boston: Houghton Mifflin, 1928), 187. Standing Bear attended a second Sioux show in Philadelphia a few weeks later. He reports that one of the Sioux, a man named Standing Elk, fell ill during the course of the show and was taken to a hospital. The show moved on without him, Standing Bear notes, and "nothing was ever again seen of Standing Elk" (188). James Welch's novel *The Heartsong of Charging Elk* (2000) recounts the similar (fictional) experience of another Sioux "show Indian" who was abandoned in a hospital in Marseilles during a European tour. It was not uncommon for Indian performers to be stranded when their show managers ran into financial trouble; Cody seems to have been more conscientious than most about providing for his performers.

21 Standing Bear, *My People the Sioux*, 179.

22 Ibid., 155, 166. References to Pratt's rank can be confusing. A career army officer, he was promoted to captain in 1883, to major in 1898, to lieutenant colonel in 1901, and to colonel in 1903, the year of his retirement. In 1904, he was made a brigadier general by an act of Congress. Although he referred to himself as brigadier general or general after 1904, others, including Standing Bear, continued to refer to him as Captain Pratt. See Robert M. Utley's introduction to Richard Henry Pratt, *Battlefield and Classroom: Four Decades with the American Indian, 1867–1904* (Lincoln: University of Nebraska Press, 1964).

23 See David Wallace Adams, *Education for Extinction: American Indians and the Boarding School Experience, 1875–1928* (Lawrence: University of Kansas Press, 1995), 192; Moses, *Wild West Shows*, chap. 8.

24 Richard Henry Pratt, *The Indian Industrial School, Carlisle Pennsylvania: Its Origin, Purposes, Progress and the Difficulties Surmounted* (Carlisle: Hamilton Library Association, 1908), 28.

25 *Booker T. Washington Papers*, vol. 2 (Urbana: University of Illinois Press, 1972), 89.

26 Daniel La France, "An Indian Boy's Story," *Independent* 55 (July 30, 1903): 1784.

27 Standing Bear, *My People the Sioux*, 277.

28 Cited in Moses, *Wild West Shows*, 258.

29 Pratt, *Indian Industrial School*, 28.

30 See Robert Rydell, *All The World's a Fair: Visions of Empire at American International Expositions, 1876–1916* (Chicago: University of Chicago Press, 1984); Frederick E. Hoxie, "Red Man's Burden," *Antioch Review* 37 (Summer 1979): 326–42; Rita G. Napier, "Across the Big Water: American Indians' Perceptions of Europe and Europeans, 1887–1906," in Christian Feest, ed., *Indians and Europeans: An Interdisciplinary Collection of Essays* (Aachen, Germany: Edition Herodot, 1987), 383–401.

31 Harvey, "The Last Race Rally of Indians," 4803, 4809.

32 Charles M. Harvey, "The Red Man's Last Roll-Call," *Atlantic Monthly* 97 (1906): 323, 330.

33 W. J. McGee, "Strange Races of Men," *World's Work* 8 (Aug. 1904): 5188, 5185, 5187.

34 *Chicago Daily News*, Sept. 26, 1923; Sept. 29, 1923.

35 E. Pauline Johnson, *The Moccasin Maker*, intro. A. Lavonne Ruoff (Norman: University of Oklahoma Press, 1998), 8.

36 Copies of two of these advertisements can be found in the SAI papers.

37 Joseph K. Griffis, *Tahan: Out of Savagery and into Civilization* (New York: George H. Doran Company, 1915), 7, 10.

38 Dan W. Peery, "The White Kiowa Captive," *Chronicles of Oklahoma* 8 (Sept. 1930): 271.

39 Johnson, *Moccasin Maker*, 14; John E. Tapia, *Circuit Chautauqua: From Rural Education to Popular Entertainment in Early Twentieth Century America* (Jefferson, N.C.: McFarland and Company, 1997), 73, 130; Louis J. Alber to the Society of American Indians, May 3, 1916, SAI papers.

40 Arthur C. Parker to Joseph K. Griffis, Nov. 11, 1911; Joseph K. Griffis to Arthur C. Parker, Jan. 6, 1912, SAI papers.

41 Griffis, *Tahan*, 258.

42 Copy included in SAI papers.

43 "Memorial to the North American Indian," *Hearings before the Congressional House Committee on the Library, May 12, 1911* (Washington, D.C.: Government Printing Office, 1911), 3.

44 Ibid., 4. Useful accounts of Dixon's three expeditions have been published in Richard Lindstrom, " 'Not from the Land Side, but from the Flag Side': Native American Responses to the Wanamaker Expedition of 1913," *Journal of Social History* 30 (Fall 1996): 209–27; Russel Lawrence Barsh, "An American Heart of Darkness: The 1913 Expedition for American Indian Citizenship," *Great Plains Quarterly* 13 (Spring 1993): 91–115; and Alan Trachtenberg, "Wanamaker Indians," *Yale Review* 86 (1998): 1–24.

45 *Wanamaker Primer on the North American Indian,* 1909, 38.

46 Alan Trachtenberg has called Dixon "a new hybrid, the lecture hall 'educator' fused with the booster and huckster," who learned from his department store experience the "role of display and performance in presenting goods in their twofold aspect as things and as moral ideas." See "Wanamaker Indians," 9.

47 *Wanamaker Primer,* 37, 36.

48 Joseph Kossuth Dixon, *The Vanishing Race: The Last Great Indian Council* (Garden City, N.Y.: Doubleday, Page, 1913), 5, 6, 8–9. Emphasis in original.

49 Ibid., 38, 222.

50 Ibid., 68, 93. Dixon's responses to the speeches of the men are consistent with a pattern of white response to Native political concerns that has been explored by Maureen Konkle. The discourse of sympathy and sentiment, Konkle observes, was often employed by nineteenth-century whites as a deliberate means of occluding or eliding the difficult political and practical issues that were paramount in the minds of Native people. See her *Writing Indian Nations: Native Intellectuals and the Politics of Historiography, 1827–1863* (Chapel Hill, N.C.: University of North Carolina Press, 2004).

51 Ibid., 205.

52 Ibid., 203, 204.

53 See Barsh, "American Heart of Darkness," 96–97.

54 Charles H. Lichtman, ed., *Official History of the Improved Order of Red Men* (Boston: Fraternity Publishing Company, 1893), 15.

55 Some contemporary reports of the ceremony give the number of Indians participating as thirty, while others say thirty-three. In his article, Barsh puts the number at thirty.

56 *New York Times,* Feb. 23, 1913; *The Indian's Friend* 25 (Mar. 1913): 2.

57 *New York Times,* Feb. 23, 1913; Feb. 24, 1913.

58 Joseph Kossuth Dixon, "The Purpose and Achievements of the Rodman Wanamaker Expedition of Citizenship to the North American Indian," papers of the Indian Rights Association.

59 Barsh and Lindstrom both give the number of reservations visited as eighty-nine; Major McLaughlin's report says ninety-nine; McLaughlin's biographer says seventy-five (Louis L. Pfaller, *James McLaughlin: The Man with an Indian Heart* [New York: Vantage Press, 1978], 311); and Dixon—whose claims are generally suspect—says in one place that his expedition visited eighty-nine *reservations* and in another that it visited 189 *tribes*.

60 Dixon, "Purpose and Achievements." Full accounts of the 1913 expedition are given by Lindstrom, Pfaller, and, especially, Barsh.

61 James McLaughlin papers.

62 Dixon, "Purpose and Achievements."

63 James McLaughlin papers.

64 Richard Lindstrom's article discusses the ways in which the Indian audiences changed the meaning of the event, "shifting its focus from the symbolic level of flags and citizenship to a more material discussion of land and the costs of citizenship" ("Not from the Land Side," 210).

65 James McLaughlin papers. Delos Lone Wolf hardly fit the profile of the benighted and romantic Indian of Dixon's fantasies and texts. He spent four years at Carlisle, graduating in 1896 at the age of twenty-six. At Carlisle, he played football and was an active participant in the YMCA and the debating society. He was also instrumental in persuading his uncle Lone Wolf and other tribal leaders to bring suit in federal court to stop the sale of tribal lands to white settlers. The suit ultimately resulted in the 1903 Supreme Court decision in *Lone Wolf v. Hitchcock,* discussed in chapter 3.

66 John Oskison to Carlos Montezuma, Mar. 31, 1913, papers of Carlos Montezuma (hereafter Montezuma papers).

67 Matthew K. Sniffen to Arthur C. Parker, Feb. 20, 1913 and May 27, 1913, SAI papers.

68 Matthew K. Sniffen, "The 'Citizenship Expedition' " (Philadelphia: Indian Rights Association), Jan. 28, 1914. Edward Curtis, the photographer that Sniffen compares favorably to Dixon, also made heavy use of the notion of the "vanishing Indian," using the term as the caption for what became probably the most well known of his photographs. The photograph, taken (and captioned) in 1904, well before Dixon used the term as the title for his own book of photographs, depicts a group of Navajo riding, single file with their backs to the camera, into the darkening distance. Curtis used the image as the centerpiece of an elaborate series of productions—Curtis called them "musicales" or "picture-operas"—that he began offering in 1911. The performances combined his photographs and commentary with music composed especially to provide an appropriately dramatic accompaniment to the images. See Mick Gidley's account in *Edward S. Curtis and the North American Indian, Incorporated* (Cambridge: Cambridge University Press, 1998), especially chapter 7.

69 *Quarterly Journal of the Society of American Indians* 1 (Jan.–Apr. 1913): 85.

70 *Quarterly Journal of the Society of American Indians* 1 (Oct.–Dec. 1913): 363; 2 (Jan.–Mar. 1914): 4.

71 "The Indian National Monument," *Southern Workman* 42 (Apr. 1913): 197.

72 "Words of Hope to the Indian," *Southern Workman* 42 (Sept. 1913): 475.

73 *Chicago Evening Post,* Dec. 8, 1913.

74 *New York Times,* Mar. 8, 1914.

75 Irene C. Beaulieu and Kathleen Woodward, eds., *Tributes to a Vanishing Race* (Chicago: privately printed, 1916), 17, 101.

76 *National Cyclopaedia of American Biography* (New York: James T. White and Company, 1932), vol. 21, p. 27.

77 Denver Convention Association to secretary of Society of American Indians, Feb. 24, 1913, SAI papers.

78 J. B. Maling to Arthur C. Parker, Mar. 22, 1913, SAI papers.

79 Arthur C. Parker to Elias M. Ammons, Mar. 28, 1913, SAI papers.

80 Richard Henry Pratt to Arthur C. Parker, May 7, 1913, SAI papers.

81 Richard Henry Pratt to Dennison Wheelock, June 18, 1913, Montezuma papers.

82 *Quarterly Journal of the Society of American Indians* 2 (Jan.–Mar. 1914): 39.

83 Parker's speech was reported in *The Indian's Friend* 23 (Jan. 1911): 11–12.

84 Pratt, *Indian Industrial School*, 29.

85 *Columbus Citizen*, Oct. 14, 1911; *Ohio State Journal*, Oct. 13, 1911; Oct. 17, 1911.

86 Caroline W. Andrus to Arthur C. Parker, Sept. 17, 1912; Parker to Andrus, Sept. 24, 1912, SAI papers.

87 *Minneapolis Morning Tribune*, Oct. 4, 1919.

88 Raymond Wilson, *Ohiyesa: Charles Eastman, Santee Sioux* (Urbana: University of Illinois Press, 1983), 151–52.

89 *Minneapolis Journal*, Oct. 3 and 5, 1919.

90 The five attorneys were Thomas Sloan (Omaha), William J. Kershaw (Menominee), Dennison Wheelock (Oneida), Robert Allen (Creek), and Arthur Beaulieu (Chippewa).

91 "Address by Father Philip Gordon," *American Indian Magazine* 7 (Fall 1919): 153; *Minneapolis Journal*, Oct. 3, 1919; "Address by Gertrude Bonnin," *American Indian Magazine* 7 (Fall 1919): 155.

92 Circular letter from F. A. McKenzie, Sept. 15, 1909, SAI papers.

CHAPTER 2. GENERAL PRINCIPLES AND UNIVERSAL INTERESTS

1 N. Scott Momaday, *The Way to Rainy Mountain* (Albuquerque: University of New Mexico Press, 1969), 3, 4.

2 *Quarterly Journal of the Society of American Indians* 1 (Apr.–June 1913), back cover.

3 Kevin Gaines, *Uplifting the Race: Black Leadership, Politics, and Culture in the Twentieth Century* (Chapel Hill: University of North Carolina Press, 1998), xiv, xx. See also his "Assimilationist Minstrelsy as Racial Uplift Ideology: James D. Corrothers's Literary Quest for Black Leadership," *American Quarterly* 45 (Sept. 1995): 341–69.

4 Ross Posnock, *Color and Culture: Black Writers and the Making of the Modern Intellectual* (Cambridge: Harvard University Press, 1998), 2, 12, 13, 21.

5 Sherman Coolidge, "The Function of the Society of American Indians," *Quarterly Journal of the Society of American Indians* 2 (July–Sept. 1914): 188.

6 Thomas F. Millard, "The Passing of the American Indian," *Forum* 34 (Jan.–Mar. 1903): 466–80; Kelly Miller, "The Ultimate Race Problem," *Atlantic Monthly* 103 (Apr. 1909): 536–42; Franz Boas, "Making the Red Faces White," *World Outlook* 6 (Jan. 1918): 6.

7 Seth K. Humphrey, *Mankind: Racial Values and the Racial Prospect* (New York: Charles Scribner's Sons, 1917), 160.

8 Gail Bederman, *Manliness and Civilization: A Cultural History of Gender and Race in the United States, 1880–1917* (Chicago: University of Chicago Press, 1995), 23; Matthew Frye

Jacobson, *Barbarian Virtues: The United States Encounters Foreign Peoples at Home and Abroad, 1876–1917* (New York: Hill and Wang, 2001), 50.

9   Ellsworth Huntington, "Climate and Civilization," *Harper's Monthly* 130 (February 1915): 370. *Webster's Third New International Dictionary* defines *civilization* as "an ideal state of human culture characterized by complete absence of barbarism and nonrational behavior, optimum utilization of physical, cultural, spiritual, and human resources, and perfect adjustment of the individual within the social framework." The last part of this definition is interesting in the current context, in that Arthur C. Parker used the SAI journal to reiterate many times, over the course of his editorship, the need for Indian people to *adjust* to their changed circumstances. It was part of his reformist mantra that, as he wrote in the first issue of the journal, "education, thrift and adjustment to conditions bring health and prosperity." *Quarterly Journal of the Society of American Indians* 1 (Jan.–Apr. 1913): 85.

10 Matthew Pratt Guterl, *The Color of Race in America, 1900–1940* (Cambridge: Harvard University Press, 2001), 16.

11 Lewis Henry Morgan, *Ancient Society* (1877; reprint, Tucson: University of Arizona Press, 1985), xxix–xxx.

12 See Francis Paul Prucha, "Scientific Racism and Indian Policy," in *Indian Policy in the United States: Historical Essays* (Lincoln: University of Nebraska Press, 1981).

13 Francis E. Leupp, *The Indian and His Problem* (New York: Charles Scribner's Sons, 1910), 42. Leupp became a freelance writer on Indian issues after his term as Commissioner of Indian Affairs ended in 1909.

14 James Mooney, "The Ghost Dance Religion and the Sioux Outbreak of 1890," *Fourteenth Annual Report of the Bureau of Ethnology,* pt. 2 (Washington, D.C.: Government Printing Office, 1896), 657. Emphasis added.

15 SAI papers.

16 *Wisconsin State Journal,* Oct. 9, 1914.

17 Matthew K. Sniffen to Arthur C. Parker, Jan. 2, 1912, SAI papers.

18 The recruitment letter is included in the SAI papers; Valentine's comments are cited in Caroline W. Andrus, "An American Indian Conference," *Southern Workman* 40 (Dec. 1911): 712. In its annual report for 1912, the Indian Rights Association listed as one of its objectives the development of "an enlightened public conscience" that could "make itself felt on those who have to do with Indian affairs, whether in Congress or in executive positions." See Indian Rights Association, *Thirtieth Annual Report* (Philadelphia, 1912), 80.

19 Lyman Abbott, "Our Indian Problem," *North American Review* 167 (Dec. 1898): 726–27.

20 J. M. Oskison, "Making an Individual of the Indian," *Everybody's Magazine* 16 (June 1907): 723.

21 Charles M. Harvey, "The Epic of the Indian," *Atlantic Monthly* 111 (Jan.–June 1913): 118.

22 Ibid., 126–28.

23 Ibid., 126.

24 Linda Kerber, "The Abolitionist Perception of the Indian," *Journal of American History* 62 (Sept. 1975): 271.

25 George Bird Grinnell, *The Indians of To-Day* (New York: Duffield and Company, 1911), 18–19.

26 Frances Campbell Sparhawk, a former Carlisle teacher and co-founder of the Indian Industries League, made the same argument as early as 1906 in an article for the *North American Review*. "It is the reservation Indian whom the white man everywhere detests," Sparhawk wrote. "But the white man quite takes to the Indian freed from the reservation yoke and walking like a man and a brother." See "The Indian's Yoke," *North American Review* 182 (Jan. 1906): 57.

27 Oskison's speech was printed in the Carlisle Indian School magazine, the *Red Man*, 4 (Jan. 1912): 204. Daniel La France, a Mohawk who worked as a nurse in New York, commented (in 1903) that he had never been aware of much prejudice directed at him by whites. "There is some, but I don't think it amounts to much. . . . I never perceived it, and I don't think I have suffered anywhere from prejudice." Interestingly, La France concluded his comment with this terse observation: "I have suffered many times from being mistaken for a Japanese." See Daniel La France, "An Indian Boy's Story," *Independent* 55 (July 30, 1903): 1787.

28 Lyman Abbott, "The Rights of Man: A Study in Twentieth Century Problems," *Outlook* 68 (June 8, 1901): 351.

29 *Southern Workman* 32 (July 1903): 312. Franz Boas, while deploring the prejudice directed against African Americans, was as pessimistic as Moton about the prospects of eliminating it from American culture. Boas wrote in 1911:

> When, finally, we consider the inferior position held by the Negro race of the United States, where the Negro lives in the closest contact with modern civilization, we must not forget that the antagonism between the races is as strong as ever and that the inferiority of the Negro race is dogmatically assumed. . . . This is a formidable obstacle to the Negro's advance and progress, even though schools and universities are open to him. We might rather wonder how much, against heavy odds, has been accomplished in a short period. It is hardly possible to predict what would be the achievements of the Negro if he were able to live with the Whites on absolutely equal terms. (Boas, *The Mind of Primitive Man* [New York: Macmillan, 1938], 15.)

30 Moton was later (in 1915) to succeed Washington, his longtime friend and intellectual ally, as principal of Tuskegee Institute. Moton was also a close friend of W. E. B. Du Bois, although the two were intellectually miles apart. Du Bois noted retrospectively that at times Moton "became to me a symbol of 'Uncle Tom' and a 'white folks nigger.'" Cited in Raymond Wolters, *Du Bois and His Rivals* (Columbia: University of Missouri Press, 2002), 132. Wolters provides a good summary of Moton's career.

31 Washington was put in charge of the dormitory for male Indian students, the Wigwam, built in 1878. The dormitory for female students, Winona Lodge, was built in 1882.

32 Booker T. Washington, *Up From Slavery: An Autobiography* (New York: A. L. Burt, 1900), 102.

33 "A Negro Who Has Sense," *Philadelphia Record*, Apr. 8, 1894.

34 Donal F. Lindsey, *Indians at Hampton Institute, 1877–1923* (Champaign: University of Illinois Press, 1995), 159–60.

35 Francis E. Leupp, *In Red Man's Land* (New York: Fleming H. Revell Company, 1914), 64.

36 Leupp, *The Indian and His Problem*, 360, 361, 42.

37 Alexander F. Chamberlain, "Negro and Indian," in Bureau of American Ethnology, *Handbook of American Indians North of Mexico*, ed. Frederick Webb Hodge, pt. 2 (Washington, D.C.: Government Printing Office, 1907), 53.

38 Richard Henry Pratt, "Why Most of Our Indians Are Dependent and Non-Citizen," paper delivered at the Lake Mohonk Conference, Oct. 16, 1914.

39 U.S. Superintendent of Indian Schools, *Course of Study for the Indian Schools of the United States, Industrial and Literary* (Washington, D.C.: Government Printing Office, 1901), 189.

40 Lindsey, *Indians at Hampton*, 38; S. C. Armstrong, *The Indian Question* (Hampton, Va.: Hampton Institute, 1883), unpaginated; Richard H. Pratt to Carlos Montezuma, Apr. 27, 1910, Montezuma papers; "Indian Leadership," *Southern Workman* 38 (Dec. 1909): 645.

41 F. F. Avery, "Indian Reservation Schools," *Southern Workman* 30 (May 1901): 251.

42 Martin S. Dworkin, ed., *Dewey on Education* (New York: Teachers College Press, 1959), 49; Jane Addams, *Democracy and Social Ethics* (New York: Macmillan, 1902), 169, 180–81.

43 "Hampton Indians' Petition to Congress," *Southern Workman* 41 (May 1912): 266.

44 Stephens is quoted in Lindsey, *Indians at Hampton*, 253. Stephens probably would have approved of a 1910 performance given at the Indian school in Phoenix—a minstrel show, with Indian students in blackface, playing Uncle Remus, Sambo, George Washington Rastus Jones, and De Li'l Pickaninny, among others. The show also featured a "Monologue by the Jew." The genteel National Indian Association, reporting on the show in its journal, was cautious in its praise of the students' accomplishments, commenting that "the presentation of negro and Hebrew characters by Indians suggests not only versatility but no small degree of ambition and—courage!" See *The Indian's Friend* 22 (Apr. 1910): 4.

45 David Levering Lewis, *W. E. B. Du Bois: Biography of a Race, 1868–1919* (New York: Henry Holt, 1993), 440.

46 Vine Deloria Jr., *Custer Died for Your Sins* (New York: Macmillan, 1969), 172. Robert Allen Warrior has attributed the SAI's studied indifference to black uplift to its effort to "corner the market on white sympathies." See his *Tribal Secrets: Recovering American Indian Intellectual Traditions* (Minneapolis: University of Minnesota Press, 1995), 13.

47 Arthur C. Parker, "Problems of Race Assimilation in America," *American Indian Magazine* 4 (Oct.–Dec. 1916): 291, 293.

48 Ibid., 296, 301.

49 Ibid., 299, 303.

50 Frederick E. Hoxie, *A Final Promise: The Campaign to Assimilate the Indians, 1880–1920* (Lincoln: University of Nebraska Press, 1984), 144.

51 Francis Paul Prucha, *Indian Policy in the United States: Historical Essays* (Lincoln: University of Nebraska Press, 1981), especially the chapters on "Scientific Racism and Indian Policy," "Indian Reform and American Protestantism, 1880–1890," and "The Decline of the Christian Reformers."

52 Lewis, *W. E. B. Du Bois,* 117.

53 The combined (active and associate) SAI membership lists for 1913 also include more than fifty employees of the Indian Bureau, most of them employed by Bureau schools. The number of Bureau employees in the SAI was a continuing source of discussion and debate, with some members, Carlos Montezuma among the most vocal of them, contending that Bureau employees had too much influence in the society. The same issue would attend the founding of the National Congress of American Indians three decades later.

54 Francis Paul Prucha, *The Great Father: The United States Government and the American Indians,* vol. 2 (Lincoln: University of Nebraska Press, 1984), 619.

55 Cited in D. S. Otis, *The Dawes Act and the Allotment of Indian Lands* (Norman: University of Oklahoma Press, 1973), 29.

56 Lyman Abbott, *Christianity and Social Problems* (New York: Johnson Reprint, 1986), 81, 134. In the same book, Abbott assigned to the church and the clergy the responsibility to "give instruction in the moral laws which govern social and industrial life,—the organized life of humanity" (364).

57 Cited in Prucha, *The Great Father,* vol. 2, 621.

58 Robert T. Handy, *A Christian America: Protestant Hopes and Historical Realities,* 2nd ed. (New York: Oxford University Press, 1984), 142.

59 Abbott, "Rights of Man," 350–51. Abbott's position was echoed by an unsigned article in *The Nation* in 1904 that announced that the "only gospel which can save what is still savable in the American Indian" is one that "declares that what the nation must do for its ward is to compel him not only to work, but to work to an economic end." One merit of this tough gospel, the article continued, is that it acknowledges unblinkingly that "some Indians will be crushed under the wheel of civilization through their own unwillingness to adapt themselves to the universal order of mankind." See "The Gospel of Work for the Indian," *The Nation* 79 (Oct. 6, 1904): 273.

60 Abbott, "Rights of Man," 351.

61 "Gospel of Work for the Indian," 273.

62 Leupp, *The Indian and His Problem,* vii. Critics of Leupp's tenure as Commissioner of Indian Affairs accused him of administering with an iron hand rather than just a steady one.

63 Vine Deloria Jr. and Clifford M. Lytle, *The Nations Within: The Past and Future of American Indian Sovereignty* (New York: Pantheon, 1984), 37–38. Roe Cloud's Lake Mohonk speech was reprinted in the *Quarterly Journal of the Society of American Indians* 2 (July–Sept. 1914): 208.

64 See Peggy Pascoe, *Relations of Rescue: The Search for Female Moral Authority in the American West, 1874–1939* (New York: Oxford University Press, 1990).

65 James McLaughlin, *My Friend the Indian* (Boston: Houghton Mifflin, 1910), 388–89.

66 Francis E. Leupp, "Improvement, not Transformation," *Southern Workman* 29 (June 1900): 365, 369.

67 Leupp, *The Indian and His Problem*, 53. Leupp's successor as Commissioner of Indian Affairs, Robert G. Valentine, essentially agreed with Leupp's position, although for more practical reasons than those given by Leupp. Valentine worried about too much haste in implementing the allotment program and opening up excess reservation lands for settlement. Expressing his faith in the Indian Service as "one great citizenship school for Indians," Valentine asked that the Service be given sufficient time to prepare its wards for citizenship, imploring the states to trust the Service and "not be too ready to discharge [the Indians] from its protecting care, at the same time that it is nevertheless advancing steadily and increasingly in the direction of taking its hands off." Significantly, this address to the states was printed in a magazine published on the West Coast, with a largely western readership. Robert G. Valentine, "Making Good Indians," *Sunset* 24 (June 1910): 602–3.

68 Fayette Avery McKenzie, "The Indian and His Problem," *Dial* 49 (July–Dec. 1910): 229.

69 Frank G. Speck, "Conservation for the Indians," *Southern Workman* 41 (June 1912): 328–32.

70 Speck had introduced Parker to Boas around 1901 and encouraged his friend to enroll in the anthropology program at Columbia. Parker declined, being at the time more interested in archaeology than in anthropology.

71 Arthur C. Parker, "Progress for the Indian," *Southern Workman* 41 (Nov. 1912): 628–35. Speck responded to Parker's accommodating stance in a paper that Parker published in the SAI's journal in 1914. Speck reiterated his position, but in stronger language this time, concluding that "anybody who advocates total tribal disintegration is manifestly advocating race murder." See "Educating the White Man Up to the Indian," *Quarterly Journal of the Society of American Indians* 2 (Jan.–Mar. 1914): 68.

72 Arthur C. Parker to Pauline Stanley, Aug. 6, 1923. Cited in Hazel W. Hertzberg, "Nationality, Anthropology, and Pan-Indianism in the Life of Arthur C. Parker (Seneca)," *Proceedings of the American Philosophical Society* 123 (Feb. 1979): 67.

CHAPTER 3. FOR THE GOOD OF THE INDIAN RACE

1 William Barrows, *The Indian's Side of the Indian Question* (Boston: D. Lothrop Company, 1887), 8, 55, 137, 188. Barrows's acknowledgment of the "dishonor" (p. 189) brought on the country by the acts of an unscrupulous few, and his sunny conviction that the right-thinking majority could fix the problems created by the reprobate minority, suggest that his book may have been written in response to the scathing indictment of white America's treatment of Indians in Helen Hunt Jackson's *A Century of Dishonor*, published in 1881. His list of those who were participating in the civilizing and Christianizing of the Indians bears some interesting (and ironic) similarities to historian Frederick Hoxie's list of those who actively supported the reduction of the Indian land base, by the opening up of Indian lands for settlement, in the 1880s: "Settlers, railroad magnates, small merchants, Populists, southerners, apostles of western expansion, and

even the Indians' new 'friends' shared a desire to destroy the 'Chinese wall' [i.e., the reservations] that separated Indians and whites." See Frederick E. Hoxie, *A Final Promise: The Campaign to Assimilate the Indians, 1880–1920* (Lincoln: University of Nebraska Press, 1984), 52.

2 Elizabeth P. Peabody, *Sarah Winnemucca's Practical Solution of the Indian Problem: A Letter to Dr. Lyman Abbott of the 'Christian Union'* (Cambridge, Mass.: John Wilson and Son, 1886), 9; Francis E. Leupp, "The Failure of the Educated American Indian," *Appleton's Booklover's Magazine* 7 (May 1906): 599; James McLaughlin, *My Friend the Indian* (New York: Houghton Mifflin, 1910), 3; Robert G. Valentine, "Making Good Indians," *Sunset* 24 (June 1910): 611.

3 Letter from F. A. McKenzie, Sept. 15, 1909, SAI papers.

4 F. A. McKenzie to Carlos Montezuma, Aug. 10, 1911, Montezuma papers.

5 "The Quarterly Journal of the Society of American Indians," *The Indian's Friend* 25 (May 1913): 10.

6 "Editorial Comment," *Quarterly Journal of the Society of American Indians* 1 (Jan.–Apr. 1913): 2.

7 Circular letter, Apr. 22, 1913, SAI papers.

8 Arthur C. Parker to Matthew K. Sniffen, Oct. 19, 1917, SAI papers; Arthur C. Parker to Pauline Stanley, Aug. 6, 1923, cited in Hazel W. Hertzberg, "Nationality, Anthropology, and Pan-Indianism in the Life of Arthur C. Parker (Seneca)," *Proceedings of the American Philosophical Society* 123 (Feb. 1979): 67.

9 Hazel W. Hertzberg, *The Search for an American Indian Identity: Modern Pan-Indian Movements* (Syracuse, N.Y.: Syracuse University Press, 1971), 134.

10 Washington Gladden, "The Race Awakening," *Quarterly Journal of the Society of American Indians* 1 (Jan.–Apr. 1913): 13, 17, 18.

11 Ibid., 13.

12 U.S. Superintendent of Indian Schools, *Course of Study for the Indian Schools of the United States, Industrial and Literary* (Washington, D.C.: Government Printing Office, 1901), 5.

13 The list of the society's objectives was printed regularly in its journal.

14 Welch's comments appeared in *Scribner's Magazine* in April 1891. They are cited in Francis Paul Prucha, *The Great Father: The United States Government and the American Indian*, vol. 2 (Lincoln: University of Nebraska Press, 1984), 644.

15 David Rich Lewis, "Reservation Leadership and the Progressive-Traditional Dichotomy: William Wash and the Northern Utes, 1865–1928," *Ethnohistory* 38 (Spring 1991): 124–48; Thomas Wildcat Alford (as told to Florence Drake), *Civilization, and the Story of the Absentee Shawnees* (Norman: University of Oklahoma Press, 1936), 81.

16 "Editorial Comment," *Quarterly Journal of the Society of American Indians* 1 (Jan.–Apr. 1913): 2.

17 Arthur C. Parker to the executive committee, Society of American Indians, Jan. 13, 1912, SAI papers.

18 Arthur C. Parker, "Certain Important Elements of the Indian Problem," *Quarterly Journal of the Society of American Indians* 2 (Jan.–Mar. 1915): 24–38. The essay was reprinted

as "The Social Elements of the Indian Problem" in the *American Journal of Sociology* 22 (Sept. 1916): 252–67.

19 F. A. McKenzie to Arthur C. Parker, Dec. 27, 1911; Arthur C. Parker to F. A. McKenzie, Jan. 14, 1912, SAI papers.

20 "The Real Value of Higher Education for the Indian," *Quarterly Journal of the Society of American Indians* 1 (July–Sept. 1913): 283.

21 R. H. Pratt, "Education of Indians," *Quarterly Journal of the Society of American Indians* 3 (Apr.–June 1915): 111, 112.

22 R. H. Pratt to Carlos Montezuma, Dec. 11, 1912, Montezuma papers.

23 Dennison Wheelock, "Not an Indian Problem but a Problem of Race Separation," *Quarterly Journal of the Society of American Indians* 1 (Oct.–Dec. 1913): 369, 371.

24 Gertrude Bonnin to Estaiene DePeltquestangue, Aug. 22, 1916, SAI papers.

25 Gertrude Bonnin to Arthur C. Parker, June 20, 1916, SAI papers.

26 Ibid. The leaflet never materialized.

27 Gertrude Bonnin to Arthur C. Parker, Dec. 19, 1916, SAI papers.

28 Gertrude Bonnin to Arthur C. Parker, Jan. 10, 1917, SAI papers.

29 Sophia Hubert to Arthur C. Parker, Sept. 26, 1914, SAI papers.

30 Rides A White Hipped Horse to Arthur C. Parker, Nov. 28, 1913, SAI papers.

31 Arthur C. Parker to Rides A White Hipped Horse, Dec. 12, 1913, SAI papers.

32 Arthur C. Parker to J. N. B. Hewitt, Aug. 30, 1913, SAI papers.

33 Maud Lundin to the Society of American Indians, Dec. 13, 1913, SAI papers; Arthur C. Parker to Honorable Cato Sells, Dec. 19, 1913, SAI papers.

34 Arthur C. Parker to Gertrude Bonnin, Mar. 12, 1917, SAI papers.

35 "Editorial Comment," *American Indian Magazine* 6 (Spring 1918): 17. The name of the journal changed from the *Quarterly Journal of the Society of American Indians* with the fourth volume, in 1916.

36 Arthur C. Parker to Rev. Sherman Coolidge, Dec. 30, 1911, SAI papers.

37 Charles A. Eastman (Ohiyesa), "The Indian's Plea for Freedom," *American Indian Magazine* 6 (Winter 1918): 164.

38 For good summaries of the legal history of the allotment program, see D. S. Otis, *The Dawes Act and the Allotment of Indian Lands* (Norman: University of Oklahoma Press, 1973); Hoxie, *A Final Promise*; Prucha, *The Great Father.*

39 Parker tells Coolidge's story in "Sherman Coolidge: A Study in the Complexities of an Indian's Legal Status," *Quarterly Journal of the Society of American Indians* 3 (Jan.–Mar. 1915): 220–23.

40 *Lone Wolf v. Hitchcock,* Supreme Court of the United States, no. 275, Jan. 5, 1903.

41 Matthew K. Sniffen, "The Record of Thirty Years: A Brief Statement of the Indian Rights Association, Its Objects, Methods, and Achievements" (Philadelphia: Indian Rights Association, 1912), 9.

42 Arthur C. Parker to the executive committee of the Society of American Indians, Jan. 13, 1912, SAI papers.

43 Arthur C. Parker, "The Legal Status of the American Indian," reprinted in the *Quarterly Journal of the Society of American Indians* 2 (July–Sept. 1914): 213–14.

44 The full details of Montezuma's life are in Peter Iverson's *Carlos Montezuma and the Changing World of American Indians* (Albuquerque: University of New Mexico Press, 1982).

45 Dorcas J. Spencer to Carlos Montezuma, Mar. 5, 1911, Montezuma papers.

46 From a speech Montezuma delivered to the Fortnightly Club of Chicago in February 1898. The speech was printed under the title "Our Treatment of the Indians from the Standpoint of One of Them" in the *Saturday Evening Post*, no. 170 (May 21, 1898): 11.

47 *Hearings before the Committee on Expenditures in the Interior Department of the House of Representatives on House Resolution no. 103, June 11, 1911* (Washington, D.C.: Government Printing Office, 1911), 385. The committee was considering the issue of funding for reservation schools.

48 Arthur C. Parker to Carlos Montezuma, Feb. 19, 1911, SAI papers; Carlos Montezuma, "What Indians Must Do," *Quarterly Journal of the Society of American Indians* 2 (Oct.–Dec., 1914): 297–98; Carlos Montezuma to Gen. R. H. Pratt, Mar. 29, 1916, Montezuma papers.

49 "Drafting Indians and Justice," *Wassaja* 2 (Oct. 1917), unpaginated; Carlos Montezuma, "Abolish the Indian Bureau," *American Indian Magazine* 7 (Spring 1919): 17, 18, 20. Montezuma's outspokenness in *Wassaja* brought him to the attention of the FBI and military intelligence. His papers contain copies of reports filed by both agencies in 1917. The author of the military intelligence report surmises that *Wassaja* is being published "with a view to inciting insurrection and disloyalty among the Indian tribes." The FBI report notes that Montezuma had married a German woman and acquired a "strong minded" German mother-in-law who had convinced him that "Germany is alright and Uncle Sam is all wrong." The writer of this report is also concerned about Montezuma's capacity to turn other Indians against the war and the country: "His opinions and beliefs would perhaps be of very little danger were it not for the fact that he is in a position to disaffect a very large number of Indians in the South West."

50 Frederick E. Hoxie, ed., *Talking Back to Civilization: Indian Voices from the Progressive Era* (Boston: Bedford/St. Martin's, 2001), 123.

51 Eastman, "The Indian's Plea for Freedom," 165.

52 [Arthur C. Parker], "Reasons Why Indians Should Join the Regular Army," *American Indian Magazine* 5 (Spring 1917): 143. Gertrude Bonnin was incensed at the idea of an all-Indian military unit. "Shame upon the Dixon-headed Walking Reservation," she wrote to Arthur Parker. "Indian Battalion! Why those false words hide the greatest scheme to utterly annihilate the Red Man, by a whole-sale slaughter!" Bonnin had earlier speculated to Parker that a similarly sinister agenda might lie behind the creation of all-black military units: "Secretly I wonder if it is not a cute idea to reduce the Negro population. This sounds like treason, so you better not quote me, unless you want me hung." Gertrude Bonnin to Arthur C. Parker, August 6, 1917 and June 20, 1917, SAI papers.

53 *Wassaja,* 2 (Sept. 1917), unpaginated.

54 Francis E. Leupp, *The Indian and His Problem* (New York: Charles Scribner's Sons, 1910), 42; Frederick H. Abbott, *The Administration of Indian Affairs in Canada* (Washington, D.C.: Board of Indian Commissioners, 1915), 29.

55 Arthur C. Parker to Fayette McKenzie, Nov. 6, 1912, SAI papers.

56 Laura Cornelius Kellogg, *Our Democracy and the American Indian* (Kansas City, Mo.: Burton Publishing Company, 1920), 59.

57 Kellogg fell into disfavor with the SAI for both moral and legal reasons. Arthur Parker wrote to J. N. B. Hewitt at the Smithsonian on Aug. 30, 1913, detailing the reasons that she had become an embarrassment to the organization:

> Mrs. Kellogg is accused of being an ex-actress who danced in the nude, and clippings are shown from theatrical papers and the Sunday supplement picturing Laura Cornelius as dancing almost in the nude for the benefit of the Indian people; from Boston to Los Angeles she is known for swindling business men out of money and I have seen affidavits and indictments issued by district attorneys and requisitions made out by United States marshals, citing her for fraud, misuse of funds and the impersonation of federal officers. (SAI papers)

Laurance M. Hauptman has defended Kellogg, pointing out that she was never convicted of any of the charges against her, that her miscalculations with money were made in the process of attempting to secure both funds and land rights for groups of reservation Indians, and that her invaluable work in documenting Iroquois history has been unfortunately obscured by her legal troubles. Hauptman also acknowledges that the archival evidence relating to Kellogg's activities is very thin. For Arthur Parker and other SAI officers, evidence of the facts of Kellogg's case were less important than the odor of scandal that her activities attached to the SAI; her name was dropped from the membership list in 1913. See Hauptman, "Designing Woman: Minnie Kellogg, Iroquois Leader," in L. G. Moses and Raymond Wilson, eds., *Indian Lives: Essays on Nineteenth-and Twentieth-Century Native American Leaders* (Albuquerque: University of New Mexico Press, 1985), 159–88.

58 "A. C. Parker Dies; Museum Expert," *New York Times*, Jan. 3, 1955. The relevant details of Parker's life are available in Joy Porter, *To Be Indian: The Life of Iroquois-Seneca Arthur Caswell Parker* (Norman: University of Oklahoma Press, 2001); Hertzberg, *Search for an American Indian Identity;* and William N. Fenton's introduction to Arthur C. Parker, *Parker on the Iroquois* (Syracuse, N.Y.: Syracuse University Press, 1968).

59 Fayette McKenzie, "The American Indian of To-day and To-morrow," *Quarterly Journal of the Society of American Indians* 1 (Oct.–Dec. 1913), 387. The essay was originally published in the *Journal of Race Development* 3 (Oct. 1912).

60 Fayette McKenzie, "The Assimilation of the American Indian," *American Journal of Sociology* 19 (May 1914): 761, 762, 770; John Dewey, "My Pedagogic Creed," in Martin S. Dworkin, ed., *Dewey on Education* (New York: Teachers College Press, 1959), 30.

61 Robert H. Lowie, *Culture and Ethnology* (New York: Basic Books, 1966), 41, 97.

62 Bureau of American Ethnology, *Handbook of American Indians North of Mexico*, ed. Frederick Webb Hodge (Washington, D.C.: Government Printing Office, 1907), pt. 1, 172.

63 Curtis M. Hinsley has argued that in its earliest days the work of anthropology done under the auspices of the Smithsonian Institution (home of the BAE) was carried out by men whose thinking was governed by religious and moral considerations: "They

called themselves scientists, but theirs was as often an aesthetic and religious exercise, and always a moral service to the nation." See *The Smithsonian and the American Indian: Making a Moral Anthropology in Victorian America* (Washington, D.C.: Smithsonian Institution Press, 1994), 84.

64 J. N. B. Hewitt, "The Teaching of Ethnology in Indian Schools," *Quarterly Journal of the Society of American Indians* 1 (Jan.–Apr. 1913): 35.

65 F. G. Speck, "Conservation for the Indians," *Southern Workman* 41 (June 1912): 331; Natalie Curtis, "Hampton's Double Mission," *Southern Workman* 34 (Oct. 1905): 544, 545.

66 Arthur C. Parker, "What Makes the Indian a Problem?" *Quarterly Journal of the Society of American Indians* 1 (Apr.–June 1913): 106.

67 Chauncey Yellow Robe to Carlos Montezuma, Mar. 27, 1915, Montezuma papers; R. H. Pratt to Carlos Montezuma, Feb. 10, 1919, Montezuma papers; Carlos Montezuma, "A Review of Commissioner Leupp's Interview in the New York Daily Tribune, Sunday, Apr. 9, 1905, on the Future of Our Indians," n.d., Montezuma papers; Carlos Montezuma to R. H. Pratt, Apr. 3. 1910, Montezuma papers; Carlos Montezuma to R. H. Pratt, July 12, 1916, Montezuma papers.

68 Porter, *To Be Indian*, 141. Michelle Wick Patterson has also remarked on "the failure of the SAI and other Native reformers to fulfill their goals and to establish a national political voice in the early twentieth century." See "Real Indian Songs: The Society of American Indians and the Use of Native American Culture as a Means of Reform," *American Indian Quarterly* 26 (Winter 2002): 62.

69 Grace Coolidge, *Teepee Neighbors* (Norman: University of Oklahoma Press, 1984), v; *Wassaja* 6 (June 1921), unpaginated.

70 Letter to Arthur C. Parker, July 11, 1911, SAI papers.

71 Arthur C. Parker, "The Editor's Viewpoint," *American Indian Magazine* 4 (Jan.–Mar. 1916): 9–10.

72 Arthur C. Parker, "Why Should the Country Heed Our Pleading?" *Quarterly Journal of the Society of American Indians* 3 (July–Sept. 1915): 166. The names he listed were the following: Sherman Coolidge, Gertrude Bonnin, Francis La Flesche, Susette La Flesche, Charles Eastman, Frank H. Wright, Charles Dagenett, Carlos Montezuma, Vincent Natalish, John Oskison, Gabe E. Parker, Marie Baldwin, Rosa La Flesche, Henry Standing Bear, Helen Clarke, Charles D. Carter, Dennison Wheelock, William J. Kershaw, Thomas Sloan, Stephen Jones, Emma Goulette, Oliver LaMere, Hiram Chase, Elvira Pike, Minnie Prophet, Bertha Thompson, Charles Kealear, Hastings Robinson, Clarence Three Stars, Joseph K. Griffis, Phillip B. Gordon, and Henry Roe Cloud.

73 Arthur C. Parker, "The Changes We Have Wrought," *American Indian Magazine* 4 (Jan.–Mar. 1916): 110–11.

74 Thomas C. Moffett, *The American Indian on the New Trail* (New York: Missionary Education Movement of the United States and Canada, 1914), 252–53; Moffett, "The Society of American Indians Is a Success," *American Indian Magazine* 4 (July–Sept. 1916): 263; Sherman Coolidge, "The Function of the Society of American Indians," *Quarterly Journal of the Society of American Indians* 2 (July–Sept. 1914): 187, 189; "Citizenship for

Indians Plea of Their Leaders," *Philadelphia Record,* Feb. 15, 1914; Charles Eastman, *The Indian To-Day* (New York: Doubleday, Page, 1915), 132.

75 Herbert Work to Arthur C. Parker, May 10, 1923, SAI papers.

76 Hoxie, *Talking Back to Civilization,* 26.

CHAPTER 4. THE PROGRESSIVE ROAD OF LIFE

1 Standing Bear determined that he was born in 1868, but the allotment records at Pine Ridge list his birth date as 1863. There is also some ambiguity surrounding Standing Bear's specific tribal identity. Some recent researchers have concluded that he was probably Brulé, but since Standing Bear refers to himself in his texts as Oglala or Lakota, I have chosen to follow his lead. See Richard N. Ellis's introduction to Standing Bear's *My People the Sioux* (Lincoln: University of Nebraska Press, 1975).

2 Charles Eastman, *Indian Boyhood* (1902; reprint, Greenwich, Conn.: Fawcett Publications, 1972), 49; Luther Standing Bear, *Land of the Spotted Eagle* (1933; reprint, Lincoln: University of Nebraska Press, 1978), 13, 15; Zitkala-Sa (Gertrude Bonnin), *American Indian Stories* (Washington, D.C.: Hayworth Publishing House, 1921), 19.

3 Arthur C. Parker to Charles A. Eastman, Nov. 3, 1911, SAI papers.

4 Elaine Goodale Eastman, *Sister to the Sioux,* ed. Kay Graber (Lincoln: University of Nebraska Press, 1978), 173.

5 Ibid., 172–73.

6 Charles A. Eastman (Ohiyesa), *From the Deep Woods to Civilization: Chapters in the Autobiography of an Indian* (1916; reprint, Lincoln: University of Nebraska Press, 1977), 117, 118, 139; Charles A. Eastman (Ohiyesa), *The Indian To-Day: The Past and Future of the First American* (New York: Doubleday, Page, 1915), 106.

7 H. David Brumble III, *American Indian Autobiography* (Berkeley: University of California Press, 1988). See also David J. Carlson, " 'Indian for a While': Charles Eastman's *Indian Boyhood* and the Discourse of Allotment," *American Indian Quarterly* 25, no. 4 (Fall 2001): 604–25; Tony Dykema-VanderArk, " 'Playing Indian' in Print: Charles A. Eastman's Autobiographical Writing for Children," *MELUS* 27, no. 2 (Summer 2002): 9–30; Penelope Myrtle Kelsey, "A 'Real Indian' to the Boy Scouts: Charles Eastman as a Resistance Writer," *Western American Literature* 38, no. 1 (2003): 30–48; Erik Peterson, " 'An Indian . . . An American': Ethnicity, Assimilation, and Balance in Charles Eastman's *From the Deep Woods to Civilization,*" in Helen Jaskoski, ed., *Early Native American Writing: New Critical Essays* (New York: Cambridge University Press, 1996).

8 Gerald Vizenor, *Manifest Manners: Postindian Warriors of Survivance* (Hanover, N.H.: University Press of New England, 1994), 51.

9 *The Indian To-Day,* 166.

10 Charles A. Eastman (Ohiyesa), "The Indian's Plea for Freedom," *American Indian Magazine* 6, no. 4 (Winter 1918): 163.

11 Charles A. Eastman (Ohiyesa), *The Soul of the Indian: An Interpretation* (Boston: Riverside Press, 1911), xii; Charles A. Eastman (Ohiyesa), *Indian Scout Talks: A Guide for Boy Scouts and Camp Fire Girls* (Boston: Little, Brown, 1914), epigraph.

12 *Soul of the Indian,* xii.

13 Gertrude Bonnin to Carlos Montezuma, Oct. 22, 1918; SAI papers.

14 Representative books published by non-Indians prior to the 1915 publication of East-man's book include William Barrows's *The Indian's Side of the Indian Question* (1887); Seth K. Humphrey's *The Indian Dispossessed* (1906); Natalie Curtis's *The Indians' Book* (1907); Fayette McKenzie's *The Indian in Relation to the White Population of the United States* (1908); Francis Leupp's *The Indian and His Problem* (1910) and *In Red Man's Land* (1914); George Bird Grinnell's *The Indians of Today* (1911); Thomas C. Moffett's *The American Indian on the New Trail* (1914); Warren K. Moorehead's *The American Indian in the United States, Period 1850–1914* (1914). The list of journal articles is very long.

15 *The Indian To-Day*, 3, 54, 119.

16 Roosevelt is cited in the *American Indian Magazine* 4, no. 4 (Oct.–Dec. 1916): 327. His opinion was widely shared among many white administrators and reformers.

17 *The Indian To-Day*, 100.

18 Ibid., 80.

19 Parker may have borrowed this formulation from Laura Cornelius Kellogg, who announced at the first SAI conference in 1911 that "I am not a new Indian, I am the old Indian adjusted to new conditions." Her comment is cited in Hazel Hertzberg, *The Search for an American Identity: Modern Pan-Indian Movements* (Syracuse: Syracuse University Press, 1971), 65.

20 Raymond Wilson, *Ohiyesa: Charles Eastman, Santee Sioux* (Urbana: University of Illinois Press, 1983), 89.

21 David I. Macleod, *Building Character in the American Boy: The Boy Scouts, YMCA, and Their Forerunners, 1870–1920* (Madison: University of Wisconsin Press, 1983), xviii.

22 Philip J. Deloria points out in his *Playing Indian* that Indian-playing in the Boy Scouts became less pronounced after 1915. In the Camp Fire Girls, on the other hand, the Indian play continued unabated.

23 *From the Deep Woods to Civilization*, 1, 5, 6.

24 *The Soul of the Indian*, 24; "The Indian's Plea for Freedom," 162.

25 *From the Deep Woods*, 2; *The Soul of the Indian*, 90–91; *The Indian To-Day*, 6.

26 *The Indian To-Day*, 159.

27 *From the Deep Woods*, 187, 188.

28 Francis La Flesche, *The Middle Five: Indian Schoolboys of the Omaha Tribe* (1900; reprint, Lincoln: University of Nebraska Press, 1978), xv.

29 Wilson, *Ohiyesa*, xi; David Reed Miller, "Charles Alexander Eastman, The 'Winner': From Deep Woods to Civilization," in Margot Liberty, ed., *American Indian Intellectuals* (St. Paul, Minn.: West Publishing, 1978), 64, 70.

30 Edward Said, *Representations of the Intellectual* (New York: Pantheon, 1994), 11, 44.

31 "America's Indian Problem," in *American Indian Stories* (Washington, D.C.: Hayworth Publishing House, 1921), 186.

32 Zitkala-Sa (Gertrude Bonnin), "The Great Spirit," in *American Indian Stories* (Washington, D.C.: Hayworth Publishing House, 1921), 106. This story was originally published in the *Atlantic Monthly* in 1902 under the title "Why I Am a Pagan."

33 These stories were written and originally published before Bonnin's conversion to Catholicism around 1909. Significantly, when she republished the stories in 1921, she

did not soften their representations of the coercive and constrictive Christianity that was part of the standard regimen of boarding school life.

34 *From the Deep Woods to Civilization*, 28.

35 "Impressions of an Indian Childhood," in *American Indian Stories*, 44.

36 Gertrude Bonnin to Carlos Montezuma, Feb. 20, 1901, Carlos Montezuma papers.

37 Gertrude Bonnin to Carlos Montezuma, Apr. 19, 1901, Montezuma papers.

38 Gertrude Bonnin to Carlos Montezuma, June 1, 1901, Montezuma papers.

39 Gertrude Bonnin to Carlos Montezuma, June 4, 1901; June 17, 1901, Montezuma papers.

40 Some of these previously unpublished stories, as well as the text of the opera on which Bonnin collaborated, have been collected and published by P. Jane Hafen in *Dreams and Thunder: Stories, Poems, and* The Sun Dance Opera (Lincoln: University of Nebraska Press, 2001). In addition to making these texts available, Hafen has provided useful information on Bonnin's life and career. Other researchers who have provided invaluable information are Cathy N. Davidson and Ada Norris, *Zitkala-Sa: American Indian Stories, Legends, and Other Writings* (New York: Penguin, 2003) and Doreen Rappaport, *The Flight of Red Bird: The Life of Zitkala-Sa* (New York: Dial, 1997). In my own discussion of Bonnin's career, I have drawn on the work of all of these scholars.

41 Gertrude Bonnin to Carlos Montezuma, Mar. 5, 1901; Sept. 4, 1901, Montezuma papers.

42 Gertrude Bonnin to Carlos Montezuma, June [?], 1901, Montezuma papers.

43 Cited in Davidson and Norris, *Zitkala-Sa*, 237, 238.

44 "An Indian Teacher among Indians," in *American Indian Stories*, 97.

45 "Reminiscences of an Educated Indian Girl," *Southern Workman* 29, no. 4 (Apr. 1900): 252, 253; *Word Carrier* 29 (Apr. 1900): 14; *Red Man* 16, no. 13 (Sept. 14, 1900): unpaginated.

46 "The Soft-Hearted Sioux," in *American Indian Stories*, 118.

47 The SAI papers contain a typed copy of this poem dated Nov. 16, 1914.

48 "The Widespread Enigma of Blue-Star Woman," in *American Indian Stories*, 173, 180.

49 Gertrude Bonnin to Arthur C. Parker, June 29, 1916; SAI papers.

50 Gertrude Bonnin to Arthur C. Parker, Dec. 19, 1916; SAI papers.

51 "Indian Woman Has Accomplished Much for Uplift of Race," *Cedar Rapids Evening Gazette* (Sept. 27, 1916), 3.

52 Davidson and Norris, *Zitkala-Sa*, 5–6.

53 *American Indian Magazine* 4, no. 1 (Jan.–Mar. 1916): 57–59.

54 In *American Indian Stories*, 155–58.

55 *Indian Helper* 15, nos. 21 (Mar. 23, 1900) and 22 (Mar. 30, 1900). Pratt explained the reason for having two school newspapers at Carlisle: the *Red Man*, in which Bonnin was castigated, was directed to the general public, including supporters of the school; the *Indian Helper*, which praised Bonnin's performances, was directed at current and past students and their families. The two papers merged later in 1900 into the *Red Man and Helper*. See Richard Henry Pratt, *Battlefield and Classroom: Four Decades with the American Indians, 1867–1904* (Lawrence: University of Kansas Press, 1995), 297.

56 The newsletter of the National Indian Association reported that "Indians and whites drove in from forty miles around" to hear Bonnin and Hanson's opera. See *The Indian's*

Friend 26, no. 3 (Dec. 1913): 1. A helpful account of Bonnin's collaboration with Hanson is given in Hafen's *Dreams and Thunder.*

57 Gertrude Bonnin to Arthur C. Parker, June 20, 1916; SAI papers.

58 Ibid.

59 Gertrude Bonnin to Carlos Montezuma, Oct. 22, 1918; SAI papers.

60 *Land of the Spotted Eagle,* 229.

61 "The Tragedy of the Sioux," reprinted in Bernd C. Peyer, ed., *The Elders Wrote: An Anthology of Early Prose by North American Indians, 1768–1931* (Berlin: Dietrich Reimer Verlag, 1982), 185, 187.

62 *Land of the Spotted Eagle,* xv.

63 Standing Bear dedicated *Land of the Spotted Eagle* to "My father, Chief Standing Bear the first, a warrior of distinction, a great leader and counsellor among his people, in later life an earnest Christian who walked the trails of peace and harmony constantly striving for the betterment of his race." He writes in the text that his father "was accounted a great man in his tribe and a chief who had the welfare of his people at heart" (98). Historians who have attempted to flesh out the life story of the elder Standing Bear by using the written records have not been able to substantiate many of the claims his son makes for him, including the claim that he was a "chief." Richard N. Ellis notes that the historical record does not provide evidence that the father was "a significant Sioux leader" and concludes that he was "probably a Brulé band leader on the Rosebud Reservation" (introduction to *My People the Sioux,* xv; foreword to *Land of the Spotted Eagle,* vii.)

64 Luther Standing Bear, *My People the Sioux,* ed. E. A. Brinninstool (Boston: Houghton Mifflin, 1928), 128, 147, 149, 152–53.

65 Ibid., 168, 184.

66 Ibid., 130.

67 Richard Henry Pratt, *The Indian Industrial School, Carlisle Pennsylvania: Its Origin, Purposes, Progress and the Difficulties Surmounted* (Carlisle PA: Hamilton Library Association, 1908), 15; Bonnin, *American Indian Stories,* 48, 85.

68 *My People the Sioux,* 166.

69 Ibid., 254, 256, 269.

70 Ibid., 285.

71 "Civilizing the Indians to a Swift Doom," *Southern Workman* 39, no. 9 (Sept. 1910): 468; *Land of the Spotted Eagle,* xv. In *The Vanishing Race,* Joseph Dixon had proclaimed his success in gaining a "close measure of the Indian mind" and persuading his Indian informants to "give to the world what the world so much craves to know—what the Indian thinks and how he feels" (8–9).

72 *Land of the Spotted Eagle,* 227–28.

73 Peyer, *The Elders Wrote,* 183.

74 *Land of the Spotted Eagle,* 90. Standing Bear dedicated *My People the Sioux* to his father, "a warrior of distinction." *Land of the Spotted Eagle,* on the other hand, is dedicated to his mother, "For it is the mothers, not the warriors, who create a people and guide their destiny."

75 Ibid., 16.

76 Ibid., 235, 234.

77 See Natalie Curtis, *The Indians' Book* (New York: Harper and Brothers, rev. ed. 1923), xxxvii, 60.

78 *Land of the Spotted Eagle,* 230.

79 *My People the Sioux,* 150, 192.

80 *Land of the Spotted Eagle,* 184.

81 Ibid., xv, xvi.

82 Ibid., 190, 191.

83 Ibid., 258.

84 Vizenor, *Manifest Manners,* 147.

85 *Land of the Spotted Eagle,* 229.

CONCLUSION

1 Paul Chaat Smith and Robert Allen Warrior have noted that the activities of the American Indian Movement in the late 1960s and early 1970s provoked a similar retrospective evaluation. They cite the 1987 remarks of Jerry Wilkinson, then executive director of the National Indian Youth Council, who criticized AIM for not focusing on specific, long-range goals but who, at the same time, praised it for "making Indians visible, for emboldening tribal leaders who had previously been afraid to criticize the government, for instilling pride in Indian people." See *Like a Hurricane: The Indian Movement from Alcatraz to Wounded Knee* (New York: New Press, 1996), 275.

2 "American Indian Culture," in Jimmie Durham, *A Certain Lack of Coherence: Writings on Art and Cultural Politics,* ed. Jean Fisher (London: Kala Press, 1993), 9.

3 Stephen E. Cornell, *The Return of the Native: American Indian Political Resurgence* (New York: Oxford University Press, 1988), 10.

4 Welch's *Killing Custer* takes on the archive directly by reexamining the historiography of the battle of the Little Big Horn in 1867. One of the earliest Indian-authored historical novels is Dallas Chief Eagle's *Winter Count,* published in 1967, which revisits the Wounded Knee massacre of 1890.

5 D'Arcy McNickle, *The Surrounded* (Albuquerque: University of New Mexico Press, 1964), 3.

6 N. Scott Momaday, *House Made of Dawn* (New York: Harper and Row, 1966), 164.

7 Sherman Alexie, "Dear John Wayne," in *The Toughest Indian in the World* (New York: Atlantic Monthly Press, 2000), 184.

8 Louis Owens, "As If an Indian Were Really an Indian," in *I Hear the Train: Reflections, Inventions, Refractions* (Norman: University of Oklahoma Press, 2001), 221.

9 Simon J. Ortiz, ed., introduction to *Speaking for the Generations* (Tucson: University of Arizona Press, 1998), xii.

10 Gloria Bird, "Breaking the Silence: Writing as Witness," 48; Luci Tapahanso, "They Moved Over the Mountain," 349. Both citations are from Ortiz, *Speaking for the Generations.*

11 Arthur C. Parker to Rides A White Hipped Horse, Dec. 12, 1913, SAI papers; Arthur C. Parker to J. N. B. Hewitt, Aug. 30, 1913, SAI papers.

12 Thomas King, introduction to *All My Relations* (Toronto: McClelland and Stewart, 1990), xii.

13 Leslie Marmon Silko, *Storyteller* (New York: Seaver Books, 1981), 7. Jace Weaver has argued, in *That the People Might Live: Native American Literatures and American Community* (New York: Oxford University Press, 1997), that the strengthening of Native communities should be the defining aim of all Native literary production.

INDEX

and native languages, 162–63
and performance, 128–29, 157–59
and progressivism, 126, 163–67
SAI, relationship to, 126
as show Indian, 24–26
and Sitting Bull, 23–24
Stories of the Sioux, 127
tribal identity, 195 n1
and white authors, 155–56, 159–61
Stephens, John Hall, 74

Taphanso, Luci, 174
Taft, William Howard, 40
Thayer, James B., 9
Tin-Tin-Meet-Sa, 37
Trachtenberg, Alan, 46

United States Board of Indian Commissioners, 115
United States v. Wong Kim Ark, 75, 178 n16
universalism
and African American uplift, 56–57
and SAI, 55–57

Valentine, Robert G., 63, 90, 189 n67
vanishing Indians, theories of, 33, 57–58, 73.
See also Dixon, Joseph Kossuth
Vizenor, Gerald, 7–8, 14, 131–32, 164, 172, 177 n13

Wannamaker, John, 23
Wannamaker, Rodman, 33, 35, 40, 47
Warrior, Robert Allen, 5, 14, 187 n46, 199 n1
Washington, Booker T.
and Hampton Institute, 25, 68–69
and race leadership, 70, 72–73
and racial prejudice, 69
Weaver, Jace, 200 n13
Welch, Herbert, 95
Welch, James, 168–69, 172–73, 180 n17, 180 n20
Wheelock, Dennison, 49
and Indian education, 101
White, Justice Edward D., 109
White Horse, 37
Wild West shows, 2–4, 22, 25, 41. *See also* Cody, Buffalo Bill
Wilson, Woodrow, 41
Winnemucca, Sarah, 4, 89, 177 n5
Womack, Craig, 5–6, 173
Women's National Indian Association, 10. *See also* National Indian Association
Woodward, Kathleen, 46
Work, Herbert, 124
World's Columbian Exposition, 1–4, 24, 26

Yellow Robe, Chauncey, 49
Yellow Robe, William Jr., 173